MW01178055

BROWNING'S ITALY

Browning's Italy

A STUDY OF
ITALIAN LIFE AND ART IN BROWNING

BY

HELEN ARCHIBALD CLARKE

Toronto
THE MUSSON BOOK COMPANY
LIMITED

Copyright, 1907, *by*
THE BAKER & TAYLOR COMPANY

Published, October, 1907

53868
3-1-34

The Plimpton Press Norwood Mass. U.S.A.

INTRODUCTION

THE inspiration for much of Robert Browning's work was found elsewhere than in Italy, yet the fact that many of his most popular shorter poems as well as his great crux "Sordello" and his great masterpiece "The Ring and the Book" blossomed from the soil of Italian life and art has brought into prominence his debt to Italian sources. Doubtless his many years of happy life with Mrs. Browning in Italy, as well as her enthusiasm for the cause of Italian independence, served to intensify the interest and delight which he felt upon his initial visit to the land that was to become one of enchantment to him.

His first journey thither was taken in 1838, with a view to becoming familiar with the scenes among which "Sordello" had been conceived. The special experience of this visit seems to have been the admiration awakened in him for the beautiful little hill-town of Asolo, — the play-kingdom of Caterina Cornaro. His first love among Italian cities he was wont to call it. So intense was his feeling for this town that he used frequently to dream of it. He described this dream, which had haunted him, to his friend, Mrs. Bronson: "I am traveling with a friend, sometimes with one person, sometimes with another, oftenest with one I do not recognize. Suddenly I see the town I love sparkling in the sun on the hillside. I cry to my companion, 'Look! look! there is Asolo! Oh, do let us go there!' The friend invariably answers, 'Impossible; we cannot stop.' 'Pray, pray, let us go there,' I entreat. 'No,' persists the friend, 'we cannot; we must go on and leave Asolo for another day,' and so I am hurried away, and wake to know that I have been dreaming it all, both pleasure and disappointment."

This deep sentiment for Asolo lasted to the end of his life, and was enshrined not only in his poetry but in the gift which the younger Browning made the town in memory of his father — namely, the establishment of the lace industry. A visitor to Asolo now will find "il poeta," as he is called, held in reverential memory. There he heard, in his early manhood, the little peasant child singing a snatch of Sordello's poetry as he climbed his way up the mountain toward the sky; here he imagined the little silk-winder Pippa scattering, all-unconscious, her uplifting influences in a "naughty world," — "so far a little candle throws its beams," — and put her into a play of which Mrs. Browning said she distinctly envied the authorship; and here, at the very last, he and his sister spent royal days with their kind American friend Mrs. Bronson. He prepared his last volume, "Asolando," for the press here, and dedicated it with most appreciative words to Mrs. Bronson. But a few short weeks later, upon the day this volume was published in England, he died in Venice.

"In a Gondola" gives his impressions of Venice received on this first visit to Italy, though the poem was directly inspired by a picture of Maclise's, "a divine Venetian work," the poet calls it, for which he was asked to write appropriate lines. These grew into the longer poem.

Another visit to Italy in 1844 is made memorable in Browning's literary life by his poem, "The Englishman in Italy." In this is given a wonderful picture of a sirocco on the plain of Sorrento. It has his usual dramatic touch. The storm is not described for itself, but, by the way, as he tries to comfort a little Italian girl, who is frightened at the black clouds, with stories of what he sees the peasant folk do when getting ready for the storm, and how nature is affected by the coming fury of wind and wave.

He has nowhere given a more charming picture of Italian scenery unless it be in the poem, "Two in the Campagna":

> "The champaign with its endless fleece
> Of feathery grasses everywhere.
> Silence and passion, joy and peace,
> An everlasting wash of air —
> Rome's ghost since her decease."

In 1846 he went to Italy with his wife, and during her life they lived most of the time at Casa Guidi in Florence, with summer excursions to the Baths of Lucca and other places and an occasional winter in Rome. Up to the time of his continued residence in Italy, Browning had written some dozen poems on Italian subjects, including all the dramas and several of the Renaissance poems: "My Last Duchess," "The Bishop Orders his Tomb at Saint Praxed's," "Pictor Ignotus," "In a Gondola."

In 1855, after nine years in Italy, he published his two volumes called "Men and Women," with a dedicatory poem to Mrs. Browning. In this, Italian subjects are still prominent, and include some of his most important work, as, for example, "Fra Lippo Lippi," "A Toccata of Galuppi's," "The Statue and the Bust," "Andrea del Sarto," "A Grammarian's Funeral."

Shortly before Mrs. Browning's death, he had found one day on a book stall, in the Piazza san Lorenzo in Florence, the original parchment-bound record of the Franceschini case, which was after several years to be transmuted into his greatest work and his last work on an Italian subject of deep significance.

This poem, with its beautiful apostrophe to his dead wife, his "Lyric Love, half angel and half bird," and its marvelous insight into the most exalted heights of a woman's soul as portrayed in Pompilia, is a superb monument to her "of whom enamored was his soul," as he elsewhere expresses his abiding devotion to her.

Unless we except "Cenciaja," "Pietro of Abano," in the "Parleyings," those with Bartoli and Furini, and a few unimportant things in "Asolando" which remind one of a sort of Italian "St. Martin's Summer," he wrote no more great Italian poems.

During the thirty years of literary activity left him, he went almost entirely to other sources for inspiration, and produced many poems which, in spite of the carping of some critics at his later work, have won as wide an appreciation as anything he has written, such as "Hervé Riel," "Caliban," "At the Mermaid," "Balaustian's Adventure," and many others.

Thus, it becomes evident that his Italian enthusiasm belonged to the days of his early manhood, when life held out to him its golden promises; to the succeeding days of the fulfilment of a rare happiness in his beloved land; and finally closed with a glorious swan-song in "The Ring and the Book" which has immortalized forever the two great passions of the poet's life — his artistic enthusiasm for Italy and his soul-love for Mrs. Browning. Of the one he wrote:

> "Open my heart and you will see
> Graved inside of it 'Italy.'"

Of the other, in Venice, many years after her death:

> "Then the cloud-rift broadens, spanning earth that's under,
> Wide our world displays its worth, man's strife and strife's success:
> All the good and beauty, wonder crowning wonder,
> Till my heart and soul applaud perfection, nothing less.
>
> "Only, at heart's utmost joy and triumph, terror
> Sudden turns the blood to ice: a chill wind disencharms
> All the late enchantment! What if all be error —
> If the halo irised round my head were, Love, thine arms."

TABLE OF CONTENTS

CHAPTER I

PAGE

The Dawn of the Renaissance 1

CHAPTER II

Glimpses of Political Life 58

CHAPTER III

The Italian Scholar 166

CHAPTER IV

The Artist and His Art 209

CHAPTER V

Pictures of Social Life 287

ILLUSTRATIONS

A Gondola . . . . *Frontispiece*

FACING PAGE

Statue of Dante in the Ufizzi, Florence 6
Arena at Verona 20
Gate of Bosari, Verona (1600 years old) 42
The Duomo, Florence 70
Porto Romano, Florence 88
Turin 114
Florence, Old and New: Old Gate and Triumphal Arch 210
The Campanile 220
Sculpture from Campanile Representing Agriculture . 224
Coronation of the Virgin, by Fra Angelico 240
Coronation of the Virgin, by Fra Lippo Lippi . . 248
Portrait of Andrea del Sarto, by Himself 262
The Annunciation, by Andrea del Sarto 268
Piazza del Popolo, Rome 326
Church of San Lorenzo, Rome 342
Statue of Duke Ferdinand, Florence 364
Venice 368
Saint Mark's, Venice. Before the Fall of the Tower 372
Interior of St. Mark's, Venice 376
The Rialto — "Shylock's Bridge," at Venice . . . 380

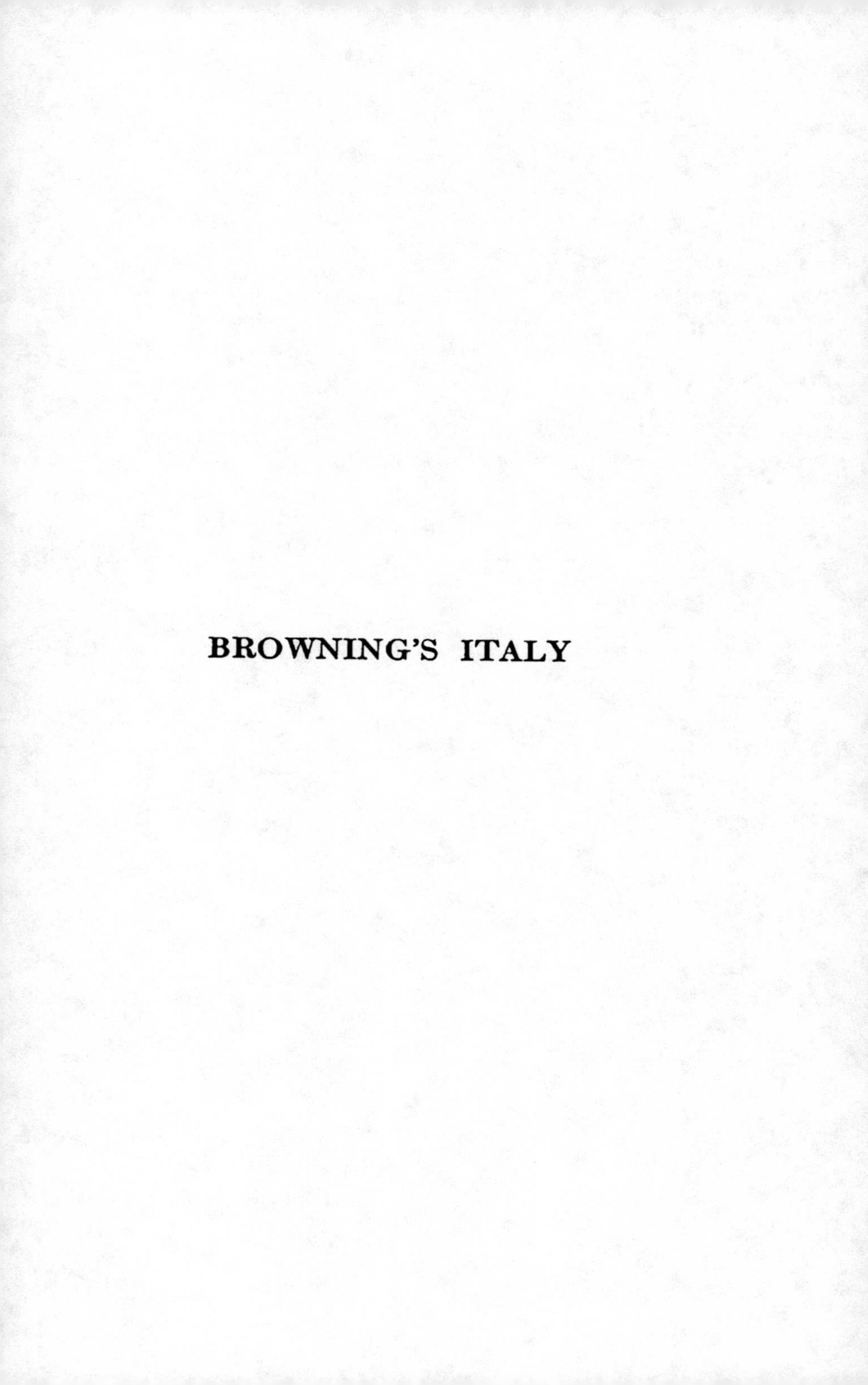

BROWNING'S ITALY

BROWNING'S ITALY

I

THE DAWN OF THE RENAISSANCE

"Love's undoing
Taught me the worth of love in man's estate,
And what proportion love should hold with power
In his right constitution: love preceding
Power, and with much power, always much more love."
— *Paracelsus.*

IN the Italy of History and Biography the name of Sordello, the Italian troubadour, is hardly known; but in the Italy of Browning he is one of the most conspicuous figures, and stands for the first faint streaks of daybreak of that great movement in art and literature known as the Italian Renaissance. He is celebrated by Browning as the forerunner of Dante, whose full dawn splendor would have blotted out this earlier, lesser light completely had it not been that the great poet himself mentions the lesser one several times in his Divine Comedy and elsewhere, with enthusiasm.

Though there is no mention of Sordello in ordinary histories, many conflicting accounts exist of him in early Italian archives, and many of the commentators of Dante have had their say about him, so that to any one burying himself in Sordello literature this poet looms up large in the perspective of his time — so large, in fact, that Justin H. Smith writes of him in "The Troubadours at Home":

"Nothing in the life or the times of Sordello was so extraordinary as the trail of glory that perpetuated his fame, and we must end as we began by exclaiming: What an extraordinary destiny!"

The real Sordello — that is, as far as he is discoverable from the conflicting accounts — was one of many Italian troubadours who flourished in the twelfth and thirteenth centuries. He was born in Goito, a quiet little town, nine or ten miles from Mantua, on the right bank of the Mincio. This town had strong walls and a castle, and here, as in Browning's poem, the young Sordello spent his early years. It is not long, however, ere he comes before the eyes of men — not as the hyper-sensitive poet, with complicated psychological makeup, which Browning depicts, but as a brawler in taverns. From this he goes on to an elopement with Cunizza, the wife of Count Richard, under peculiar circumstances. Sordello had attached himself to the Court of Richard, which was held both in Mantua and Verona, and soon became the close friend of this liberal and cultured Count. But Ecelin, at first a friend of Richard's, — the two having married sisters, — later desired to injure his brother-in-law, and so arranged with Sordello that he should run away with Richard's wife. Later we see him carrying off a lady without the knowledge of her family and marrying her. Thereupon the lady's family, the Strassos, joined with the partisans of Count Richard and waged such persistent warfare against him that he found it necessary to protect himself with a large troop.

Then we hear of him journeying through Italy and France, Spain and Portugal, preaching the doctrine of pleasure wherever he goes, and evidently following his own preachments if we may trust accounts. Drifting to Provence again, after a stay at Rodez, he attaches himself to Charles of Anjou, and becomes prominent in public affairs. When Charles invaded Italy, to seize the crown of Naples and Sicily, Sordello assisted him and received as his reward no less than five castles. Toward the last of his life he falls into pleasant relations with the Pope, and turns his attention from love-poems to a long poem of a didactic nature in which he tells young nobles how to win God and the world. Justin H. Smith rather fiercely describes him as a "bold, unprincipled, licentious, and unflinchingly practical adventurer," who yet left a remarkable impress upon his own age and the ages to come. He sums up his career with graphic force as a "man who won his fame by singing in a foreign tongue upon a foreign soil, who was enriched by fighting against Italy for a Gallic oppressor, and who in spite of this is mentioned by Dante as the ideal patriot, the embodiment of Italian aspirations. This error so thoroughly planted throve on the ignorance of Dante's commentators, and still more upon the inventive ability of Aliprandi; and eventually Eméric David thought that he found three distinct men in the inflated volumes of his legend."

So much for the real Sordello! Browning's imagination was evidently fired by Dante's enthusiasm, and in creating his character of Sordello the poet seized upon any hints in the accounts that best fitted into his conception of the sort of person the forerunner of Dante should be, taking his cue from Dante's reference to Sordello in the sixth book of the "Purgatorio," and from a prose writing, "De Vulgari Eloquentia." The passage in the "Purgatorio" is as follows:

"'But yonder there behold! a soul that stationed
All, all alone is looking hitherward;
It will point out to us the quickest way.'
We came up onto it; O Lombard soul,
How lofty and disdainful thou didst bear thee,
And grand and slow in moving of thine eyes.

"Nothing whatever did it say to us,
But let us go our way, eyeing us only
After the manner of a couchant lion;
Still near to it Virgilius drew, entreating
That it would point us out the best ascent;
And it replied not unto his demand,
But of our native land and of our life
It questioned us; and the sweet Guide began:
'Mantua,'— and the shade, all in itself recluse,
Rose tow'rds him from the place where first it was,
Saying: 'O Mantuan, I am Sordello
Of thine own land!' and one embraced the other.

"That noble soul was so impatient, only
At the sweet sound of his own native land,
To make its citizen glad welcome there."

In the "De Vulgari Eloquentia," Dante declares that Sordello excelled in all kinds of composition and that he helped to form the Tuscan tongue by some happy attempts which he made in the dialects of Cremona,

Brescia, and Verona — cities not far removed from Mantua.

From such meager material as this Browning evolves a being who comprises in his own soul all the complex possibilities of the coming quickening of the human mind and spirit which was so remarkable a feature of the intellectual and artistic life of the fourteenth, fifteenth and sixteenth centuries and which, taking its rise in Italy, made Italy the beacon light for the rest of Europe.

Dante's feeling for Sordello is intensified tenfold in the modern poet's attitude, who thus shows forth the relation of Sordello to Dante, as he conceives it and as he develops it in his poem.

"For he — for he,
Gate-vein of this hearts' blood of Lombardy,
(If I should falter now) — for he is thine!
Sordello, thy forerunner, Florentine!
A herald-star I know thou didst absorb
Relentless into the consummate orb
That scared it from its right to roll along
A sempiternal path with dance and song
Fulfilling its allotted period,
Serenest of the progeny of God —
Who yet resigns it not! His darling stoops
With no quenched lights, desponds with no blank troops
Of disenfranchised brilliances, for, blent
Utterly with thee, its shy element
Like thine upburneth prosperous and clear.

Statue of Dante in the Ufizzi, Florence.

Still, what if I approach the august sphere
Named now with only one name, disentwine
That under-current soft and argentine
From its fierce mate in the majestic mass
Leavened as the sea whose fire was mixt with glass
In John's transcendent vision, — launch once more
That lustre? Dante, pacer of the shore
Where glutted hell disgorgeth filthiest gloom,
Unbitten by its whirring sulphur-spume —
Or whence the grieved and obscure waters slope
Into a darkness quieted by hope;
Plucker of amaranths grown beneath God's eye
In gracious twilights where his chosen lie, —
I would do this! If I should falter now!"

The Sordello of Browning has the latent power to be a creator in poetry and a leader in the cause of patriotism, but so many conflicting forces contend for mastery within him that his life is spent mostly in unraveling the problems of his soul. The tangled strands of Sordello's psychology, as Browning has made him, have been the despair of many readers and the joy of the few who have had the patience to untangle the strands and receive the reward of a full revelation of the soul-struggles of this sensitive, vacillating and tortured being. For both classes of readers he has thus attained an immortality more lasting than any bestowed upon him by Aliprandi, or other verbose Chroniclers.

To add to the complexities of the poem, Sordello has been placed by Browning in the historical setting of a period distinguished for its chaotic political conditions. Guelf and Ghibelline are names with which we become familiar at school, but they seldom are more than names, and when we pick up a poem wherein these names and the political struggles they stand for are talked of with the familiarity with which we might discuss the last dog show, the effect is bewildering indeed.

Yet, in spite of all this, there are clear, sharp-cut pictures scattered throughout the poem, and one may gain through the poet's eyes many a vivid glimpse of the life and social conditions of thirteenth century Italy.

The birthplace of Sordello is introduced to us in the following beautiful description:

"In Mantua territory half is slough,
Half pine-tree forest; maples, scarlet oaks
Breed o'er the river-beds; even Mincio chokes
With sand the summer through: but 'tis morass
In winter up to Mantua walls. There was,
Some thirty years before this evening's coil,
One spot reclaimed from the surrounding spoil,
Goito; just a castle built amid
A few low mountains; firs and larches hid
Their main defiles, and rings of vineyard bound

The rest. Some captured creature in a pound,
Whose artless wonder quite precludes distress,
Secure beside in its own loveliness,
So peered with airy head, below, above,
The castle at its toils, the lapwings love
To glean among at grape-time."

The poet then proceeds to the inside of the castle where he represents Sordello as having passed his boyhood.

"Pass within.
A maze of corridors contrived for sin,
Dusk winding-stairs, dim galleries got past,
You gain the inmost chambers, gain at last
A maple-panelled room; that haze which seems
Floating about the panel, if there gleams
A sunbeam over it, will turn to gold
And in light-graven characters unfold
The Arab's wisdom everywhere; what shade
Marred them a moment, those slim pillars made,
Cut like a company of palms to prop
The roof, each kissing top entwined with top,
Leaning together; in the carver's mind
Some knot of bacchanals, flushed cheek combined
With straining forehead, shoulders purpled, hair
Diffused between, who in a goat-skin bear
A vintage; graceful sister-palms! But quick
To the main wonder, now. A vault, see; thick
Black shade about the ceiling, though fine slits
Across the buttress suffer light by fits
Upon a marvel in the midst. Nay, stoop —
A dullish gray-streaked cumbrous font, a group
Round it, — each side of it, where'er one sees, —

Upholds it; shrinking Caryatides
Of just-tinged marble like Eve's lilied flesh
Beneath her maker's finger when the fresh
First pulse of life shot brightening the snow.
The font's edge burthens every shoulder, so
They muse upon the ground, eyelids half closed;
Some, with meek arms behind their backs disposed,
Some, crossed above their bosoms, some, to veil
Their eyes, some, propping chin and cheek so pale,
Some, hanging slack an utter helpless length
Dead as a buried vestal whose whole strength
Goes when the grate above shuts heavily.
So dwell these noiseless girls, patient to see,
Like priestesses because of sin impure
Penanced forever, who resigned endure,
Having that once drunk sweetness to the dregs.
And every eve, Sordello's visit begs
Pardon for them: constant as eve he came
To sit beside each in her turn, the same
As one of them, a certain space: and awe
Made a great indistinctness till he saw
Sunset slant cheerful through the buttress-chinks,
Gold seven times globed; surely our maiden shrinks
And a smile stirs her as if one faint grain
Her load were lightened, one shade less the strain
Obscured her forehead, yet one more bead slipt
From off the rosary whereby the crypt
Keeps count of the contritions of its charge?
Then with a step more light, a heart more large,
He may depart, leave her and every one
To linger out the penance in mute stone."

I am told by an authority in Italian art that such a fountain could not have existed in Italy in Sordello's time since caryatid figures were not introduced from Greece until the fifteenth century. The poet refers to this fountain again later on as a Messina Marble,

"Like those Messina marbles Constance took
Delight in, or Taurello's self conveyed
To Mantua for his mistress, Adelaide, —
A certain font with caryatides
Since cloistered at Goito."

However that may be, their use by Browning as a subtly suggestive force in the education of the mind of the young Sordello is much more effective than if he had taken him through a University course such as he might have had even in those early days.

The rest of his education was derived from nature.

" . . . beyond the glades
On the fir-forest border, and the rim
Of the low range of mountain, was for him
No other world: but this appeared his own
To wander through at pleasure and alone.
The castle, too, seemed empty; far and wide
Might he disport; only the northern side
Lay under a mysterious interdict —
Slight, just enough remembered to restrict
His roaming to the corridors, the vault
Where those font-bearers expiate their fault,
The maple-chamber, and the little nooks
And nests, and breezy parapet that looks

Over the woods to Mantua: there he strolled.
Some foreign women-servants, very old,
Tended and crept about him — all his clue
To the world's business and embroiled ado
Distant a dozen hill-tops at the most."

Passing from the particular individual life described here we may next get a view of Sordello upon his first contact with the social life of the time when, wandering one day beyond his usual range, he comes upon a Court of Love where Palma, the girl he has caught a glimpse of in the castle, is to choose her minstrel. A vision of her draws him on until he chances upon a "startling spectacle."

"Mantua, this time! Under the walls — a crowd
Indeed, real men and women, gay and loud
Round a pavilion. How he stood!"

. . . .

"What next? The curtains see
Dividing! She is there; and presently
He will be there — the proper You, at length —
In your own cherished dress of grace and strength:

. . . .

It was a showy man advanced; but though
A glad cry welcomed him, then every sound
Sank and the crowd disposed themselves around,
— 'This is not he! Sordello felt; while, 'Place
For the best Troubadour of Boniface!'
Hollaed the Jongleurs, — 'Eglamor, whose lay
Concludes his patron's Court of Love to-day!'

. . . .

. . . Has he ceased
And, lo, the people's frank applause half done,
Sordello was beside him, had begun
(Spite of indignant twitchings from his friend
The Trouvere) the true lay with the true end,
Taking the other's names and time and place
For his. On flew the song, a giddy race,
After the flying story; word made leap
Out word, rhyme — rhyme; the lay could barely keep
Pace with the action visibly rushing past:
Both ended. Back fell Naddo more aghast
Than some Egyptian from the harassed bull
That wheeled abrupt and, bellowing, fronted full
His plague, who spied a scarab 'neath the tongue,
And found 'twas Apis' flank his hasty prong
Insulted. But the people — but the cries,
The crowding round, and proffering the prize!
— For he had gained some prize. He seemed to shrink
Into a sleepy cloud, just at whose brink
One sight withheld him. There sat Adelaide,
Silent; but at her knees the very maid
Of the North Chamber, her red lips as rich,
The same pure fleecy hair; one weft of which,
Golden and great, quite touched his cheek as o'er
She leant, speaking some six words and no more.
He answered something, anything; and she
Unbound a scarf and laid it heavily
Upon him, her neck's warmth and all. Again
Moved the arrested magic; in his brain
Noises grew, and a light that turned to glare,
And greater glare, until the intense flare
Engulfed him, shut the whole scene from his sense.
And when he woke 'twas many a furlong thence,
At home; the sun shining his ruddy wont;

The customary birds'-chirp; but his front
Was crowned — was crowned! Her scented scarf around
His neck! Whose gorgeous vesture heaps the ground?
A prize? He turned, and peeringly on him
Brooded the women-faces, kind and dim,
Ready to talk — 'The Jongleurs in a troop
Had brought him back, Naddo, and Squarcialupe
And Tagliafer; how strange! a childhood spent
In taking, well for him, so brave a bent!
Since Eglamor,' they heard, 'was dead with spite,'
And Palma chose him for her minstrel."

In calling this poetical contest in which Sordello engaged a Court of Love, Browning has adopted a term which should properly be applied to a court where difficult questions in the rigid etiquette of chivalric love were decided. Though we read of such Courts in literature recent investigators of the subject declare that no such Courts existed, the first mention of them occurring in a book by Martial of Auvergne three hundred years later than they were said to have flourished.

Justin H. Smith in a note to his "Troubadours at Home," points out that the silence of the troubadours is especially convincing against the alleged Courts, because we often see them feeling the need of such a tribunal and finding themselves compelled to choose their own arbiters. Further, these arbiters were men rather oftener than women, whereas the Courts were supposed to have consisted of women only.

Browning really has in mind the poetical tournaments of the Middle Ages, held at a Court where a presiding lady acted as judge, awarding the laurel crown and other prizes, usually rich raiment, as the poet intimates, to the poet who sang best — all the contestants taking the same theme.

Palma, who figures here, is Browning's substitution for the Cunizza of the biographies. She is the betrothed of Count Richard, but loves Sordello who turns out to be the son of Taurello, head of the Ghibelline party, according to our poet. As we shall see later, she determines to marry Sordello but his death prevents it.

A stirring historical picture is brought before us in this description of a scene in Verona, later in the life of Sordello, where he reaches the turning point in his career.

"Lo, the past is hurled
In twain: up-thrust, out-staggering on the world.
Subsiding into shape, a darkness rears
Its outline, kindles at the core, appears
Verona. 'Tis six hundred years and more
Since an event. The Second Friedrich wore
The purple, and the Third Honorius filled
The holy chair. That autumn eve was stilled:
A last remains of sunset dimly burned

O'er the far forests, like a torch-flame turned
By the wind back upon its bearer's hand
In one long flare of crimson; as a brand,
The woods beneath lay black. A single eye
From all Verona cared for the soft sky.
But, gathering in its ancient market-place,
Talked group with restless group; and not a face
But wrath made livid, for among them were
Death's staunch purveyors, such as have in care
To feast him. Fear had long since taken root
In every breast, and now these crushed its fruit,
The ripe hate, like a wine: to note the way
It worked while each grew drunk! Men grave and gray
Stood, with shut eyelids, rocking to and fro,
Letting the silent luxury trickle slow
About the hollows where a heart should be;
But the young gulped with a delirious glee
Some foretaste of their first debauch in blood
At the fierce news: for, be it understood,
Envoys apprised Verona that her prince,
Count Richard of Saint Boniface, joined since
A year with Azzo, Este's Lord, to thrust
Taurello Salinguerra, prince in trust
With Ecelin Romano, from his seat
Ferrara, — over zealous in the feat
And stumbling on a peril unaware,
Was captive, trammelled in his proper snare,
They phrase it, taken by his own intrigue.
Immediate succor from the Lombard league
Of fifteen cities that affect the Pope,
For Azzo, therefore, and his fellow-hope
Of the Guelf cause, a glory overcast!
Men's faces, late agape, are now aghast.
'Prone is the purple pavis; Este makes

Mirth for the devil where he undertakes
To play the Ecelin; as if it cost
Merely your pushing by to gain a post
Like his! The patron tells ye, once for all,
There be sound reasons that preferment fall
On our beloved.' . . .
'Duke o' the Rood, why not?'

This passage places before us a crisis in the struggles of the Guelfs and the Ghibellines. It will be worth while to pause a moment here to try and gain a clear notion of the historical events that form the background of the poem.

Various origins of the terms Guelf and Ghibelline have been suggested, but the most authentic is probably that sanctioned by Cabot's History of Italy, which traces their derivation to Germany. Here they had been the rallying words of faction for more than half a century before they appeared on Italian soil. The name of Guelf belonged to an illustrious family, several of whom had been dukes of Bavaria in the tenth and eleventh centuries. The heiress of the last of these intermarried with a younger son of the house of Este, a noble family settled near Padua, and the owners of great estates on each bank of the lower Po. The name of Ghibelline is supposed to have been derived from a village in Franconia, whence Conrad the Salic came, the progenitor, through females, of the Suabian emperors. At the election of Lothaire in 1125, the Suabian family were disappointed of what they considered almost an hereditary possession; and at this time a hostility appears to have commenced between them and the house of Guelf, which was nearly related to Lothaire. The elder branch of this house flourished in Italy. When, about the year 1200, the cities of Lombardy wanted some designations by which they could distinguish the two leading parties, and though full of mutual animosity had no general subject of contention, they chose these appellations. Generally speaking, the Guelfs were on the side of the Pope and the Ghibellines on the side of the Emperor.

At the time when the second Frederick wore the purple, and the third Honorius was Pope, the contest between Pope and Emperor was nearing that climax which was to end in the downfall of the temporal power in Italy.

Frederick II was one of the most remarkable figures in Italian history, and though himself doomed to destruction, he as much as Dante was the torch-bearer of the coming intellectual awakening. If Sordello was the forerunner of Dante, Frederick might well have been called the forerunner of the Medicis. The description given of him by Sedgwick in his "Short History of Italy" brings his qualities before us vividly. "Frederick himself is the central figure of the period. In his lifetime he excited love and hate to extravagance and he still excites the enthusiasm of scholars." Dante Gabriel Rossetti places him among the poets in Dante's circle. Sedgwick goes on "His is the most interesting Italian personality between St. Francis and Dante, for though he inherited the Hohenstauffen vigor and energy, he got his chief traits from his Sicilian mother. Poet, lawgiver, soldier, statesman, he was the wonder of the world. Impetuous, terrible, voluptuous, refined, he was a kind of Cæsarian Byron. In most ways he outstripped contemporary thought, in many ways he outstripped contemporary sympathy. He was sceptical of the Athanasian creed, of Communal freedom, and of other things which his Italian countrymen believed devoutly while they were sceptical of the divine right of the Empire, of the blessing of a strong central government, and of other matters which he believed!"

After several years of skirmishing, the

hatred of Frederick II and his policy among the Guelf cities of Lombardy, broke out in a protracted war. Among the Lombardy cities engaged in this warfare the most important to us is the city of Verona. It falls into a group along with Vicenza, Padua, and Treviso — all inclined to Guelf interests. But there was a powerful body of small nobility who had fortified themselves in the hilly country in the neighborhood, and who had never been forced to quit their fortresses or to reside within the walls. These attached themselves to the side of the Emperor. Among those who became important in the civil feuds of that time, the Ecelins were conspicuous, and, as we shall see later, Ezzellino da Romano or Ecelin III was of so ferocious a nature, that even his supporters turned against him. The Ecelin mentioned in this passage was the father of Ecelin III, Alberic and Palma, his wife being the Adelaide of the poem. Ecelin II, called the hillcat, was the representative of the Emperor and head of the Ghibelline party, but in 1223 he divided his lands between his two sons and himself became a monk. Browning represents him at this time as dozing at Oliero,

"with dry lips
Telling upon his perished finger-tips

Arena at Verona.

> How many ancestors are to depose
> Ere he be Satan's Viceroy when the doze
> Deposits him in hell."

Taurello Salinguerra was Ecelin's chief lieutenant, and head of the Ghibelline party at Ferrara. Opposed to these Ghibelline leaders were Azzo VII, Marquis of Este and Ancona, and Count Richard of St. Boniface, Prince of Verona. History explains that the Marquises of Este were by far the most powerful nobles in eastern Lombardy, and about the end of the twelfth century began to be considered the heads of the church party in their neighborhood. They were frequently chosen for the chief magistrate or Podestà, by the cities of Romagna, and in 1208 the people of Ferrara set the fatal example of sacrificing their freedom for tranquillity by electing Azzo VII, Marquis of Este, as their lord or sovereign.

Such was the general state of affairs — all that ordinary history usually goes into, when the event happened that Browning describes in this passage, and for the history of which we may glean a little in Muratori's "Annals," made accessible by W. M. Rossetti's translations. Browning describes the life of Taurello leading up to this event in a passage in Book IV, where he tells how Taurello dwelt at Ferrara, representing, of course, the side of the Emperor. The Estes did not interfere with him until Linguetta Marchesalla, left heiress of her house, was about to be married to Taurello. The Guelfs of Ravenna, afraid that if this marriage was consummated, Ferrara would fall into the hands of Taurello, attacked Ferrara and carried off the bride. Azzo VI was invited to the city, and while Taurello was sent off hunting, entered with the bride Linguetta. Taurello took refuge in the court of Sicily, ruled over at that time by Henry (VI). He married Retrude, of Henry's family, and suddenly returned to Ferrara, powerfully befriended by Ecelin and the Emperor. He built a finè palace for his bride. But Azzo and Boniface, afraid of trouble, took the initiative, and attacked Taurello and Ecelin when conferring together at Vicenza, where Ecelin was Podestà. Here Retrude was mortally wounded and her child supposed to be lost; but the Guelfs were at last repulsed and Taurello became only second in control to Ecelin.

At the time of the episode described in the passage quoted from the poem, Azzo VII had succeeded to the Azzo who stole the young Taurello's bride. He, according to

Muratori, resided frequently in Ferrara, as being head of the Guelf faction and possessing here great plenty of property and vassals, — one of whom was Salinguerra, himself, head of the Ghibellines. It was ill brooked by his adherents that Salinguerra and his partisans should enjoy the best offices of the Republic. Consequently, in the month of August (1221), taking up arms they assailed the party of Salinguerra, and after a severe fight they forced him to abandon the city. Or, as Muratori adds, "This Guelf success led to a treaty which resulted in an agreement reinstating the Guelfs." The next year (according to Browning, next week) Salinguerra returned and Azzo with his Guelfic party had to quit the city. To recover from this affront the Marquis got together an army collected at Rovigo and from his other states, and from Lombardy and the march of Verona, and went to pitch his camp under Ferrara. This was in 1222. In 1224 there was a renewed attack with an army, collected "from his own states and from his friends in Mantua, Padua, and Verona, bent upon vengeance." The siege was ended by the capture of Boniface as described in the poem, and of which Muratori gives this account:

"The astute Salinguerra exerted himself so much by affectionate letters and embassies that he induced Count Richard of San Bonifazio, with a certain number of horsemen, to enter Ferrara under the pretext of concluding a friendly pact. But, on entering, he was at once made prisoner with all his company; and therefore the Marquis of Este, disappointed, retired from the siege."

In the poem this bit of history is further enlarged upon by an envoy.

"Taurello," quoth an envoy, "as in wane
Dwelt at Ferrara. Like an osprey fain
To fly but forced the earth his couch to make
Far inland, till his friend the tempest wake,
Waits he the Kaiser's coming; and as yet
That fast friend sleeps, and he too sleeps: but let
Only the billow freshen, and he snuffs
The aroused hurricane ere it enroughs
The sea it means to cross because of him.
Sinketh the breeze? His hope-sick eye grows dim;
Creep closer on the creature! Every day
Strengthens the Pontiff; Ecelin, they say,
Dozes now at Oliero, with dry lips
Telling upon his perished finger-tips
How many ancestors are to depose
Ere he be Satan's Viceroy when the doze
Deposits him in hell. So, Guelfs rebuilt
Their houses; not a drop of blood was spilt
When Cino Bocchimpane chanced to meet
Buccio Virtù — God's wafer, and the street

Is narrow! Tutti Santi, think, a-swarm
With Ghibellins, and yet he took no harm!
This could not last. Off Salinguerra went
To Padua, Podestà, 'with pure intent,'
Said he, 'my presence, judged the single bar
To permanent tranquillity, may jar
No longer' — so! his back is fairly turned!
The pair of goodly palaces are burned,
The gardens ravaged, and our Guelfs laugh, drunk
A week with joy. The next, their laughter sunk
In sobs of blood, for they found, some strange way,
Old Salinguerra back again — I say,
Old Salinguerra in the town once more
Uprooting, overturning, flame before,
Blood fetlock-high beneath him. Azzo fled;
Who 'scaped the carnage followed; then the dead
Were pushed aside from Salinguerra's throne,
He ruled once more Ferrara, all alone,
Till Azzo, stunned awhile, revived, would pounce
Coupled with Boniface, like lynx and ounce
On the gorged bird. The burghers ground their teeth
To see troop after troop encamp beneath
I' the standing corn thick o'er the scanty patch
It took so many patient months to snatch
Out of the marsh; while just within their walls
Men fed on men. At length Taurello calls
A parley; 'let the Count wind up the war!
Richard, light-hearted as a plunging star,
Agrees to enter for the kindest ends
Ferrara, flanked with fifty chosen friends,
No horse-boy more, for fear your timid sort
Should fly Ferrara at the bare report.
Quietly through the town they rode, jog-jog;
'Ten, twenty, thirty, — curse the catalogue

Of burnt Guelf houses! Strange, Taurello shows
Not the least sign of life' — whereat arose
A general growl: 'How? With his victors by?
I and my Veronese? My troops and I?
Receive us, was your word?' So jogged they on,
Nor laughed their host too openly: once gone
Into the trap!" —

The story of the especial relations of Frederick II to the Pope forms an interesting chapter in the great struggle of Pope and Emperor, and is thus touched upon by Browning:

"When the new Hohenstauffen dropped the mask,
Flung John of Brienne's favor from his casque,
Forswore crusading, had no mind to leave
Saint Peter's proxy leisure to retrieve
Losses to Otho and to Barbaross,
Or make the Alps less easy to recross,
And, thus confirming Pope Honorius' fear,
Was excommunicate that very year.
'The triple-bearded Teuton come to life!'
Groaned the Great League; and, arming for the strife,
Wide Lombardy, on tiptoe to begin,
Took up, as it were Guelf or Ghibellin,
Its cry: what cry?
'The Emperor to come!'"

It has been hinted that the popes, though honestly desirous of reconquering Jerusalem, yet also had a sneaking feeling that the best way to keep Frederick out of mischief in

Italy would be to keep him occupied in the holy land. Frederick made all sorts of promises, that he would go on a crusade, and that he would keep the crowns of Germany and the Two Sicilies separate. He did not go on a crusade, and he secured the two crowns for himself and his heir. Upon his renewed promise that he would go on a crusade, Pope Honorius crowned him Emperor in 1220. Three years passed and Frederick with his crowns safely on his head still neglected his trip to Jerusalem. When Gregory IX succeeded he was exceedingly angry at the Emperor's procrastination, and Frederick at last actually set forth, under difficult conditions, too, for a pestilence had killed many of the soldiers, but in a few days it was learned that he had put about and disembarked in Italy.

Gregory's wrath now broke forth in an encyclical letter, which he sent off to various bishops in Frederick's dominions. It dwelt at length upon the Papal side of the matter and ended up with "Yet, lest like dumb dogs who cannot bark, We should seem to defer to man against God and take no vengeance upon him, the Emperor Frederick who has wrought such ruin on God's people, We, though unwilling, do publicly pronounce him excommunicated, and command that he be by all completely shunned, and that you and other prelates who shall hear of this, publicly publish his excommunications. And, if his contumacy shall demand, more grave proceeding shall be taken." From Sicily to Scotland this ban was published. Frederick, nothing daunted, wrote to the kings of Europe his side of the matter, and expressing the opinion that the Roman Church was so consumed with avarice and greed that, not satisfied with her own Church property, she was not ashamed to disinherit emperors, kings, and princes, and make them tributary.

Peace was, however, outwardly maintained, the Emperor went on a crusade and succeeded so well that he had himself crowned King of Jerusalem.

The Ecclesiastics were becoming terribly worried over his desire to put the temporal power above the spiritual power, especially when he was known to hob-nob so intimately with the Saracens.

Finally, the Lombard cities formed a league, and revolted. Frederick marched against them and won a victory in 1237. All the Guelfs in Italy now arose against him. The Pope did his share with his thunders of excommunication, and at a Council held at

Lyons deprived Frederick of his imperial crown. Then an anti-emperor was set up. He was defeated later at Padua, and his son Enzio was captured and spent twenty-three years in prison, there dying. Finally, in 1250, Frederick himself died, to the joy of Papal Italy.

In Count Richard's Palace at Verona, Sordello and Palma are together the night of Richard's capture. Another vivid picture gives this imaginary situation, for which, as the Poet himself says, the historical pictures are merely the setting.

"The same night wears. Verona's rule of yore
Was vested in a certain Twenty-four;
And while within his palace these debate
Concerning Richard and Ferrara's fate,
Glide we by clapping doors, with sudden glare
Of cressets vented on the dark, nor care
For aught that's seen or heard until we shut
The smother in, the lights, all noises but
The carroch's booming: safe at last! Why strange
Such a recess should lurk behind a range
Of banquet-rooms? Your finger — thus — you push
A spring, and the wall opens, would you rush
Upon the banqueters, select your prey,
Waiting (the slaughter-weapons in the way
Strewing this very bench) with sharpened ear
A preconcerted signal to appear;
Or if you simply crouch with beating heart,
Bearing in some voluptuous pageant part

To startle them. Nor mutes nor masquers now;
Nor any . . . does that one man sleep whose brow
The dingy lamp-flame sinks and rises o'er?
What woman stood beside him? not the more
Is he unfastened from the earnest eyes
Because that arras fell between! Her wise
And lulling words are yet about the room,
Her presence wholly poured upon the gloom
Down even to her vesture's creeping stir.
And so reclines he, saturate with her,
Until an outcry from the square beneath
Pierces the charm: he springs up, glad to breathe,
Above the cunning element, and shakes
The stupor off as (look you) morning breaks
On the gay dress, and, near concealed by it,
The lean frame like a half-burnt taper, lit
Erst at some marriage-feast, then laid away
Till the Armenian bridegroom's dying day,
In his wool wedding-robe."

Although this scene is near the end of Sordello's life, it is presented in the first book of the poem, after which Browning takes us back to the childhood of Sordello, telling of the events of his life and of the progress of his soul until the scene at first described is again reached. We take from the Camberwell edition of Robert Browning the following summary of the steps in his development. The first step is when he awakes from the dream-life, described in the first book, spent in the old castle and woods of Goito, during which he exerted his powers of imagination within himself for his private pleasure. He lives here as a child, not knowing who he is, in the castle belonging to the Ecelins, where Adelaide, wife of Ecelin II is living, and also Palma, the daughter of Ecelin II and Agnes Este. The second step follows when suddenly brought into contact with the outside world at Palma's Court of Love, there he wins the crown from the troubadour, Eglamore, is made Palma's minstrel; and thereafter exerting his powers over his fellows as a minstrel in Mantua, he finally finds that his skill is insufficient to keep himself supreme while he is swaying others for his own pleasure. He cannot make them recognize in him the power behind his song. The attempt to assert himself through his poetry finally brings himself and his art into utter conflict. He loves Palma, but she is the betrothed of Count Richard, as Taurello learns much to his surprise from Ecelin. Adelaide, having fallen sick, Old Ecelin lost heart, and fell deeper into the clutches of the Church. He writes Salinguerra of the betrothal of his sons Ecelin III and Alberic, to Beatrix, Este's sister, and to Richard's Giglia, and of Palma as Richard's prospective bride; these alliances joining the Guelf and Ghibelline parties. This, with the news of Adelaide's death reached Taurello as he was about to sail with the Emperor to the Crusades. At once he set out, but reached Ecelin's side only to find out that the marriages of the sons had been consummated, that Ecelin was himself absorbed in making his peace before dying, and that Palma only was left him at Goito. Taurello at once goes to Mantua, where he had lived for a time with Retrude, and where his family had its origin, and the Mantuans prepared to greet him with ceremony. Sordello is to take the opportunity to win laurels for himself as Minstrel, but his power deserts him, and excuses are made to Taurello for his non-appearance. He also finds out at this time that he is the son of a poor archer, Elcorte, who had perished in the attack upon Ecelin, in which he had saved Adelaide and the young Ecelin, leaving his son Sordello to be gratefully reared by his chief's family in Adelaide's private retreat, Goito. This story of Sordello's birth was found by Mrs. Caroline H. Dall, among old chronicles in the Canadian Parliament library, which relate that Sordello was "born in the Mantuan territory, of a poor knight named Elcorte." He began to write songs early and was attached to the Court of St.

Boniface, and the lover of his wife eloping with her!

The third step in his development is described in Book III. He seeks loneliness with nature at Goito once more, and determines to experience life itself now, instead of living merely for art's sake. Then he is summoned by Palma to Verona. The next day at evening he reaches Verona — the moment and scene sketched at the beginning of the poem have arrived. He resolves, under her inspiration to make his art tributary to the life of others instead of making them, through his art, tributary to himself.

The fourth step described in Book IV follows as a result of his new contact, at Ferrara, with two unreconciled social influences: the career of power exemplified in Salinguerra, and the suffering life of the people. Having determined to devote himself to uplifting the masses, it devolves upon him to find an efficient way to serve them. Concluding that the Guelf and Ghibelline policy are equally hard upon them, the only solution of the question he finds is the suggestion Rome gives of a universal and continuing city sheltering all mankind.

Pursuing this clue toward a way of serving the people, in Book V he seeks to act upon it by reconciling the two opposite influences he has just recognized, attempting to use his poetic gift to persuade Salinguerra to champion the Guelf cause, since that serves Rome's. In doing this, Salinguerra's sudden conferring of the Emperor's badge upon Sordello, and Palma's revelation that he is Salinguerra's son, brings upon himself the burden of the decision he is urging upon the old soldier. Sordello's struggle over the decision described in Book VI results, finally, in a conquest over his own personal self-seeking, and he dies stamping the imperial badge beneath his foot, but in a failure to seize the one chance of centuries, to pacify the war of Barons against People, to reconcile in his own person the conflicting influences of individual and social welfare.

So, it will be seen, Browning brings together the artistic and political issues of the time. Sordello is brought into close personal contact with the Ghibelline cause by being made the lost son of Taurello and Retrude. He represents Adelaide, alone, as knowing of this, and keeping Sordello's birth secret because she was afraid of his superiority to her own son. Finding himself by birth a Ghibelline, by sympathy a Guelf, and with the opportunity to win preferment in the Emperor's cause, he triumphs spiritually over the temptation.

In the sketch of the real Sordello, it developed that he joined the forces of Charles of Anjou and helped him secure the throne of the Two Sicilies. What, at first sight, appears so unpatriotic has a different color if we look a little more closely into the history of the time, and really brings him more into touch with Sordello as Browning has represented him.

Of the two sons of Ecelin II, between whom he had divided his possessions, Ezzelino was destined to play the most important part in the struggles between Pope and Emperor. After Richard had been re-instated in his city of Verona, as Muratori says, "only a few months passed ere many nobles and leading men of his faction in that city, corrupted by Salinguerra's money, united with the Montecchi, Ghibellines, and expelled him. Then it was that Ezzelino da Romana, who in closest league with Salinguerra bore a part in these negotiations, hurried to Verona to reenforce the Montecchi, and began to exercise some little authority in the city." Soon this man was to become what Burckhard describes as a usurper of the most peculiar kind. "He stands as the representative of no system of government or administration, for all his activity was wasted in struggles for supremacy in the eastern part of upper Italy; but as a political type he was a figure of no less importance for the future than his imperial protector Frederick. The conquests and usurpations which had hitherto taken place in the Middle Ages rested on real or pretended inheritance and other such claims, or else were effected against unbelievers and excommunicated persons. Here for the first time the attempt was openly made to found a throne by wholesale murder and endless barbarities, by the adoption, in short, of any means with a view to nothing but the end pursued. None of his successors, not even Cæsar Borgia, rivaled the colossal guilt of Ezzelino; but the example once set was not forgotten, and his fall led to no return of justice among the nations, and served as no warning to future transgressors. Frederick and Ezzelino were, and remain for Italy, the great political phenomena of the thirteenth century."

Against this outrageous tyrant, Pope Alexander IV preached a crusade. It was so much the custom at that time for rulers to indulge in any tyrannies they wished to perpetrate, that advances against him could only be made on political grounds.

Alexander stirred up the Guelfic cities to attack him. He was a good soldier and had Ghibelline alliances, and he defended himself bravely. But while he was ravaging the territory of a Guelfic neighbor, the enemy took Padua. Great was the horror when upon opening the dungeon where his maimed and starving prisoners were kept, they came upon a crowd of helpless children, which had been blinded by this cruel fiend. Even his Ghibelline allies deserted him, and joining the Guelfs turned their arms against him, and finally, brought to bay, he killed himself.

Such a fiend as this did not help the cause of the Empire, and after the death of Frederick, already recorded, the Hohenstauffens went quickly to their ruin. Manfred, an illegitimate son of Frederick's, first acting as regent for Conradin, the lawful heir, then tried to establish himself in the Two Sicilies as King. The Popes, however, determined to destroy this last of the "Vipers' brood" as they called the Hohenstauffens, so they invited the French prince, Charles of Anjou, to come and depose Manfred. A crusade against Manfred was proclaimed, and with an army furnished by the Pope,

Charles defeated and killed him. Charles was enthusiastically welcomed by Guelfic Italy, and was given the crown of the Two Sicilies. Conradin, a lad only sixteen years old came down in the hope of regaining his kingdom, but he, too, was defeated, taken prisoner, and after a mock trial for treason put to death. Thus the Popes prevented the union of the Two Sicilies with the Empire.

From this it will be seen that the really patriotic side, the side most allied to the cause of the people was the side against the Emperor; and just as Browning's Sordello saw that the Guelfs furnished a better implement with which to work for the people than the Emperor's faction, so may the real Sordello have regarded Charles of Anjou as a weapon against tyranny, as he was certainly regarded by the Guelfs, and this no doubt is the reason why Dante lauded him as a patriot.

Historical glimpses of the sketches just given, enlivened by the poet's imagination, may be gained from the following passages:

"The tale amounts
To this: when at Vicenza both her counts
Banished the Vivaresi kith and kin,
Those Maltraversi hung on Ecelin,
Reviled him as he followed; he for spite
Must fire their quarter, though that self-same night

Among the flames young Ecelin was born
Of Adelaide, there too, and barely torn
From the roused populace hard on the rear,
By a poor archer when his chieftain's fear
Grew high; into the thick Elcorte leapt,
Saved her, and died; no creature left except
His child to thank. And when the full escape
Was known — how men impaled from chine to nape
Unlucky Prata, all to pieces spurned
Bishop Pistore's concubines, and burned
Taurello's entire household, flesh and fell,
Missing the sweeter prey — such courage well
Might claim reward. The orphan, ever since,
Sordello, had been nurtured by his prince
Within a blind retreat.

. . . .

"Meanwhile the world rejoiced ('tis time explain)
Because a sudden sickness set it free
From Adelaide. Missing the mother-bee,
Her mountain-hive Romano swarmed; at once
A rustle-forth of daughters and of sons
Blackened the valley. 'I am sick too, old,
Half-crazed I think; what good's the Kaiser's gold
To such an one? God help me! for I catch
My children's greedy sparkling eyes at watch —
"He bears that double breastplate on," they say,
"So many minutes less than yesterday!"
Beside, Monk Hilary is on his knees
Now, sworn to kneel and pray till God shall please
Exact a punishment for many things
You know, and some you never knew; which brings
To memory, Azzo's sister Beatrix
And Richard's Giglia are my Alberic's
And Ecelin's betrothed; the Count himself

Must get my Palma: Ghibellin and Guelf
Mean to embrace each other.' So began
Romano's missive to his fighting man
Taurello — on the Tuscan's death, away -
With Friedrich sworn to sail from Naples' bay
Next month for Syria. Never thunder-clap
Out of Vesuvius' throat, like this mishap
Startled him. 'That accursed Vicenza! I
Absent, and she selects this time to die!
Ho, fellows, for Vicenza!' Half a score
Of horses ridden dead, he stood before
Romano in his reeking spurs: too late —
'Boniface urged me, Este could not wait,'
The chieftain stammered; 'let me die in peace —
Forget me! Was it I who craved increase
Of rule? Do you and Friedrich plot your worst
Against the Father: as you found me first
So leave me now. Forgive me! Palma, sure,
Is at Goito still. Retain that lure —
Only be pacified!'
The country rung
With such a piece of news: on every tongue,
How Ecelin's great servant, congeed off,
Had done a long day's service, so, might doff
The green and yellow, and recover breath
At Mantua, whither, — since Retrude's death,
(The girlish slip of a Sicilian bride
From Otho's house, he carried to reside
At Mantua till the Ferrarese should pile
A structure worthy her imperial style,
The gardens raise, the statues there enshrine,
She never lived to see) — although his line
Was ancient in her archives and she took
A pride in him, that city, nor forsook

Her child when he forsook himself and spent
A prowess on Romano surely meant
For his own growth — whither he ne'er resorts
If wholly satisfied (to trust reports)
With Ecelin. So, forward in a trice
Were shows to greet him. 'Take a friend's advice,'
Quoth Naddo, to Sordello 'nor be rash
Because your rivals (nothing can abash
Some folks) demur that we pronounced you best
To sound the great man's welcome; 'tis a test,
Remember!'

. . . .

"One more day,
One eve — appears Verona! Many a group,
(You mind) instructed of the osprey's swoop
On lynx and ounce, was gathering — Christendom
Sure to receive, whate'er the end was, from
The evening's purpose cheer or detriment,
Since Friedrich only waited some event
Like this, of Ghibellins establishing
Themselves within Ferrara, ere, as King
Of Lombardy, he'd glad descend there, wage
Old warfare with the Pontiff, disengage
His barons from the burghers, and restore
The rule of Charlemagne, broken of yore
By Hildebrand.

I' the palace, each by each,
Sordello sat and Palma; little speech
At first in that dim closet, face with face
(Despite the tumult in the market-place)
Exchanging quick low laughters: now would rush
Word upon word to meet a sudden flush,
A look left off, a shifting lips' surmise —
But for the most part their two histories

Ran best through the locked fingers and linked arms.
And so the night flew on with its alarms
Till in burst one of Palma's retinue;
'Now, Lady!' gasped he. Then arose the two
And leaned into Verona's air, dead-still.
A balcony lay black beneath until
Out, 'mid a gush of torchfire, gray-haired men
Came on it and harangued the people: then
Sea-like that people surging to and fro
Shouted, 'Hale forth the carroch — trumpets, ho,
A flourish! Run it in the ancient grooves!
Back from the bell! Hammer — that whom behooves
May hear the League is up! Peal — learn who list,
Verona means not first of towns break tryst
To-morrow with the League!'
                                        Enough. Now turn —
Over the eastern cypresses: discern!
Is any beacon set a-glimmer?
                                        Rang
The air with shouts that overpowered the clang
Of the incessant carroch, even: 'Haste —
The candle 's at the gateway! ere it waste,
Each soldier stand beside it, armed to march
With Tiso Sampier through the eastern arch!'
Ferrara's succored, Palma!"

Here is a fine picture of Ferrara during the struggle in which Richard had been seized, and following it a little later, a description of Taurello's palace, the one he had built for Retrude, and in which Richard is imprisoned. The description shows Browning in one of his most poetic moods.

Gate of Bosari, Verona. (1600 years old.)

"Meantime Ferrara lay in rueful case;
The lady-city, for whose sole embrace
Her pair of suitors struggled, felt their arms
A brawny mischief to the fragile charms
They tugged for — one discovering that to twist
Her tresses twice or thrice about his wrist
Secured a point of vantage — one, how best
He 'd parry that by planting in her breast
His elbow spike — each party too intent
For noticing, howe'er the battle went,
The conqueror would but have a corpse to kiss.
'May Boniface be duly damned for this!'
— Howled some old Ghibellin, as up he turned,
From the wet heap of rubbish where they burned
His house, a little skull with dazzling teeth:
'A boon, sweet Christ — let Salinguerra seethe
In hell forever, Christ, and let myself
Be there to laugh at him!' — moaned some young Guelf
Stumbling upon a shrivelled hand nailed fast
To the charred lintel of the doorway, last
His father stood within to bid him speed.
The thoroughfares were overrun with weed
— Docks, quitchgrass, loathly mallows no man plants.
The stranger, none of its inhabitants
Crept out of doors to taste fresh air again,
And ask the purpose of a splendid train
Admitted on a morning; every town
Of the East League was come by envoy down
To treat for Richard's ransom: here you saw
The Vicentine, here snowy oxen draw
The Paduan carroch, its vermilion cross
On its white field. A-tiptoe o'er the fosse
Looked Legate Montelungo wistfully
After the flock of steeples he might spy

In Este's time, gone (doubts he) long ago
To mend the ramparts: sure the laggards know
The Pope's as good as here! They paced the streets
More soberly. At last, 'Taurello greets
The League,' announced a pursuivant, — 'will match
Its courtesy, and labors to dispatch
At earliest Tito, Friedrich's Pretor, sent
On pressing matters from his post at Trent,
With Mainard Count of Tyrol, — simply waits
Their going to receive the delegates.'"

. . . .

"Our dropping Autumn morning clears apace,
And poor Ferrara puts a softened face
On her misfortunes. Let us scale this tall
Huge foursquare line of red brick garden-wall
Bastioned within by trees of every sort
On three sides, slender, spreading, long and short;
Each grew as it contrived, the poplar ramped,
The fig-tree reared itself, — but stark and cramped,
Made fools of, like tamed lions: whence, on the edge,
Running 'twixt trunk and trunk to smooth one ledge
Of shade, were shrubs inserted, warp and woof,
Which smothered up that variance. Scale the roof
Of solid tops, and o'er the slope you slide
Down to a grassy space level and wide,
Here and there dotted with a tree, but trees
Of rarer leaf, each foreigner at ease,
Set by itself: and in the centre spreads,
Borne upon three uneasy leopards' heads,
A laver, broad and shallow, one bright spirt
Of water bubbles in. The walls begirt
With trees leave off on either hand; pursue
Your path along a wondrous avenue
Those walls abut on, heaped of gleamy stone,

With aloes leering everywhere, gray-grown
From many a Moorish summer: how they wind
Out of the fissures! likelier to bind
The building than those rusted cramps which drop
Already in the eating sunshine. Stop,
You fleeting shapes above there! Ah, the pride
Or else despair of the whole country-side!
A range of statues, swarming o'er with wasps,
God, goddess, woman, man, the Greek rough-rasps
In crumbling Naples marble — meant to look
Like those Messina marbles Constance took
Delight in, or Taurello's self conveyed
To Mantua for his mistress, Adelaide,
A certain font with caryatides
Since cloistered at Goito; only, these
Are up and doing, not abashed, a troop
Able to right themselves — who see you, stoop
Their arms o' the instant after you! Unplucked
By this or that, you pass; for they conduct
To terrace raised on terrace, and, between,
Creatures of brighter mould and braver mien
Than any yet, the choicest of the Isle
No doubt. Here, left a sullen breathing-while,
Up-gathered on himself the Fighter stood
For his last fight, and, wiping treacherous blood
Out of the eyelids just held ope beneath
Those shading fingers in their iron sheath,
Steadied his strengths amid the buzz and stir
Of the dusk hideous amphitheatre
At the announcement of his over-match
To wind the day's diversion up, dispatch
The pertinacious Gaul: while, limbs one heap,
The Slave, no breath in her round mouth, watched leap
Dart after dart forth, as her hero's car

Clove dizzily the solid of the war
— Let coil about his knees for pride in him.
We reach the farthest terrace, and the grim
San Pietro Palace stops us.
Such the state
Of Salinguerra's plan to emulate
Sicilian marvels, that his girlish wife
Retrude still might lead her ancient life
In her new home: whereat enlarged so much
Neighbors upon the novel princely touch
He took, — who here imprisons Boniface.
Here must the Envoys come to sue for grace;
And here, emerging from the labyrinth
Below, Sordello paused beside the plinth
Of the door-pillar."

Wholly imaginative is the scene where Sordello tries to persuade Taurello to give up the Ghibelline side for the Guelf side. Despite the fact that his arguments fail to convince, Taurello suddenly throws the imperial badge on Sordello's neck, with the idea that he, once being Palma's husband, will bear her burdens as head of the Romano house.

It will be remembered that Ecelin II retired to a monastery, and married his two sons to Guelf wives and proposed to marry Palma to a Guelf husband.

Ecelin has also given his best land to the Pope as a sop to allow him to divide the rest of it between his sons, so Taurello's work of thirty years is lost, and he feels a younger person is needed to hold up the Ghibelline cause. Palma, not yet married to Richard, is his only hope of a head to the Romano house. The climax of the scene is Palma's revelation that Sordello is really Taurello's son.

"My poor Sordello! what may we extort
By this, I wonder? Palma's lighted eyes
Turned to Taurello who, long past surprise,
Began, 'You love him — what you'd say at large
Let me say briefly. First, your father's charge
To me, his friend, peruse: I guessed indeed
You were no stranger to the course decreed.
He bids me leave his children to the saints:
As for a certain project, he acquaints
The Pope with that, and offers him the best
Of your possessions to permit the rest
Go peaceably — to Ecelin, a stripe
Of soil the cursed Vicentines will gripe,
— To Alberic, a patch the Trevisan
Clutches already; extricate, who can,
Treville, Villarazzi, Puissolo,
Loria and Cartiglione! — all must go,
And with them go my hopes. 'Tis lost, then! Lost
This eve, our crisis, and some pains it cost
Procuring; thirty years — as good I'd spent
Like our admonisher! But each his bent
Pursues: no question, one might live absurd
One's self this while, by deed as he by word
Persisting to obtrude an influence where
'Tis made account of, much as . . . nay, you fare
With twice the fortune, youngster! — I submit,
Happy to parallel my waste of wit

With the renowned Sordello's: you decide
A course for me. Romano may abide
Romano, — Bacchus! After all, what dearth
Of Ecelins and Alberics on earth?
Say there's a prize in prospect, must disgrace
Betide competitors, unless they style
Themselves Romano? Were it worth my while
To try my own luck! But an obscure place
Suits me — there wants a youth to bustle, stalk
And attitudinize — some fight, more talk,
Most flaunting badges — how, I might make clear
Since Friedrich's very purposes lie here
— Here, pity they are like to lie! For me,
With station fixed unceremoniously
Long since, small use contesting; I am but
The liegeman — you are born the lieges — shut
That gentle mouth now! or resume your kin
In your sweet self; were Palma Ecelin
For me to work with! Could that neck endure
This bauble for a cumbrous garniture,
She should . . . or might one bear it for her? Stay —
I have not been so flattered many a day
As by your pale friend — Bacchus! The least help
Would lick the hind's fawn to a lion's whelp:
His neck is broad enough — a ready tongue
Beside — too writhled — but, the main thing, young —
I could . . . why, look ye!'

And the badge was thrown
Across Sordello's neck: 'This badge alone
Makes you Romano's Head — becomes superb
On your bare neck, which would, on mine, disturb
The pauldron,' said Taurello. A mad act,
Nor even dreamed about before — in fact,
Not when his sportive arm rose for the nonce —

But he had dallied overmuch, this once
With power: the thing was done, and he, aware
The thing was done, proceeded to declare —
(So like a nature made to serve, excel
In serving, only feel by service well!)
— That he would make Sordello that and more.
'As good a scheme as any. What's to pore
At in my face?' he asked — 'ponder instead
This piece of news; you are Romano's Head!
One cannot slacken pace so near the goal,
Suffer my Azzo to escape heart-whole
This time! For you there's Palma to espouse —
For me, one crowning trouble ere I house
Like my compeer.'
On which ensued a strange
And solemn visitation; there came change
O'er every one of them; each looked on each:
Up in the midst a truth grew, without speech.
And when the giddiness sank and the haze
Subsided, they were sitting, no amaze,
Sordello with the baldric on, his sire
Silent, though his proportions seemed aspire
Momently; and, interpreting the thrill, —
Right at its ebb, — Palma was found there still
Relating somewhat Adelaide confessed
A year ago, while dying on her breast, —
Of a contrivance that Vicenza night
When Ecelin had birth. 'Their convoy's flight,
Cut off a moment, coiled inside the flame
That wallowed like a dragon at his game
The toppling city through — San Biagio rocks!
And wounded lies in her delicious locks
Retrude, the frail mother, on her face,
None of her wasted, just in one embrace

Covering her child: when, as they lifted her,
Cleaving the tumult, mighty, mightier
And mightiest Taurello's cry outbroke,
Leapt like a tongue of fire that cleaves the smoke,
Midmost to cheer his Mantuans onward — drown
His colleague Ecelin's clamor, up and down
The disarray: failed Adelaide see then
Who was the natural chief, the man of men?
Outstripping time, her infant there burst swathe,
Stood up with eyes haggard beyond the scathe
From wandering after his heritage
Lost once and lost for aye — and why that rage,
That deprecating glance? A new shape leant
On a familiar shape — gloatingly bent
O'er his discomfiture; 'mid wreaths it wore,
Still one outflamed the rest — her child's before
'Twas Salinguerra's for his child: scorn, hate,
Rage now might startle her when all too late!
Then was the moment! — rival's foot had spurned
Never that House to earth else! Sense returned —
The act conceived, adventured and complete,
They bore away to an obscure retreat
Mother and child — Retrude's self not slain'
(Nor even here Taurello moved) 'though pain
Was fled: and what assured them most 'twas fled,
All pain, was, if they raised the pale hushed head
'Twould turn this way and that, waver awhile,
And only settle into its old smile —
(Graceful as the disquieted water-flag
Steadying itself, remarked they, in the quag
On either side their path) — when suffered look
Down on her child. They marched: no sign once shook
The company's close litter of crossed spears
Till, as they reached Goito, a few tears

Slipped in the sunset from her long black lash,
And she was gone. So far the action rash;
No crime. They laid Retrude in the font,
Taurello's very gift, her child was wont
To sit beneath — constant as eve he came
To sit by its attendant girls the same
As one of them. For Palma, she would blend
With this magnific spirit to the end,
That ruled her first; but scarcely had she dared
To disobey the Adelaide who scared
Her into vowing never to disclose
A secret to her husband, which so froze
His blood at half-recital, she contrived
To hide from him Taurello's infant lived,
Lest, by revealing that, himself should mar
Romano's fortunes. And, a crime so far,
Palma received that action: she was told
Of Salinguerra's nature, of his cold
Calm acquiescence in his lot! But free
To impart the secret to Romano, she
Engaged to repossess Sordello of
His heritage, and hers, and that way doff
The mask, but after years, long years: while now,
Was not Romano's sign-mark on that brow?'
Across Taurello's heart his arms were locked:
And when he did speak 'twas as if he mocked
The minstrel, 'who had not to move,' he said,
'Nor stir — should fate defraud him of a shred
Of his son's infancy? much less his youth!'
(Laughingly all this) — 'which to aid, in truth,
Himself, reserved on purpose, had not grown
Old, not too old — 'twas best they kept alone
Till now, and never idly met till now;'
— Then, in the same breath, told Sordello how

All intimations of this eve's event
Were lies, for Friedrich must advance to Trent,
Thence to Verona, then to Rome, there stop,
Tumble the Church down, institute a-top
The Alps a Prefecture of Lombardy:
— 'That's now! — no prophesying what may be
Anon, with a new monarch of the clime,
Native of Gesi, passing his youth's prime
At Naples. Tito bids my choice decide
On whom' . . .
'Embrace him, madman!' Palma cried,
Who through the laugh saw sweat-drops burst apace,
And his lips blanching: he did not embrace
Sordello, but he laid Sordello's hand
On his own eyes, mouth, forehead."

Sordello's struggle over the decision thus forced upon him causes his sudden death, which is wonderfully touched upon in these lines:

"What has Sordello found?
Or can his spirit go the mighty round,
End where poor Eglamor begun? So, says
Old fable, the two eagles went two ways
About the world: where, in the midst, they met,
Though on a shifting waste of sand, men set
Jove's temple. Quick, what has Sordello found?
For they approach — approach — that foot's rebound
Palma? No, Salinguerra though in mail;
They mount, have reached the threshold, dash the veil
Aside — and you divine who sat there dead,
Under his foot the badge: still, Palma said,
A triumph lingering in the wide eyes,

Wider than some spent swimmer's if he spies
Help from above in his extreme despair,
And, head far back on shoulder thrust, turns there
With short quick passionate cry: as Palma pressed
In one great kiss, her lips upon his breast,
It beat.
By this, the hermit-bee has stopped
His day's toil at Goito: the new-cropped
Dead vine-leaf answers, now 'tis eve, he bit,
Twirled so, and filed all day: the mansion's fit,
God counselled for. As easy guess the word
That passed betwixt them, and become the third
To the soft small unfrighted bee, as tax
Him with one fault — so, no remembrance racks
Of the stone maidens and the font of stone
He, creeping through the crevice, leaves alone.
Alas, my friend, alas Sordello, whom
Anon they laid within that old font-tomb,
And, yet again, alas!"

The poet in expressing his own opinion of Sordello refers to the fame which was accorded him by the Chroniclers of Mantua, among them Aliprandi, who is responsible for the legend that he belonged to the Visconti family. To Browning's mind, however, the best that can be said of him is that he wrote poetry in the Tuscan dialect, which he has heard a little barefoot child in Asolo sing.

"Is there no more to say? He of the rhymes —
Many a tale, of this retreat betimes,
Was born: Sordello die at once for men?

The Chronclers of Mantua tired their pen
Telling how *Sordello Prince Visconti* saved
Mantua, and elsewhere notably behaved —
Who thus, by fortune ordering events,
Passed with posterity, to all intents,
For just the god he never could become.
As Knight, Bard, Gallant, men were never dumb
In praise of him: while what he should have been,
Could be, and was not — the one step too mean
For him to take, — we suffer at this day
Because of: Ecelin had pushed away
Its chance ere Dante could arrive and take
That step Sordello spurned, for the world's sake:
He did much — but Sordello's chance was gone.
Thus, had Sordello dared that step alone,
Apollo had been compassed — 'twas a fit
He wished should go to him, not he to it
— As one content to merely be supposed
Singing or fighting elsewhere, while he dozed
Really at home — one who was chiefly glad
To have achieved the few real deeds he had,
Because that way assured they were not worth
Doing, so spared from doing them henceforth —
A tree that covets fruitage and yet tastes
Never itself, itself. Had he embraced
Their cause then, men had plucked Hesperian fruit
And, praising that, just thrown him in to boot
All he was anxious to appear, but scarce
Solicitous to be. A sorry farce
Such life is, after all! Cannot I say
He lived for some one better thing? this way. —
Lo, on a heathy brown and nameless hill
By sparkling Asolo, in mist and chill,
Morning just up, higher and higher runs

A child barefoot and rosy. See! the sun's
On the square castle's inner-court's low wall
Like the chine of some extinct animal
Half turned to earth and flowers; and through the haze
(Save where some slender patches of gray maize
Are to be overleaped) that boy has crossed
The whole hill-side of dew and powder-frost
Matting the balm and mountain camomile.
Up and up goes he, singing all the while
Some unintelligible words to beat
The lark, God's poet, swooning at his feet,
So worsted is he at 'the few fine locks
Stained like pale honey oozed from topmost rocks
Sun-blanched the livelong summer,' — all that's left
Of the Goito lay!"

For detailed analysis and criticism of the psychical development of Sordello, the description of which fills up the greater part of the poem, the reader must go elsewhere. Our concern here is merely to show what use the poet has made of the historical conditions of that age in building up a setting for the poem. Historians usually dwell principally upon the fights between Pope and Emperor to gain the ascendancy, giving little or no attention to the third element in the evolving life of the time — namely the dawning perception of the people that their rights are really the divine rights; not those of Pope nor those of Emperor. Browning makes his Sordello see this by means of his own growth from an individualist, bent upon obtaining power and glory for himself, to a socialist type, in its broad sense, desirous of helping the masses of the people to rise to better conditions. Sordello, in his own person, stands as a symbol of this awakening tendency that constituted as much an element in the Renaissance movement as the outburst of a desire for learning or the blossoming of great artistic talents. The human race had been something like a tightly closed cauldron of seething metals, which, reaching the boiling point, burst off the lid, and the vapors escaped first in chaotic masses, but finally to take shape in forms both beautiful and hideous, some of them fixed, and some ever changing their aspects. Sordello's failure to grasp the truth he saw when put to the test — because his heart could not stand the strain, typifies the fact that the time was not yet ripe for the fruition of the wavering, ever changing, yet upward growing ideal of democracy. It is picturesque for Browning to declare that we suffer to this day for the step Sordello did not take — this step being that he should have had the courage to serve the cause of the people through Ghibelline means. But in spite of the opinion of Mr. Bryce that had the emperors seen their opportunity, and been strong enough to improve it they might have been in part, at least, the pioneers of the reformation, it is decidedly doubtful whether the impulse of the people themselves was strong enough in these chaotic times to give the needed support to any one single individual for the building up of a more democratic civilization. The truth which Sordello saw then has in all the centuries since been striving for full recognition, and still there are thousands upon thousands unready for it, and still we have faith that this truth will finally come into its own. But that Sordello, or any other single arm, could have struck any very telling blows for the people at that time is to say the least, problematical, for like Sordello, nations and peoples are obliged to learn by bitter experience that love is best, and democracy is only another name for social love.

II

GLIMPSES OF POLITICAL LIFE

"A people is but the attempt of many
To rise to the completer life of one;
And those who live as models for the mass
Are singly of more value than they all."

— *Luria.*

IN four out of the seven dramas written by Browning, he has given through the optic glass of his own vision a characteristic view of some phase of political life in Italy.

With the exception of "King Victor and King Charles" — a tolerably accurate portrayal of an actual series of events in one of the side issues of Italian History, these plays have for atmosphere known historical conditions in the midst of which move beings of the poet's own imagination, such as might have existed.

To begin with "Luria," which chronologically comes first, the scene is Florence, the date 14—, a sufficiently vague date to allow one's imagination to range through the whole of the fifteenth century in conjuring up the setting of the play. Accordingly if we say that, broadly speaking, "Luria" stands for fifteenth century Florentine civilization, we shall come near hitting the mark.

The central event of the play is a war between Florence and Pisa. The history of the century has two wars between Florence and Pisa to show, one near the beginning of the century, 1406, and one near the end, about 1494. No events in either of these wars can be found exactly parallel to those Browning describes, yet he has taken hints from both to build up his imaginary situation.

This was the century of the Medicis in Florence and of Savonarola, the first standing for much that was good and for much that was bad in the Renaissance spirit, the second, for much that was good and something that was bad in the religious attitude of the age.

It is impossible here to go into the details of the fierce struggles which were constantly waged at this time, as well as earlier and later, between the antagonistic forces of the human spirit, the desire for freedom at odds with the desire for power making the much boasted liberty of Florence little more than a shadow, and the desire for pleasure at war with religious aspiration leading to license on the one hand and finally to religious persecution on the other. Yet out of this well nigh indescribable chaos arose industry and commerce, intellectual power and art which will be the amazement of mankind to the end of time; for did not Florence give the world Dante and Giotto and Michael Angelo as well as nourishing the Medici and Savonarola! While her great commerce was the envy of all nations. Mrs. Oliphant in her "Makers of Florence" writes: "It is curious to step out of the disturbed and turbulent city life, in which nobles and commons, poets, historians, and philosophers, were revolving in a continual turmoil, now up, now down, falling and rising and falling again, with all the bitter hopes and fears natural amid vicissitudes so painful, into the artist world where no such ups or downs seem to have existed, but where work went on placidly, whatever happened. Enough for them (the artists) that it was all to be theirs afterwards, and that when the factions and the families had done their worst and torn each other to pieces, and all the Magnificoes had had their day, they were to pass every one of them, and leave the silent painter, the patient worker in stone, omnipotent in the city which has come to belong to them — to be its princes and its potentates for ever and ever." And again, "Internal conflicts, which showed not only in the public square and public palace, but which convulsed every petty alley and made a fortress of every street corner; and external assault by neighboring cities, by marauding emperors, by now one, now another league of belligerent towns, backed up by bands of mercenaries, kept up such a continual commotion that the existence of the shop, the manufactory, or the studio behind seems almost incredible. Yet that background of calm to all these fierce contentions seems to have appeared entirely natural to the Florentines. Trade flourished among them, not only as it does among ourselves, underneath the brilliant surface on which the great and wealthy and non-laboring keep up a princely show, but in the hands of the very men who formed the surface of Florentine life: the same men who negotiated with princes, and led armies, and had a share in all the imperial affairs of Europe, yet returned to their banking houses or their woolen manufactories unchanged, talking of the *bottega,* the business which gave them their standing, with the most perfect satisfaction and content in that source of their fortune."

That there was no love lost between

Florence and Pisa would be understandable in such an age upon the mere ground that they were rival free cities with similar aims and ambitions, but there was an even more vital reason. Pisa was near the sea and possessed a fine port "Porto Pisana," and what would Florence do with her vast commercial relations in the event of Pisa and other Italian ports, Sienna and Genoa, combining to boycott Florence and prevent her from getting her goods to market! The policy of Florence had always been to fan the flames of rivalry and jealousy between these cities, but the fatal moment at last arrived. The cities all came under one ruler, Visconti; Florence was facing the ruin she had always dreaded when the tyrant Visconti luckily for her died. As one historian puts it, "They recovered as from the indulgence in a long slumber; and the reduction of Pisa from that moment became the first object of their ambition." The war of 1406 resulted in a victory over Pisa and the commerce of Florence was put on a firm foundation. But the two cities did not, after the manner of the old fairy-tales, live happy ever after. A hint of the relations between them may be gained from Machiavelli. "Pisa," he says, "should have participated in all the rights and privileges of Florence and thus have been attached by companionship, or else after the Roman fashion its walls should have been destroyed; but it never should have been coerced by citadels, which are useless in the occupation of a conquered town and injurious to a native one." At last the time was ripe. The unsatisfactory rule of Piero de' Medici had brought about civil discord in Florence and weakened it so that Pisa began to think of throwing off the yoke, and finally with the help of Charles VIII of France accomplished it. Just at this moment Piero de' Medici was banished, and later Charles VIII retired from the scene after making things very uncomfortable for Florence. Freed from these disturbing influences, however, Florence was able to improve the internal condition of affairs and then turn her attention to the reconquering of Pisa. Thus came about the second war. Certain details given in the history of both these wars have been used by Browning in the development of his situation.

For example, we read in Napier's history, "The Florentine camp was accordingly pitched at San Piero on the river side a little below the town, under the Florentine commissioner, Maso degli Albizzi, but more especially Gino Capponi." Besides these commissioners were the commanders, with whom history records Florence had difficulties. The army was first commanded by Jacopo Salviati, a Florentine citizen who after some useful and active service was superseded by Bertoldo degli Orsini: but this general, showing more rapacity than soldiership, displeased the Florentines and was ordered to resign his command to Obizzo da Monte Carelli. Two other commanders, Sforza da Cotignola and Tartaglia, showed such a spirit of rivalry toward each other that they were placed in distinct and distant commands with their separate forces. The attack of the Florentine forces on Pisa was repulsed, but the Pisans were so closely invested by land and sea that famine drove them to capitulation, though it was done through the secret negotiations of their commander, Gambacorta, who made such good terms for himself, that his actions might be regarded as distinctly treasonable.

Of the second war, ninety years later, we read that "Ercole Bentivoglio and other condottieri were engaged with a large body of troops which under the direction of Piero Capponi and Francesco Valori, as Florentine commissaries, recovered almost all the Pisan territory from a badly armed and undisciplined peasantry, the sole defenders as yet assembled beyond the walls of Pisa; so that in a short time Vico Pisano, Cascina, and Buti were the only places that still sustained her independence." Again we read, "Lucca and Sienna although afraid to declare themselves openly against Florence sent succours clandestinely to Pisa; the first supplied her with grain and three hundred soldiers, the second with troops alone. Ludovico the Moor, who had at first encouraged the Pisan revolt, although afraid openly to violate his engagements with Florence, referred the Pisans to Genoa, which, notwithstanding its dependence on Milan, still retained a certain liberty of national action." Later we read that notwithstanding his aid to Pisa, Ludovico "maintained an amiable intercourse with Florence" and "now exhibited more unequivocal signs of friendship by intimating that he wished to restore Pisa to Florentine dominion." To this Malpiero adds that "Ludovico secretly offered before this to assist Florence if she would continue the subsidy of 60,000 florins that she had paid to his brother Galeazzo, and that Florence alarmed by the interference of Venice consented."

It gives one an instructive glimpse into the workings of a poet's mind to see what he has done with such hints as these in the making of his play.

We find the Florentine forces encamped between Florence and Pisa, with Braccio, a Florentine Commissary, and Luria, a Moor, the commander of the Florentine forces. Around these chief characters are grouped Jacopo, Luria's secretary, Husain, Luria's Moorish friend, Puccio, the old Florentine commander, now Luria's chief officer, Tiburzio, commander of the Pisans, and Domizia, a noble Florentine lady and a spy, a position frequently given to women at that time.

At first sight it would look as if Browning had taken from history the suggestion of a Moor interested in Florentine and Pisan affairs and made him the Florentine commander. Ludovico was of course actually not a Moor, the name being merely a pseudonym, bestowed upon him because of his dark complexion. One is tempted to draw a parallel here with the Christopher Moro who has been brought forward by some as furnishing hints to Shakespeare for his Othello. His name was also derived from his complexion. Ludovico was an Italian of the Sforza family and the Duke of Milan, and his interest in Florentine and Pisan affairs was all with the end in view of making them subject to Milan. Perhaps Browning had in mind, however, his double dealing with Florence and Pisa, when he makes the Pisan commander, Tiburzio, offer Luria the command of the Pisan forces, after revealing to him the underhanded intentions of the Florentines to indite and try him off hand as soon as the battle is won.

The plot in the play hangs upon the integrity of Luria, and Browning, instead of making him what the commanders and rulers of that day only too frequently were — utterly selfish, scheming and untrustworthy, has made him stand firm amidst suspicion and treachery. The question may very well be asked why the poet chose to make this paragon of military honor and virtue a Moor?

One feels upon first reading Luria as if Browning desired to vindicate the character of the Moor against all the insults heaped upon it in Shakespeare's "Othello," and had undertaken to show how supreme could be the action of an Oriental nature when placed in the most trying circumstances. Luria like Othello is a mercenary captain. Mercenary troops were the chief soldiers up to the fifteenth century, and mercenary captains were also frequent — one of the most noted in Florentine history being the Englishman, Sir John Hawkwood; but no Moorish captain flourishes in the pages of Florentine history.

Moors there had been in plenty in Sicily in the days of Frederick II. He had colonies at Nocera and Luceria, and fought all his battles with Moorish troops. Learned Moors and Moorish ladies thronged his court, and through his close association with Moorish culture, which was in most respects far ahead of European culture, he stands out as one of the intellectual pioneers in the Renaissance movement, a fact already mentioned in Part I. But, as Draper points out, "In the eye of Rome all this was abomination. Were human laws to take the precedence of the law of God? Was this new-born product of the insolence of human intellect — this so-called science — to be brought into competition with theology, the heaven descended? Frederick and his parliaments, his laws and universities, his libraries, his statues, his pictures and sonnets were denounced." But, as Draper goes on to say, the fall of Frederick was not followed by the destruction of the influences he represented. These not only survived him, but were destined in the end to overcome the power which had transiently overthrown them.

While the Moors are not prominent in Italian history after this, there is every reason to suppose that there were many of them still in Italy at the time of this play, so that Browning would be quite justified in having a Moorish captain, though it is a little doubtful if the Florentines would have entrusted their forces to a so-called barbarian. In connection with this subject it is interesting to note that as early as 812 the Moors not only attacked Corsica and Sardinia, but in order to revenge a defeat which they had suffered from a Frankish general invaded Nice in the Narbonese Gaul and Civita Vecchia in Tuscany. This comes near Florence; but still nearer to Florence did they come in the twelfth century, according to a writer of that time who reproaches Pisa with the Jews, the Arabians and other monsters of the sea who thronged in her streets.

With a poet's prerogative, Browning has taken a universal view of the forces at work in historical development, rather than an individual view of persons acting in the midst of historical events. His portrayal of the noble Luria has all the sympathy which we might expect from a Frederick II who appreciated the fine qualities of intellect and heart, possessed by the Moors. The Florentines in the play have all the suspicion and the latent hatred which the Church engendered in its attitude toward the Moors, while the complete triumph of Luria in winning the love of his Florentines may symbolize the final union of Oriental and Occidental ideals as it has been realized in later centuries.

The Poet foreshadows this idea in Luria's fancy that the Duomo might be finished with a Moorish front, a sketch of which he makes. Braccio's remarks upon seeing this drawing in the tent sum up the whole situation.

Brac. I see —
A Moorish front, nor of such ill design!
Lapo, there's one thing plain and positive;
Man seeks his own good at the whole world's cost.
What? If to lead our troops, stand forth our chiefs,
And hold our fate, and see us at their beck,
Yet render up the charge when peace return,
Have ever proved too much for Florentines,
Even for the best and bravest of ourselves —
If in the struggle when the soldier's sword
Should sink its point before the statist's pen,
And the calm head replace the violent hand,
Virtue on virtue still have fallen away
Before ambition with unvarying fate,
Till Florence' self at last in bitterness
Be forced to own such falls the natural end,
And, sparing further to expose her sons
To a vain strife and profitless disgrace,
Declare, "The foreigner, one not my child,

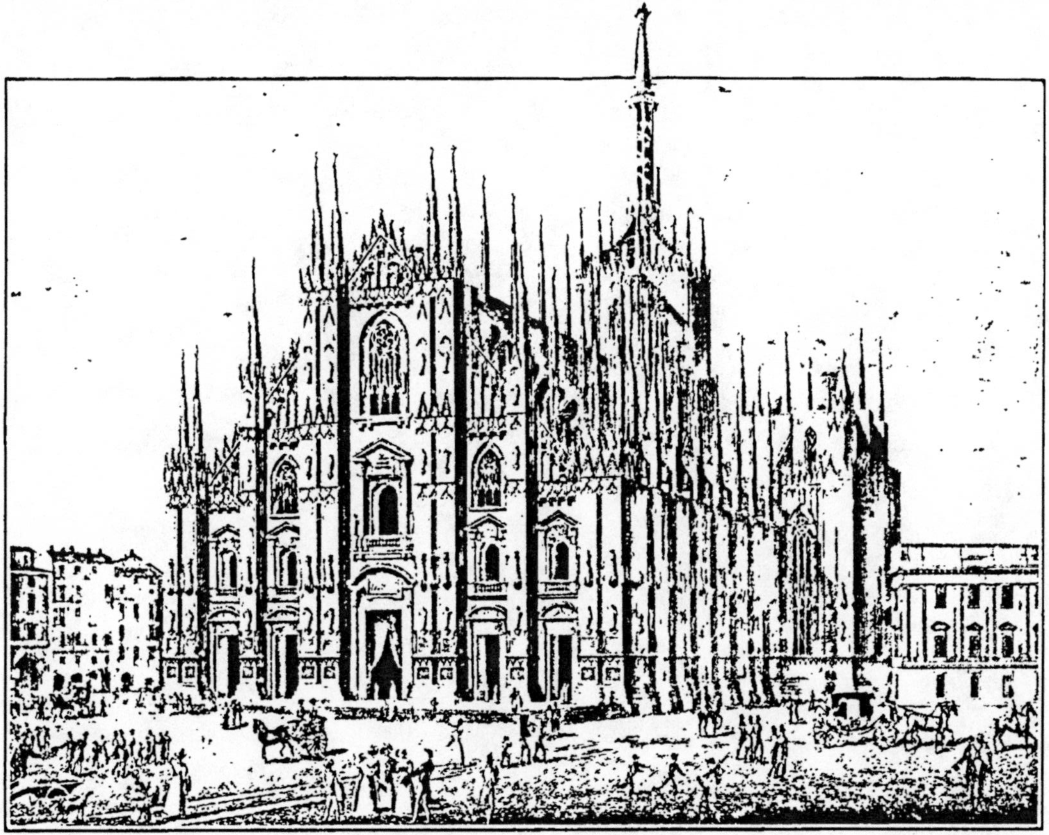

THE DUOMO, FLORENCE.

Shall henceforth lead my troops, reach height by height
The glory, then descend into the shame;
So shall rebellion be less guilt in him,
And punishment the easier task for me:"
— If on the best of us such brand she set,
Can I suppose an utter alien here,
This Luria, our inevitable foe,
Confessed a mercenary and a Moor,
Born free from many ties that bind the rest
Of common faith in Heaven or hope on earth,
No past with us, no future, — such a spirit
Shall hold the path from which our stanchest broke,
Stand firm where every famed precursor fell?
My Lapo, I will frankly say, these proofs
So duly noted of the man's intent,
Are for the doting fools at home, not me.
The charges here, they may be true or false:
— What is set down? Errors and oversights,
A dallying interchange of courtesies
With Pisa's General, — all that, hour by hour,
Puccio's pale discontent has furnished us,
Of petulant speeches, inconsiderate acts,
Now overhazard, overcaution now;
Even that he loves this lady who believes
She outwits Florence, and whom Florence posted
By my procurement here, to spy on me,
Lest I one minute lose her from my sight —
She who remembering her whole House's fall,
That nest of traitors strangled in the birth,
Now labors to make Luria (poor device
As plain) the instrument of her revenge!
— That she is ever at his ear to prompt
Inordinate conceptions of his worth,
Exorbitant belief in worth's reward,

And after, when sure disappointment follows,
Proportional rage at such a wrong —
Why, all these reasons, while I urge them most,
Weigh with me less than least; as nothing weigh.
Upon that broad man's-heart of his, I go:
On what I know must be, yet while I live
Shall never be, because I live and know.
Brute-force shall not rule Florence! Intellect
May rule her, bad or good as chance supplies:
But intellect it shall be, pure if bad,
And intellect's tradition so kept up.
Till the good come — 'twas intellect that ruled,
Not brute-force bringing from the battlefield
The attributes of wisdom, foresight's graces
We lent it there to lure its grossness on;
All which it took for earnest and kept safe
To show against us in our market-place,
Just as the plumes and tags and swordsman's-gear
(Fetched from the camp where, at their foolish best,
When all was done they frightened nobody)
Perk in our faces in the street, forsooth,
With our own warrant and allowance. No!
The whole procedure's overcharged, — its end
In too strict keeping with the bad first step.
To conquer Pisa was sheer inspiration?
Well then, to perish for a single fault;
Let that be simple justice! There, my Lapo!
A Moorish front ill suits our Duomo's body:
Blot it out — and bid Luria's sentence come!

Another glimpse of Florentine ways is given in the part of Domizia who is bent upon revenge for the destruction of her family. Such incidents were of frequent occurrence in

Florence. She hopes to make Luria the instrument of her revenge, knowing that Florence will turn against him, she looks for him to take his revenge and destroy Florence.

One after another temptations to turn against Florence assail Luria. First comes Tiburzio armed with a letter disclosing the intended treachery of the Florentines, to offer him the leadership of the Pisan forces. Read how Luria acts:

Tib. Luria, you know the peril imminent
On Pisa, — that you have us in the toils,
Us her last safeguard, all that intercepts
The rage of her implacablest of foes
From Pisa: if we fall to-day, she falls.
Though Lucca will arrive, yet, 'tis too late.
You have so plainly here the best of it,
That you must feel, brave soldier as you are,
How dangerous we grow in this extreme,
How truly formidable by despair.
Still, probabilities should have their weight:
The extreme chance is ours, but, that chance failing,
You win this battle. Wherefore say I this?
To be well apprehended when I add,
This danger absolutely comes from you.
Were you, who threaten thus, a Florentine . . .
Lur. Sir, I am nearer Florence than her sons.
I can, and have perhaps obliged the State,
Nor paid a mere son's duty.
Tib. Even so.
Were you the son of Florence, yet endued
With all your present nobleness of soul,

No question, what I must communicate
Would not detach you from her.
Lur. Me, detach?
Tib. Time urges. You will ruin presently
Pisa, you never knew, for Florence' sake
You think you know. I have from time to time
Made prize of certain secret missives sent
From Braccio here, the Commissary, home:
And knowing Florence otherwise, I piece
The entire chain out, from these its scattered links.
Your trial occupies the Signory;
They sit in judgment on your conduct now.
When men at home inquire into the acts
Which in the field e'en foes appreciate . . .
Brief, they are Florentines! You, saving them,
Seek but the sure destruction saviors find.
Lur. Tiburzio!
Tib. All the wonder is of course.
I am not here to teach you, nor direct,
Only to loyally apprise — scarce that.
This is the latest letter, sealed and safe,
As it left here an hour ago. One way
Of two thought free to Florence, I command.
The duplicate is on its road; but this, —
Read it, and then I shall have more to say.
Lur. Florence!
Tib. Now, were yourself a Florentine,
This letter, let it hold the worst it can,
Would be no reason you should fall away.
The mother city is the mother still,
And recognition of the children's service
Her own affair; reward — there's no reward!
But you are bound by quite another tie.
Nor nature shows, nor reason, why at first

A foreigner, born friend to all alike,
Should give himself to any special State
More than another, stand by Florence' side
Rather than Pisa; 'tis as fair a city
You war against, as that you fight for — famed
As well as she in story, graced no less
With noble heads and patriotic hearts:
Nor to a stranger's eye would either cause,
Stripped of the cumulative loves and hates
Which take importance from familiar view,
Stand as the right and sole to be upheld.
Therefore, should the preponderating gift
Of love and trust, Florence was first to throw,
Which made you hers, not Pisa's, void the scale, —
Old ties dissolving, things resume their place,
And all begins again. Break seal and read!
At least let Pisa offer for you now!
And I, as a good Pisan, shall rejoice,
Though for myself I lose, in gaining you,
This last fight and its opportunity;
The chance it brings of saving Pisa yet,
Or in the turn of battle dying so
That shame should want its extreme bitterness.
Lur. Tiburzio, you that fight for Pisa now
As I for Florence . . . say my chance were yours!
You read this letter, and you find . . . no, no!
Too mad!
Tib. I read the letter, find they purpose
When I have crushed their foe, to crush me: well?
Lur. You, being their captain, what is it you do?
Tib. Why, as it is, all cities are alike;
As Florence pays you, Pisa will pay me.
I shall be as belied, whate'er the event,
As you, or more: my weak head, they will say

Prompted this last expedient, my faint heart
Entailed on them indelible disgrace,
Both which defects ask proper punishment.
Another tenure of obedience, mine!
You are no son of Pisa's: break and read!
Lur. And act on what I read? What act were fit?
If the firm-fixed foundation of my faith
In Florence, who to me stands for mankind,
— If that break up and, disimprisoning
From the abyss . . . Ah friend, it cannot be!
You may be very sage, yet — all the world
Having to fail, or your sagacity,
You do not wish to find yourself alone!
What would the world be worth? Whose love be sure?
The world remains: you are deceived!
Tib. Your hand!
I lead the vanguard. — If you fall, beside,
The better, I am left to speak! For me,
This was my duty, nor would I rejoice
If I could help, it misses its effect;
And after all you will look gallantly
Found dead here with that letter in your breast.
Lur. Tiburzio — I would see these people once
And test them ere I answer finally!
At your arrival let the trumpet sound:
If mine return not then the wonted cry
It means that I believe — am Pisa's!
Tib. Well!
[*Goes.*
Lur. My heart will have it he speaks true! My blood
Beats close to this Tiburzio as a friend.
If he had stept into my watch-tent, night
And the wild desert full of foes around,
I should have broke the bread and given the salt

Secure, and, when my hour of watch was done,
Taken my turn to sleep between his knees
Safe in the untroubled brow and honest cheek.
Oh world, where all things pass and naught abides,
Oh life, the long mutation — is it so?
Is it with life as with the body's change?
— Where, e'en though better follow, good must pass,
Nor manhood's strength can mate with boyhood's grace,
Nor age's wisdom, in its turn, find strength,
But silently the first gift dies away,
 And though the new stays, never both at once.
Life's time of savage instinct o'er with me,
It fades and dies away, past trusting more,
As if to punish the ingratitude
With which I turned to grow in these new lights,
And learned to look with European eyes.
Yet it is better, this cold certain way,
Where Braccio's brow tells nothing, Puccio's mouth,
Domizia's eyes reject the searcher: yes!
For on their calm sagacity I lean,
Their sense of right, deliberate choice of good,
Sure, as they know my deeds, they deal with me.
Yes, that is better — that is best of all!
Such faith stays when mere wild belief would go.
Yes — when the desert creature's heart, at fault
Amid the scattering tempest's pillared sands,
Betrays its step into the pathless drift —
The calm instructed eye of man holds fast
By the sole bearing of the visible star,
Sure that when slow the whirling wreck subside,
The boundaries, lost now, shall be found again, —
The palm-trees and the pyramid over all.
Yes: I trust Florence: Pisa is deceived.

(*Enter* BRACCIO, PUCCIO, *and* DOMIZIA.)

Brac. Noon's at an end: no Lucca? You must fight.
Lur. Do you remember, ever, gentle friends,
I am no Florentine?
Dom. It is yourself
Who still are forcing us, importunately,
To bear in mind what else we should forget.
Lur. For loss! — for what I lose in being none!
No shrewd man, such as you yourselves respect,
But would remind you of the stranger's loss
In natural friends and advocates at home,
Hereditary loves, even rivalships
With precedent for honor and reward.
Still, there's a gain, too! If you take it so,
The stranger's lot has special gain as well.
Do you forget there was my own far East
I might have given away myself to, once,
As now, to Florence and for such a gift,
Stood there like a descended deity?
There, worship waits us: what is it waits here?
[*Shows the letter.*
See! Chance has put into my hand the means
Of knowing what I earn, before I work.
Should I fight better, should I fight the worse,
With payment palpably before me? See!
Here lies my whole reward! Best learn it now
Or keep it for the end's entire delight?
Brac. If you serve Florence as the vulgar serve,
For swordsman's pay alone, — break seal and read!
In that case, you will find your full desert.
Lur. Give me my one last happy moment, friends!
You need me now, and all the graciousness
This letter can contain will hardly balance
The after-feeling that you need no more.
This moment . . . oh, the East has use with you!

Its sword still flashes — is not flung aside
With the past praise, in a dark corner yet!
How say you? 'Tis not so with Florentines —
Captains of yours: for them, the ended war
Is but a first step to the peace begun:
He who did well in war, just earns the right
To begin doing well in peace, you know:
And certain my precursors, — would not such
Look to themselves in such a chance as mine,
Secure the ground they trod upon, perhaps?
For I have heard, by fits, or seemed to hear,
Of strange mishap, mistake, ingratitude,
Treachery even. Say that one of you
Surmised this letter carried what might turn
To harm hereafter, cause him prejudice:
What would he do?

Dom. [*Hastily.*] Thank God and take revenge!
Hurl her own force against the city straight!
And, even at the moment when the foe
Sounded defiance . . .

[TIBURZIO's *trumpet sounds in the distance.*

Lur. Ah, you Florentines!
So would you do? Wisely for you, no doubt!
My simple Moorish instinct bids me clench
The obligation you relieve me from,
Still deeper! [*To* PUC.] Sound our answer, I should say,
And thus: — [*Tearing the paper.*] — The battle! That solves every doubt.

When Luria, having won the battle and taken Tiburzio prisoner, learns the full measure of Florentine intention against him, he exclaims

Lur. Hear them! All these against one foreigner!
And all this while, where is, in the whole world,
To his good faith a single witness?
Tib. [*Who has entered unseen during the preceding dialogue.*] Here!
Thus I bear witness, not in word but deed.
I live for Pisa; she's not lost to-day
By many chances — much prevents from that!
Her army has been beaten, I am here,
But Lucca comes at last, one happy chance!
I rather would see Pisa three times lost
Than saved by any traitor, even by you;
The example of a traitor's happy fortune
Would bring more evil in the end than good; —
Pisa rejects the traitor, craves yourself!
I, in her name, resign forthwith to you
My charge, — the highest office, sword and shield!
You shall not, by my counsel, turn on Florence
Your army, give her calumny that ground —
Nor bring one soldier: be you all we gain!
And all she'll lose, — a head to deck some bridge,
And save the cost o' the crown should deck the head.
Leave her to perish in her perfidy,
Plague-stricken and stripped naked to all eyes,
A proverb and a by-word in all mouths!
Go you to Pisa! Florence is my place —
Leave me to tell her of the rectitude,
I, from the first, told Pisa, knowing it.
To Pisa!
Dom. Ah my Braccio, are you caught?
Brac. Puccio, good soldier and good citizen,
Whom I have ever kept beneath my eye,
Ready as fit, to serve in this event
Florence, who clear foretold it from the first —

Through me, she gives you the command and charge
She takes, through me, from him who held it late!
A painful trial, very sore, was yours:
All that could draw out, marshal in array
The selfish passions 'gainst the public good —
Slights, scorns, neglects, were heaped on you to bear:
And ever you did bear and bow the head!
It had been sorry trial, to precede
Your feet, hold up the promise of reward
For luring gleam; your footsteps kept the track
Through dark and doubt: take all the light at once!
Trial is over, consummation shines;
Well have you served, as well henceforth command!
Puc. No, no . . . I dare not! I am grateful, glad;
But Luria — you shall understand he's wronged:
And he's my captain — this is not the way
We soldiers climb to fortune: think again!
The sentence is not even passed, beside!
I dare not: where's the soldier could?
Lur. Now, Florence —
Is it to be? You will know all the strength
O' the savage — to your neck the proof must go?
You will prove the brute nature? Ah, I see!
The savage plainly is impassible —
He keeps his calm way through insulting words,
Sarcastic looks, sharp gestures — one of which
Would stop you, fatal to your finer sense,
But if he stolidly advance, march mute
Without a mark upon his callous hide,
Through the mere brushwood you grow angry with,
And leave the tatters of your flesh upon,
— You have to learn that when the true bar comes,
The murk mid-forest, the grand obstacle,
Which when you reach, you give the labor up,

Nor dash on, but lie down composed before,
— He goes against it, like the brute he is:
It falls before him, or he dies in his course.
I kept my course through past ingratitude:
I saw — it does seem, now, as if I saw,
Could not but see, those insults as they fell,
— Ay, let them glance from off me, very like,
Laughing, perhaps, to think the quality
You grew so bold on, while you so despised
The Moor's dull mute inapprehensive mood,
Was saving you: I bore and kept my course,
Now real wrong fronts me: see if I succumb!
Florence withstands me? I will punish her.

At night my sentence will arrive, you say.
Till then I cannot, if I would, rebel
— Unauthorized to lay my office down,
Retaining my full power to will and do:
After — it is to see. Tiburzio, thanks!
Go; you are free: join Lucca! I suspend
All further operations till to-night.
Thank you, and for the silence most of all!
[*To* BRAC.] Let my complacent bland accuser go
Carry his self-approving head and heart
Safe through the army which would trample him
Dead in a moment at my word or sign!
Go, sir, to Florence; tell friends what I say —
That while I wait my sentence, theirs waits them!
[*To* DOM.] You, lady, — you have black Italian eyes!
I would be generous if I might: oh, yes —
For I remember how so oft you seemed
Inclined at heart to break the barrier down
Which Florence finds God built between us both.
Alas, for generosity! this hour

Asks retribution: bear it as you may,
I must — the Moor — the savage, — pardon you!
Puccio, my trusty soldier, see them forth!

Later he is visited by Husain, then Domizia, both urging him to take his revenge on Florence.' But he is loyal even unto death.

Lur. Thus at the last must figure Luria, then!
Doing the various work of all his friends,
And answering every purpose save his own.
No doubt, 'tis well for them to wish; but him —
After the exploit what were left? Perchance
A little pride upon the swarthy brow,
At having brought successfully to bear
'Gainst Florence' self her own especial arms, —
Her craftiness, impelled by fiercer strength
From Moorish blood than feeds the northern wit.
But after! — once the easy vengeance willed,
Beautiful Florence at a word laid low
— (Not in her domes and towers and palaces,
Not even in a dream, that outrage!) — low,
As shamed in her own eyes henceforth forever,
Low, for the rival cities round to laugh,
Conquered and pardoned by a hireling Moor!
— For him, who did the irreparable wrong,
What would be left, his life's illusion fled, —
What hope or trust in the forlorn wide world?
How strange that Florence should mistake me so!
Whence grew this? What withdrew her faith from me?
Some cause! These fretful-blooded children talk
Against their mother, — they are wronged, they say —
Notable wrongs her smile makes up again!
So, taking fire at each supposed offence,

They may speak rashly, suffer for their speech:
But what could it have been in word or deed
Thus injured me? Some one word spoken more
Out of my heart, and all had changed perhaps.
My fault, it must have been, — for, what gain they?
Why risk the danger? See, what I could do!
And my fault, wherefore visit upon them,
My Florentines? The notable revenge
I meditated! To stay passively,
Attend their summons, be as they dispose!
Why, if my very soldiers keep the rank,
And if my chieftains acquiesce, what then?
I ruin Florence, teach her friends mistrust,
Confirm her enemies in harsh belief,
And when she finds one day, as find she must,
The strange mistake, and how my heart was hers,
Shall it console me, that my Florentines
Walk with a sadder step, in graver guise,
Who took me with such frankness, praised me so,
At the glad outset? Had they loved me less,
They had less feared what seemed a change in me.
And after all, who did the harm? Not they!
How could they interpose with those old fools
I' the council? Suffer for those old fools' sake —
They, who made pictures of me, sang the songs
About my battles? Ah, we Moors get blind
Out of our proper world, where we can see!
The sun that guides is closer to us! There —
There, my own orb! He sinks from out the sky!
Why, there! a whole day has he blessed the land,
My land, our Florence all about the hills,
The fields, and gardens, vineyards, olive-grounds,
All have been blest — and yet we Florentines,
With souls intent upon our battle here,

Found that he rose too soon, or set too late,
Gave us no vantage, or gave Pisa much —
Therefore we wronged him! Does he turn in ire
To burn the earth that cannot understand?
Or drop out quietly, and leave the sky,
His task once ended? Night wipes blame away.
Another morning from my East shall spring
And find all eyes at leisure, all disposed
To watch and understand its work, no doubt.
So, praise the new sun, the successor praise,
Praise the new Luria and forget the old!
[*Taking a phial from his breast.*
— Strange! This is all I brought from my own land
To help me: Europe would supply the rest,
All needs beside, all other helps save one!
I thought of adverse fortune, battle lost,
The natural upbraiding of the loser,
And then this quiet remedy to seek
At end of the disastrous day. [*He drinks.*
'Tis sought!
This was my happy triumph-morning: Florence
Is saved: I drink this, and ere night, — die! Strange!

In the last act, through his proved nobility he wins the hearts and undying allegiance of his Florentines, who learn only when too late that the restitution they would make has been put by Luria, himself, beyond their power. Tiburzio and Braccio, the rival leaders, both bear witness to his worth:

Tib. I return
From Florence: I serve Pisa, and must think

By such procedure I have served her best.
A people is but the attempt of many
To rise to the completer life of one;
And those who live as models for the mass
Are singly of more value than they all.
Such man are you, and such a time is this,
That your sole fate concerns a nation more
Than much apparent welfare: that to prove
Your rectitude, and duly crown the same,
Imports us far beyond to-day's event,
A battle's loss or gain: man's mass remains, —
Keep but God's model safe, new men will rise
To take its mould, and other days to prove
How great a good was Luria's glory. True —
I might go try my fortune as you urged,
And, joining Lucca, helped by your disgrace,
Repair our harm — so were to-day's work done;
But where leave Luria for our sons to see?
No, I look farther. I have testified
(Declaring my submission to your arms)
Her full success to Florence, making clear
Your probity, as none else could: I spoke,
And out it shone!

Lur. Ah — until Braccio spoke!

Brac. Till Braccio told in just a word the whole —
His lapse to error, his return to knowledge:
Which told . . . Nay, Luria, *I* should droop the head,
I whom shame rests with! Yet I dare look up,
Sure of your pardon now I sue for it,
Knowing you wholly. Let the midnight end!
'Tis morn approaches! Still you answer not?
Sunshine succeeds the shadow passed away;
Our faces, which phantasmal grew and false,
Are all that felt it: they change round you, turn

Truly themselves now in its vanishing.
Speak, Luria! Here begins your true career:
Look up, advance! All now is possible
Fact's grandeur, no false dreaming! Dare and do!
And every prophecy shall be fulfilled
Save one — (nay, now your word must come at last)
— That you would punish Florence!
Hus. [*Pointing to* LURIA's *dead body.*] That is done.

Whether there ever existed in the flesh such great and noble Moors as Englishmen have liked to portray — men like Shakespeare's "Othello," Scott's "Saladin," Browning's "Luria" it is impossible to say, yet we do certainly know that the Moors possessed a refinement and culture which put Europe to shame at the time of the Crusades, and long after, and that their influence was one of the great civilizing influences of the Middle Ages in Europe, spreading from Spain into Southern France and from thence to Sicily and Italy. Striking examples of the stage they had reached is seen in the fact that in Cordova one could walk ten miles on a paved street at night lighted by lamps, seven hundred years before they had even dreamed of one street lamp in London, or in Paris that streets needed other paving than mud; and in the common schools, geography was taught with a globe, when the rest of Europe considered it blasphemous to regard the earth as anything but flat.

With the exception of the reference to the Duomo, Luria's mention of her "domes and towers and palaces," and the lines given at the close, this play does not show us any pictures of the Florence of that day, though be it said, it differed much from the Florence of to-day. The Ponta Vecchio, alone, with its ancient buildings shows a complete bit of the Florence of the Middle Ages.

Wide streets have been made and many of the dismal fort-like palaces have been modified. The walls no longer exist, though some of the old gates have been left standing as monuments, an illustration of one of which we give, Porto Romano, through which we may think of Luria as often passing.

If we imagine Luria to be the captain of the Pisan war of 1406, there was no Pitti Palace with its treasures, no Riccardi, no Strozzi, but if we imagine the date to be 1495, all these would have been built or building. The Ufizzi, however, would not yet be in existence. Luria might go to church in San Marco, San Lorenzo, Santa Croce, or San Michele, but evidently his devotion was given to the great Cathedral Santa Maria del Fiore which he longed to have had com-

Porto Romano. Florence.

pleted with a Moorish front. At that time, the façade of this Cathedral was built only a third of the way up. They had in those days a curious fashion of leaving the façade of their cathedrals until the last, with the idea of making it the crowning glory of the building. Unfortunately, it frequently happened that the façade was never built at all.

In the present instance the façade was finally completed as late as 1887, the original building having been begun in 1298. The history of this cathedral is interesting, taking us back as it does to the very dawn of Italian art. The decree of the city read "The wisest men of this city do hereby opine and resolve that the Republic will undertake nothing unless with a determination that the performance shall be commensurate with the grandeur of the idea, which has emanated from the whole community." It was begun by Arnolfo di Cambio who died in 1300. The work stopped for thirty years and then Giotto was appointed Master Builder, and assisted by Andrea Pisano he continued the Cathedral according to Arnolfo's designs.

The first façade was attributed to Giotto, but it seems investigations lately made have revealed the fact that it was not begun until twenty years after Giotto's death, and that it was the joint design of several artists, Neri di Fioravante, Benci, Cione, Francesco Salsetti, Andrea Orcagna, Taddeo Gaddi, and Nicolo Tommasi. The design was Gothic, with columns and niches containing statues of the Madonna and Child, of saints and prophets and Florentine citizens.

We may imagine Luria gazing upon this unfinished façade and in 1490, if we choose, sympathizing with the Guild of Wool in its decision that the design for this façade being contrary to architectural rules, its reconstruction would be resolved upon. A meeting was held in the Cathedral at which many artists attended, but in spite of the fact that Lorenzo de' Medici was in favor of the plan, no satisfactory decision was reached and not until 1575 was the order finally issued for its demolition. Some of the frescos and statues were carried inside the Cathedral, and a new façade begun which was also condemned. A final interesting bit of information in relation to the Cathedral was unearthed not long ago by Mr. Ernest Radford, who found a sketch for a Moorish front in a small museum in Florence. Browning, however, did not know of this and wrote to Dr. Furnivall of the London Browning Society, that he "never heard nor dreamed there had been any such notion at any time of a Moorish Front for the Duomo, it was altogether a fancy of my own illustrative of the feelings natural to Luria and Braccio, each after his kind."

During this fifteenth century the dome of the Cathedral, designed by Brunelleschi, was in process of construction. This architect conceived the idea of an octagonal cupola to rest upon the dome raised above the roof, in 1417, and in 1420 he was accepted as architect. To borrow Mrs. Oliphant's picturesque phraseology: "Thus day by day, the great dome swelled out over the shining marble walls and rose against the beautiful Italian sky. Nothing like it had been seen before by living eyes. The solemn grandeur of the Pantheon at Rome was indeed known to many, and San Giovanni was in some sort an imitation of that; but the immense structure of the cupola, so justly poised, springing with such majestic grace from the familiar walls to which it gave new dignity, flattered the pride of the Florentines as something unique, besides delighting the eyes and imagination of so beauty-loving a race. With that veiled and subtle pride, which takes the shape of pious fear, some even pretended to tremble, lest it should be supposed to be too near an emulation of the blue vault above, and that Florence was competing with heaven; others, with the delightful magniloquence of the time, declared that the hills around the city were scarcely higher than the beautiful Duomo; and Vasari himself has a doubt that the heavens were envious, so persistent were the storms amid which the cupola arose."

This Florence Luria loved so well that he would fain delay the battle that was to give it peace:

"I wonder, do you guess why I delay
Involuntarily the final blow
As long as possible? Peace follows it!
Florence at peace, and the calm studious heads
Come out again, the penetrating eyes;
As if a spell broke, all's resumed, each art
You boast, more vivid that it slept awhile.
'Gainst the glad heaven, o'er the white palace-front
The interrupted scaffold climbs anew;
The walls are peopled by the painter's brush;
The statue to its niche ascends to dwell.
The present noise and trouble have retired
And left the eternal past to rule once more;
You speak its speech and read its records plain,
Greece lives with you, each Roman breathes your friend:
But Luria — where will then be Luria's place?"

In the "Soul's Tragedy," the connection with actual history is still more remote. It is dated with the same delightful vagueness as

"Luria," simply 15—. It may easily be conjectured, however, that it is Italy after the Sack of Rome, Italy under the yoke of foreign rule, that Italy which was described by Englishmen from the court of Henry VIII as full of greater wretchedness than was to be found anywhere else in Christendom. The best towns were either in ruins or depopulated. The plain between Vercelli and Pavia, fifty miles in length, once so fertile in grains and vines was reduced to a desert. The fields were uncultivated. They saw "not the shadow" of a human creature except three poor women gathering a few grapes.

The political events responsible for this state of affairs are brought before the reader with such clearness and terseness by Sedgwick in a passage in his Italian History that we cannot do better than quote it in full:

"The struggle between the Barbarians of France and Spain for Mastery in Italy was practically decided by the battle of Pavia (1525) in which the French King lost all but life and honor. France was most reluctant to acquiesce in defeat, and from time to time marched her troops across the Alps into unfortunate Piedmont, sometimes of her own motion, and sometimes at the invitation of an Italian state; but the Spanish grip was too strong to be shaken off. From this time on Italian politics were determined by the pleasure of foreign kings. Two treaties between France and Spain, that of Cambria (1529) and that of Cateau-Cambresis (1559) embodied the results of their bargains and their wars. The sum and substance of them was a practical abandonment by France of her Italian claims, and the map of Italy was drawn to suit Spain.

"Milan was governed by Spanish governors, Naples and Sicily by Spanish viceroys. The business of a Spanish viceroy, then as always, was to raise money. Taxes were oppressive. It was said that in Sicily the royal officials nibbled, in Naples they ate, and in Milan they devoured. In addition to regular taxes, special imports were laid on various occasions, — when a new king succeeded to the throne, when a royal heir was born, when war was waged against the Lutherans in Germany, or the pirates in Africa."

The Pope's Legate, Ogniben, in this play remarks more than once that he has known three-and-twenty leaders of revolt. It is not surprising that such conditions should lead to the springing up of patriots and saviours of their country, who thirsted for the blood of their tyrants and not unfrequently murdered them. Florence itself was the scene of such a murder. Alessandro de' Medici, grandson of Lorenzo the Magnificent, was placed at the head of the government with the title of "Duke of the Republic." He proved himself, Napier relates, "the most detestable of tyrants, maintained absolute power by the help of foreign mercenaries, and, having disgraced his reign by the commission of every crime known even in that depraved age, was murdered in his bed, after a reign of seven years, by his cousin, Lorenzino. The latter probably hoped to pose as a saviour of his country, but lost his self confidence and fled, leaving Florence once more without a government. Now would have been the time to proclaim a republic; but the oligarchy which had been the minister of Alessandro's crimes did not dare to face the popular indignation, and contrived, by means of the soldiers of the late duke, to place another Medici upon the throne before the people in general had recovered from the surprise into which Lorenzino's action had thrown them."

The Prelate of the play, the clever Ogniben, has all the marks of the culture of the clergy of the Renaissance, with an added sense of integrity which might well mark a man belonging to the time of the Catholic revival. This renewal of moral feeling strangely enough went hand in hand with the political degeneration. Before the foreign invasions the prelates of Rome were conspicuous for their shameless dissoluteness. There seemed to be no crime of which they were not capable. But, to quote Sedgwick again: "At the end of the century (the sixteenth) the Papacy stood erect and vigorous, shorn indeed of universal empire, but reestablished, the Order of Jesus (founded by Ignatius Loyola, and vowed to poverty, chastity, and obedience to the Papacy) at its right, the Holy Inquisition at its left, draped in piety by the council of Trent, and hobnobbing on even terms with Kings.

"The same spirit that caused the Reformation in the North, started the Catholic Revival in the South. A wave comparable to the old movement for Church reform in Hildebrand's time, swept over the Catholic Church, and lifted the reformers within the church into power. The South emulated the North. Catholic zeal rivaled Protestant ardor. Bigotry followed zeal. Moreover, a reformed Papacy found ready allies. The logical consequence of Protestantism was personal independence in religion, and the next logical step was personal independence in politics. Protestant subjects, more especially when their rulers were Catholic, tended to become disobedient; and monarchs, who stood for absolutism, found themselves drawn close to an absolute and conservative Pope. The Kings of Spain and the Popes of Rome became friends and allies."

Such we may suppose to be the political conditions in which Chiappino, the hero of "A Soul's Tragedy" and a leader of revolt, lived his little day. The play does not exist for the sake of these conditions, but in order that this particular leader of revolt may show whereof he is made. He turns out to be a patriot of very poor stuff indeed — a man, bent upon his own gain, which he hides under a cloak of righteousness, deceiving not only to others but to himself. He could slay a tyrant and with the turn of fortune become himself a tyrant, and produce logical arguments to prove that it is a sign of his own extraordinary development, and probably believe them, for an egotist of this type sincerely believes any interpretation of himself which will bolster him up in serving his own ends.

As a matter of fact, Chiappino did not kill the tyrant of the play, who was struck down by his friend Luitolfo. He helps his friend to escape and takes the deed upon himself — not in his inmost soul because he wants to save his friend, but because he wants the glory; proved by the fact that, when the populace infests the house of Luitolfo, and instead of arresting Chiappino, proclaim him their saviour, he does not disabuse them, but takes the triumph which should have been his friend's.

(*Enter the* POPULACE.)

Ch. I killed the Provost!

The Populace. [*Speaking together.*] 'Twas Chiappino, friends!

Our savior! The best man at last as first!
He who first made us feel what chains we wore,
He also strikes the blow that shatters them,
He at last saves us — our best citizen!
— Oh, have you only courage to speak now?
My eldest son was christened a year since
"Cino" to keep Chiappino's name in mind —
Cino, for shortness merely, you observe!
The city's in our hands. The guards are fled.
Do you, the cause of all, come down — come up —
Come out to counsel us, our chief, our king,
Whate'er rewards you! Choose your own reward!
The peril over, its reward begins!
Come and harangue us in the market-place!

Eu. Chiappino?

Ch. Yes — I understand your eyes!
You think I should have promptlier disowned
This deed with its strange unforeseen success,

In favor of Luitolfo. But the peril,
So far from ended, hardly seems begun.
To-morrow, rather, when a calm succeeds,
We easily shall make him full amends:
And meantime — if we save them as they pray,.
And justify the deed by its effects?
Eu. You would, for worlds, you had denied at once.
Ch. I know my own intention, be assured!
All's well. Precede us, fellow-citizens!

Before this he had shown forth his nature in his subtle insinuations that his love for Luitolfo's betrothed, Eulalia, was greater than his friend's. He sings his own praises to Eulalia in the following manner after she assures him that she has never loved him:

Ch. That's sad. Say what I might,
There was no help from being sure this while
You loved me. Love like mine must have return,
I thought: no river starts but to some sea.
And had you loved me, I could soon devise
Some specious reason why you stifled love,
Some fancied self-denial on your part,
Which made you choose Luitolfo; so, excepting
From the wide condemnation of all here,
One woman. Well, the other dream may break!
If I knew any heart, as mine loved you,
Loved me, though in the vilest breast 'twere lodged,
I should, I think, be forced to love again:
Else there's no right nor reason in the world.

In the end his nature is completely exposed by the Pope's legate, Ogniben, whose astuteness in showing the weak points in Chiappino's philosophy may be sixteenth century Italian, but certainly could not be more up to date if it had been written in the twentieth century instead of in the first part of the nineteenth.

Everything appears to go smoothly with Chiappino for a time, he has been engaged to his friend's betrothed and is about to be installed as Provost when Ogniben begins his arraignment of him. This part of the play is written in prose. Browning, very fittingly, having divided Chiappino's life into two parts, first, the poetry of it, then the prose.

Enter CHIAPPINO *and* EULALIA

Eu. We part here, then? The change in your principles would seem to be complete.

Ch. Now, why refuse to see that in my present course I change no principles, only re-adapt them and more adroitly? I had despaired of what you may call the material instrumentality of life; of ever being able to rightly operate on mankind through such a deranged machinery as the existing modes of government: but now, if I suddenly discover how to inform these perverted institutions with fresh purpose, bring the functionary limbs once more into immediate communication with, and subjection to, the soul I am about to bestow on them — do you see? Why should one desire to invent, as long as it remains possible to renew and transform? When all further hope of the old organization shall be extinct, then, I grant you, it may be time to try and create another.

Eu. And there being discoverable some hope yet in the hitherto much-abused old system of absolute government by a Provost here, you mean to take your time about endeavoring to realize those visions of a perfect State we once heard of?

Ch. Say, I would fain realize my conception of a palace, for instance, and that there is, abstractedly, but a single way of erecting one perfectly. Here, in the market-place is my allotted building-ground; here I stand without a stone to lay, or a laborer to help me, — stand, too, during a short day of life, close on which the night comes. On the other hand, circumstances suddenly offer me (turn and see it!) the old Provost's house to experiment upon — ruinous, if you please, wrongly constructed at the beginning, and ready to tumble now. But materials abound, a crowd of workmen offer their services; here exists yet a Hall of Audience of originally noble proportions, there a Guest-chamber of symmetrical design enough: and I may restore, enlarge, abolish or unite these to heart's content. Ought I not make the best of such an opportunity, rather than continue to gaze disconsolately with folded arms on the flat pavement here, while the sun goes slowly down, never to rise again? Since you cannot understand this nor me, it is better we should part as you desire.

Eu. So, the love breaks away too!

Ch. No, rather my soul's capacity for love widens — needs more than one object to content it, — and, being better instructed, will not persist in seeing all the component parts of love in what is only a single part, — nor in finding that so many and so various loves are all united in the love of a woman, — manifold uses in one instrument, as the savage has his sword, staff, sceptre and idol, all in one club-stick. Love is a very compound thing. The intellectual part of my love I shall give to men, the mighty dead or the illustrious living; and determine to call a mere sensual instinct by as few fine names as possible. What do I lose?

Eu. Nay, I only think, what do I lose? and, one more word — which shall complete my instruction — does friendship go too? What of Luitolfo, the author of your present prosperity?

Ch. How the author?

Eu. That blow now called yours . . .

Ch. Struck without principle or purpose, as by a blind natural operation: yet to which all my thought and life directly and advisedly tended. I would have struck it, and could not: he would have done his utmost to avoid striking it, yet did so. I dispute his right to that deed of mine — a final action with him, from the first effect of which he fled away, — a mere first step with me, on which I base a whole mighty superstructure of good to follow. Could he get good from it?

Eu. So we profess, so we perform!

(*Enter* OGNIBEN. EULALIA *stands apart.*)

Ogniben. I have seen three-and-twenty leaders of revolts. By your leave, sir! Perform? What does the lady say of performing?

Ch. Only the trite saying, that we must not trust profession, only performance.

Ogni. She'll not say that, sir, when she knows you longer; you'll instruct her better. Ever judge of men by their professions! For though the bright moment of promising is but a moment and cannot be prolonged, yet, if sincere in its moment's extravagant goodness, why, trust it and know the man by it, I say — not by his performance; which is half the world's work, interfere as the world needs must, with its accidents and circumstances: the profession was purely the man's own. I judge people by what they might be, — not are, nor will be.

Ch. But have there not been found, too, performing natures, not merely promising?

Ogni. Plenty. Little Bindo of our town, for instance,

promised his friend, great ugly Masaccio, once, "I will repay you!" — for a favor done him. So, when his father came to die, and Bindo succeeded to the inheritance, he sends straightway for Masaccio and shares all with him — gives him half the land, half the money, half the kegs of wine in the cellar. "Good," say you: and it is good. But had little Bindo found himself possessor of all this wealth some five years before — on the happy night when Masaccio procured him that interview in the garden with his pretty cousin Lisa — instead of being the beggar he then was, — I am bound to believe that in the warm moment of promise he would have given away all the wine-kegs and all the money and all the land, and only reserved to himself some hut on a hilltop hard by, whence he might spend his life in looking and seeing his friend enjoy himself: he meant fully that much, but the world interfered. — To our business! Did I understand you just now within-doors? You are not going to marry your old friend's love, after all?

Ch. I must have a woman that can sympatize with, and appreciate me, I told you.

Ogni. Oh, I remember! You, the greater nature, needs must have a lesser one (— avowedly lesser — contest with you on that score would never do) — such a nature must comprehend you, as the phrase is, accompany and testify of your greatness from point to point onward. Why, that were being not merely as great as yourself, but greater considerably! Meantime, might not the more bounded nature as reasonably count on your appreciation of it, rather? — on your keeping close by it, so far as you both go together, and then going on by yourself as far as you please? Thus God serves us.

Ch. And yet a woman that could understand the whole of me, to whom I could reveal alike the strength and the weakness —

Ogni. Ah, my friend, wish for nothing so foolish! Worship your love, give her the best of you to see; be to her like the western lands (they bring us such strange news of) to the Spanish Court; send her only your lumps of gold, fans of feathers, your spirit-like birds, and fruits and gems! So shall you, what is unseen of you, be supposed altogether a paradise by her, — as these western lands by Spain: though I warrant there is filth, red baboons, ugly reptiles and squalor enough, which they bring Spain as few samples of as possible. Do you want your mistress to respect your body generally? Offer her your mouth to kiss: don't strip off your boot and put your foot to her lips! You understand my humor by this time? I help men to carry out their own principles: if they please to say two and two make five, I assent, so they will but go on and say, four and four make ten.

Ch. But these are my private affairs; what I desire you to occupy yourself about, is my public appearance presently: for when the people hear that I am appointed Provost, though you and I may thoroughly discern — and easily, too— the right principle at bottom of such a movement, and how my republicanism remains thoroughly unaltered, only takes a form of expression hitherto commonly judged (and heretofore by myself) incompatible with its existence, — when thus I reconcile myself to an old form of government instead of proposing a new one —

Ogni. Why, you must deal with people broadly. Begin at a distance from this matter and say, — New truths, old truths! sirs, there is nothing new possible to be revealed to us in the moral world; we know all we shall ever know: and it is for simply reminding us, by their various respective expedients, how we do know this and the other matter, that men get called prophets, poets and the like. A philosopher's life is spent in discovering that, of the half-dozen truths he knew when a child, such an one is a lie, as the world states it in set terms; and then, after a weary lapse of years, and plenty of hard thinking, it becomes a truth again after all, as he happens to newly consider it and view it in a different relation with the others: and so he re-states it, to the confusion of somebody else in good time. As for adding to the original stock of truths, — impossible! Thus, you see the expression of them is the grand business: — you have got a truth in your head about the right way of governing people, and you took a mode of expressing it which now you confess to be imperfect. But what then? There is truth in falsehood, falsehood in truth. No man ever told one great truth, that I know, without the help of a good dozen of lies at least, generally unconscious ones. And as when a child comes in breathlessly and relates a strange story, you try to conjecture from the very falsities in it what the reality was, — do not conclude that he saw nothing in the sky, because he assuredly did not see a flying horse there as he says, — so, through the contradictory expression, do you see, men should look painfully for, and trust to arrive eventually at, what you call the true principle at bottom. Ah, what an answer is there! to what will it not prove applicable? — "Contradictions? Of course there were," say you!

Ch. Still, the world at large may call it inconsistency, and what shall I urge in reply?

Ogni. Why, look you, when they tax you with tergiversation or duplicity, you may answer — you begin to perceive that, when all's done and said, both great parties in the State, the advocators of change in the present system of things, and the opponents of it, patriot and anti-patriot, are found working together for the common good; and that in the midst of their efforts for and against its progress, the world somehow or other still advances: to which result they contribute in equal proportions, those who spend their life in pushing it onward, as those who give theirs to the business of pulling it back. Now, if you found the world stand still between the opposite forces, and were glad, I should conceive you: but it steadily advances, you rejoice to see! By the side of such a rejoicer, the man who only winks as he keeps cunning and quiet, and says, "Let yonder hot-headed fellow fight out my battle: I, for one, shall win in the end by the blows he gives, and which I ought to be giving," — even he seems graceful in his avowal, when one considers that he might say, "I shall win quite as much by the blows our antagonist gives him, blows from which he saves me — I thank the antagonist equally!" Moreover, you may enlarge on the loss of the edge of party-animosity with age and experience . . .

Ch. And naturally time must wear off such asperities: the bitterest adversaries get to discover certain points of similarity between each other, common sympathies — do they not?

Ogni. Ay, had the young David but sat first to dine on his cheeses with the Philistine, he had soon discovered an abundance of such common sympathies. He of Gath, it is recorded, was born of a father and mother, had brothers and sisters like another man, — they, no more than the sons of Jesse, were used to eat each other. But, for the sake of one broad antipathy that had existed from the beginning, David slung the stone, cut off the giant's head, made a spoil of it, and after ate his cheeses alone, with the better appetite, for all I can learn. My friend, as you, with a quickened eyesight, go on discovering much good on the worse side, remember that the same process should proportionably magnify and demonstrate to you the much more good on the better side! And when I profess no sympathy for the Goliaths of our time, and you object that a large nature should sympathize with every form of intelligence, and see the good in it, however limited, — I answer, "So I do; but preserve the proportions of my sympathy, however finelier or widelier I may extend its action." I desire to be able, with a quickened eyesight, to descry beauty in corruption where others see foulness only; but I hope I shall also continue to see a redoubled beauty in the higher forms of matter, where already everybody sees no foulness at all. I must retain, too, my old power of selection, and choice of appropriation, to apply to such new gifts; else they only dazzle instead of enlightening me. God has his archangels and consorts with them: though he made too, and intimately sees what is good in, the worm. Observe, I speak only as you profess to think and so ought to speak: I do justice to your own principles, that is all.

Ch. But you very well know that the two parties do, on occasion, assume each other's characteristics. What more disgusting, for instance, than to see how promptly the newly emancipated slave will adopt, in his own favor, the very measures of precaution, which pressed soreliest on himself as institutions of the tyranny he has just escaped from? Do the classes, hitherto without opinion, get leave to express it? there follows a confederacy immediately, from which — exercise your individual right and dissent, and woe be to you!

Ogni. And a journey over the sea to you! That is the generous way. Cry — "Emancipated slaves, the first excess, and off I go!" The first time a poor devil, who has been bastinadoed steadily his whole life long, finds himself let alone and able to legislate, so, begins pettishly, while he rubs his soles, "Woe be to whoever brings anything in the shape of a stick this way!" — you, rather than give up the very innocent pleasure of carrying one to switch flies with, — you go away, to everybody's sorrow. Yet you were quite reconciled to staying at home while the governors used to pass, every now and then, some such edict as, "Let no man indulge in owning a stick which is not thick enough to chastise our slaves, if need require!" Well, there are pre-ordained hierarchies among us, and a profane vulgar subjected to a different law altogether; yet I am rather sorry you should see it so clearly: for, do you know what is to — all but save you at the Day of Judgment, all you men of genius? It is this: that, while you generally began by pulling down God, and went on to the end of your life in one effort at setting up your own genius in his place, — still, the last, bitterest concession wrung with the utmost unwillingness from the experience of the very loftiest of you, was invariably — would one think it? — that the rest of mankind, down to the lowest of the mass, stood not, nor ever could stand, just on a level and equality with yourselves. That will be a point in the favor of all such, I hope and believe.

Ch. Why, men of genius are usually charged, I think, with doing just the reverse; and at once acknowledging the natural inequality of mankind, by themselves participating in the universal craving after, and deference to, the civil distinctions which represent it. You wonder they pay such undue respect to titles and badges of superior rank.

Ogni. Not I (always on your own ground and showing, be it noted!) Who doubts that, with a weapon to brandish, a man is the more formidable? Titles and badges are exercised as such a weapon, to which you and I look up wistfully. We could pin lions with it moreover, while in its present owner's hands it hardly prods rats. Nay, better than a mere weapon of easy mastery and obvious use, it is a mysterious divining-rod that may serve us in undreamed-of ways. Beauty, strength, intellect — men often have none of these, and yet conceive pretty accurately what kind of advantages they would bestow on the possessor. We know at least what it is we make up our mind to forego, and so can apply the fittest substitute in our power. Wanting beauty, we cultivate good-humor; missing wit, we get riches: but the mystic unimaginable operation of that gold collar and string of Latin names which suddenly turned poor stupid little peevish Cecco of our town into natural lord of the best of us — a Duke, he is now — there indeed is a virtue to be reverenced!

Ch. Ay, by the vulgar: not by Messere Stiatta the poet, who pays more assiduous court to him than anybody.

Ogni. What else should Stiatta pay court to? He has talent, not honor and riches: men naturally covet what they have not.

Ch. No; or Cecco would covet talent, which he has not, whereas he covets more riches, of which he has plenty, already.

Ogni. Because a purse added to a purse makes the holder twice as rich: but just such another talent as Stiatta's, added to what he now possesses, what would that profit him? Give the talent a purse indeed, to do something with! But lo, how we keep the good people waiting! I only desired to do justice to the noble sentiments which animate you, and which you are too modest to duly enforce. Come, to our main business: shall we ascend the steps? I am going to propose you for Provost to the people; they know your antecedents, and will accept you with a joyful unanimity: whereon I confirm their choice. Rouse up! Are you nerving yourself to an effort? Beware the disaster of Messere Stiatta we were talking of! who, determining to keep an equal mind and constant face on whatever might be the fortune of his last new poem with our townsmen, heard too plainly "hiss, hiss, hiss," increase every moment. Till at last the man fell senseless: not perceiving that the portentous sounds had all the while been issuing from between his own nobly clenched teeth, and nostrils narrowed by resolve.

Ch. Do you begin to throw off the mask? — to jest with me, having got me effectually into your trap?

Ogni. Where is the trap, my friend? You hear what I engage to do, for my part: you, for yours, have only to fulfil your promise made just now within doors, of professing unlimited obedience to Rome's authority in my person.

And I shall authorize no more than the simple re-establishment of the Provostship and the conferment of its privileges upon yourself: the only novel stipulation being a birth of the peculiar circumstances of the time.

Ch. And that stipulation?

Ogni. Just the obvious one — that in the event of the discovery of the actual assailant of the late Provost . . .

Ch. Ha!

Ogni. Why, he shall suffer the proper penalty, of course; what did you expect?

Ch. Who heard of this?

Ogni. Rather, who needed to hear of this?

Ch. Can it be, the popular rumor never reached you . . .

Ogni. Many more such rumors reach me, friend, than I choose to receive: those which wait longest have best chance. Has the present one sufficiently waited? Now is its time for entry with effect. See the good people crowding about yonder palace-steps — which we may not have to ascend, after all! My good friends! (nay, two or three of you will answer every purpose) — who was it fell upon and proved nearly the death of your late Provost? His successor desires to hear, that his day of inauguration may be graced by the act of prompt, bare justice we all anticipate. Who dealt the blow that night, does anybody know?

Luit. [*Coming forward*]. I!

All. Luitolfo!

Luit. I avow the deed, justify and approve it, and stand forth now, to relieve my friend of an unearned responsibility. Having taken thought, I am grown stronger: I shall shrink from nothing that awaits me. Nay, Chiappino — we are friends still: I dare say there is some proof of your superior nature in this starting aside, strange as it seemed at first. So, they tell me, my horse is of the right stock, because a shadow in the path frightens him into a frenzy, makes him dash my brains out. I understand only the dull mule's way of standing stockishly, plodding soberly, suffering on occasion a blow or two with due patience.

Eu. I was determined to justify my choice, Chiappino; to let Luitolfo's nature vindicate itself. Henceforth we are undivided, whatever be our fortune.

Ogni. Now, in these last ten minutes of silence, what have I been doing, deem you? Putting the finishing stroke to a homily of mine, I have long taken thought to perfect, on the text, "Let whoso thinketh he standeth, take heed lest he fall." To your house, Luitolfo! Still silent, my patriotic friend? Well, that is a good sign, however. And you will go aside for a time? That is better still. I understand: it would be easy for you to die of remorse here on the spot and shock us all, but you mean to live and grow worthy of coming back to us one day. There, I will tell everybody; and you only do right to believe you must get better as you get older. All men do so: they are worst in childhood, improve in manhood, and get ready in old age for another world. Youth, with its beauty and grace, would seem bestowed on us for some such reason as to make us partly endurable till we have time for really becoming so of ourselves, without their aid; when they leave us. The sweetest child we all smile on for his pleasant want of the whole world to break up, or suck in his mouth, seeing no other good in it — would be rudely handled by that world's inhabitants, if he retained those angelic infantine desires when he had grown six feet high, black and bearded. But, little by little, he sees fit to forego claim after claim on the world, puts up with a less and less share of its good as his proper portion; and when the octogenarian asks barely a sup of gruel and a fire of dry sticks, and thanks you as for his full allowance and right in the common good of life, — hoping nobody may murder him, — he who began by asking and expecting the whole of us to

bow down in worship to him, — why, I say he is advanced, far onward, very far, nearly out of sight like our friend Chiappino yonder. And now — (ay, good-by to you! He turns round the northwest gate: going to Lugo again? Good-by!) — And now give thanks to God, the keys of the Provost's palace to me, and yourselves to profitable meditation at home! I have known *Four*-and-twenty leaders of revolts.

The drama, "King Victor and King Charles," like "Strafford," is a true historical play in which the poet has used imagination only in the development of real historical personages, into whose mouths he puts language, doubtless true to their natures, if not such as they ever actually uttered.

The episode in history which he has dramatized is the story of the relation between Victor, King of Sardinia and his son Charles, afterwards king.

The accounts of Victor Amadeus II are somewhat contradictory and confused, but the poet with a poet's privilege has seized those points which would tell best dramatically. Gathering these up from the histories of Voltaire, Costa da Beauregard, and Gallenga, the story runs as follows:

Victor was born in 1666 and succeeded his father under the regency of his mother in 1675. He had a warlike and brilliant career and succeeded in building up for himself an independent kingdom. In 1713, by the treaty of Utrecht, Savoy was recognized as an independent state and he was made King of Sicily, but soon exchanged this title for that of king of Sardinia. Later events having made it probable that the Bourbons would return to Italy again, Victor and all the other European monarchs became anxious at the prospect. Victor received propositions from both France and Austria to join with them in case of a rupture. After having wavered between them for some time, he finally made secret engagements with both. In June, 1730, he received from the Emperor of Austria a sum of money, with the promise that he and his descendants should be governors of Milan *in perpetuo* if he would never separate his interests from those of Austria. A few days after, the Spanish Minister, having had a secret audience with him, made him flattering offers if he would declare himself for the Bourbons. He accepted this offer also, but at last, seeing that his intrigues were about to be discovered, decided to abdicate, affecting a philosophic love of repose which was far from his character, as proved by his attempt later to remount the throne. According to Gallenga in his history of Piedmont, the later years of

Victor were crowned with unprecedented prosperity, and his abdication was really due to weariness of the world and a doting fondness for his new bride, while his desire to return to rule was due to the ennui he suffered in his retreat at Chambéry and the ambition of the Marchioness, who had set her heart on being queen.

The story is told a little differently by Lord Orrery in one of his letters from Italy, and, as he had actually seen King Charles and heard the story related as the gossip of the time, it may be interesting to quote from this letter, which also gives glimpses of Turin and the palace as it existed at that time:

"The city of Turin, dear sir, is not large, nor can it in any sense be called magnificent. The same may be said of the King's palace, most part of the outward building being old and unfinished. The royal apartments of Turin consist of a great number of small rooms, many of them indeed only closets; but so delicately fitted up, so elegantly furnished and so properly adorned, that, in passing from room to room, the whole appears a fairy castle. Amidst all these exquisite decorations, not one effeminate toy, not one Chinese dragon nor Indian monster is to be seen.

TURIN.

"Almost every room in the palace is filled with pictures, none indifferent; most of them by the best Flemish masters. The whole collection, except a very small number, belonged to prince Eugene and were bought after his death by the present King of Sardinia. The floors of the King's apartments are inlaid, and so nicely kept that you view yourself as you walk upon them. The chapel, which opens into the great church, is not answerable to any other part of the palace. It is clean, but it is heavy and dismal. The pillars are of black marble. The lamps and tapers give little light and less cheerfulness. At the first entrance it appears like a melancholy mausoleum.

"The king in his younger days is said to have been of a gay and sprightly disposition; but soon after the death of his father he contracted a more serious behavior, which is now growing apace into the melancholy of devotion.

"One particular anecdote of the Sardinian monarch was related to me, as a certain truth. If the eagerness of the chase happens accidentally to lead him near Montcallier, he turns his eyes and horse as fast as possible from the castle. His father died there under such circumstances as must affect a son.

"Victor Amadeus, father of the present King of Sardinia, had made a considerable figure in the annals of Europe. He had appeared a great soldier, and was known to be a great politician. In the decline of his life, the latter part of that character was not a little sullied. He involved himself in a disadvantageous treaty with France, and he degraded his royalty by a marriage. The lady, whom he chose for his wife, in the same private manner that the famous Maintenon had been chosen by Lewis XIV, was called Madam de Sebastien. She was the widow of an officer of that name. She had been maid of honor to the King's mother. She was at that time extremely handsome, but always of an intriguing, ambitious temper. The King had paid his addresses to her not unsuccessfully in his youth. Now finding himself absolutely constrained to fulfil his impolitic engagements with France, he determined to resign his crown to his son, who being under no such engagements, might openly repair the injudicious step which his father had taken. On one and the same day Amadeus delivered up his crown and married his former mistress, whom he had not long before created Marchioness di Spigno, a town in Italy in the duchy of

Montferat. His abdication was public; his marriage was private. The King and the Marchioness immediately retired to Chambéry. The young King soon acted the part in which he had been fully instructed by his father, mingling with it a scene or two of his own. He discarded King Victor's ministers and favorites, but still maintained all the outward tokens of duty and respect, which he owed his father, who soon grew impatient and weary of retirement, and wished to return to business, power and a throne. His new consort was equally desirous to taste the splendor of a crown, and to command in the circle of a court. They both repented, not of their marriage, but of their retreat.

"Chambéry, in its utmost magnificence, was too melancholy a situation and had too much the air of a prison to calm and alleviate the struggles of such restless minds. The King and the lady kept up a constant correspondence with the discontented Piedmontese, especially those in Turin. A plot was formed. The King was to dethrone his son, and to reassume the reins of government. Measures to this end were taken with all possible secrecy. The King complained of the air of Chambéry. His son attended to his complaint with the deepest filial attachment.

Amadeus was permitted to approach nearer to the capital. He came to Rivoli, that hunting seat which I mentioned in my last. The air of Rivoli disagreed with him. He was suffered to come still nearer, and was lodged at his own request in the castle of Montcallier, a noble palace within a very little distance of Turin. There the embers of ambition soon kindled into a flame. The fire was on the point of breaking out when the heat of it began to be felt by the young king and his ministers. They had only time to stop Amadeus as he was going into his coach under a pretence of visiting, but with a resolution of seizing the citadel of Turin. In a moment he became his son's prisoner in the castle of Montcallier. His wife was abruptly torn from him. They met no more. He was treated with respect, but guarded with the closest strictness. He often desired to see his son. The interview was promised, but the promise was not performed. Rage, grief and disappointment ended, in less than two years, the life of this unhappy prince, whose sunset was excessively languid in comparison of his meridian glory.

"Affairs of state probably constrained the present king to act as he did; but deep has been the impression which his father's catastrophe has left on his mind. Perhaps the late King extorted from his son a private promise of restoring the crown. Policy and majesty soon put a stop to the designs, if any, of answering that promise."

Here Browning deliberately departs from history and causes Charles to return the crown to his father. Loyalty and love to his father are the ruling impulses of Charles's life as the poet portrays him, and while he also has loyalty and love to his subjects, when these two come in conflict his devotion to his father conquers.

Beauregard emphasizes this filial devotion in his account of the scene between the father and son upon the former's resignation of the crown. "He called his son to him, and declared to him his design. The young prince, astonished, troubled, fearing perhaps that this overture was only a trap in order to prove him, said to the King all that was proper to turn him from such a design. He prayed the King, if he really thought a time of repose was necessary to his health, to confer upon him the temporary exercise of authority, reserving the right to re-take the crown when he thought proper. He ended by throwing himself at his father's feet and conjuring him to change his resolution."

For the character of d'Ormea, the Minister in this play, the poet took a hint from Voltaire. "He was a man without birth, whom Victor found in utter misery. This minister had rendered him the service of ending the differences with the Court of Rome, which had existed during a great part of his reign. He obtained for him a more favorable agreement than Victor had been able to obtain for himself." Of him, Blondel says, "he had more mind, more transcendent qualities, above all, more audacity and confidence in himself, than any of the other ministers. It is certain he had all the favor of King Victor. He had many enemies, having, while he was manager of the finances, brought about the reunion of the fiefs with the domain, and treated with the Court of Rome. The nobility and clergy hated him."

In the play there are but four characters, Victor, Charles, d'Ormea, and Polyxena, the wife of Charles. The historical events are in reality merely the factors by means of which the natures of these four individuals reveal themselves.

Charles is made at first of a timid, vacillating nature, but the help and encouragement of his wife, combined with the sudden thrusting of power upon him make a man of him and he governs so well that he is much beloved by his people. Victor is an almost exact picture of the historical Victor, astute and unscrupulous, while d'Ormea, at first the match of his master in all underhanded schemes for self-advancement, is really won over to rectitude by the fine, unselfish nature of Charles.

To illustrate the masterful handling of his material by the poet we give the scene of Victor's abdication and the scene of his retaking of the Crown.

KING VICTOR

PART II

Enter KING VICTOR, *bearing the regalia on a cushion, from his apartment. He calls loudly —*

D'Ormea! — for patience fails me, treading thus
Among the obscure trains I have laid, — my knights
Safe in the hall here — in that anteroom,
My son, — D'Ormea, where? Of this, one touch —
[*Laying down the crown.*
This fireball to these mute black cold trains — then
Outbreak enough!
[*Contemplating it.*] To lose all, after all!
This, glancing o'er my house for ages — shaped,
Brave meteor, like the crown of Cyprus now,
Jerusalem, Spain, England, every change
The braver, — and when I have clutched a prize
My ancestry died wan with watching for,

To lose it! — by a slip, a fault, a trick
Learnt to advantage once and not unlearned
When past the use, — "just this once more" (I thought)
"Use it with Spain and Austria happily,
And then away with trick!" An oversight
I'd have repaired thrice over, any time
These fifty years, must happen now! There's peace
At length; and I, to make the most of peace,
Ventured my project on our people here,
As needing not their help: which Europe knows,
And means, cold-blooded, to dispose herself
(Apart from plausibilities of war)
To crush the new-made King — who ne'er till now
Feared her. As Duke, I lost each foot of earth
And laughed at her: my name was left, my sword
Left, all was left! But she can take, she knows,
This crown, herself conceded . . .
That's to try,
Kind Europe! — My career's not closed as yet!
This boy was ever subject to my will,
Timid and tame — the fitter! — D'Ormea, too —
What if the sovereign also rid himself
Of thee, his prime of parasites? — I delay!
D'Ormea!

(*As* D'ORMEA *enters, the King seats himself.*)

My son, the Prince — attends he?

D'O. Sir,
He does attend. The crown prepared! — it seems
That you persist in your resolve.

Victor. Who's come?
The chancellor and the chamberlain? My knights?

D'O. The whole Annunziata? If, my liege,
Your fortune had not tottered worse than now . . .

Vic. Del Borgo has drawn up the schedules? mine —

My son's, too? Excellent! Only, beware
Of the least blunder, or we look but fools.
First, you read the Annulment of the Oaths;
Del Borgo follows . . . no, the Prince shall sign;
Then let Del Borgo read the Instrument:
On which, I enter.
D'O. Sir, this may be truth;
You, sir, may do as you affect — may break
Your engine, me, to pieces: try at least
If not a spring remain worth saving! Take
My counsel as I've counselled many times!
What if the Spaniard and the Austrian threat?
There's England, Holland, Venice — which ally
Select you?
Vic. Aha! Come, D'Ormea, — "truth"
Was on your lip a minute since. Allies?
I've broken faith with Venice, Holland, England
— As who knows if not you?
D'O. But why with me
Break faith — with one ally, your best, break faith?
Vic. When first I stumbled on you, Marquis — 'twas
At Mondovi — a little lawyer's clerk . . .
D'O. Therefore your soul's ally! — who brought you through
Your quarrel with the Pope, at pains enough —
Who simply echoed you in these affairs!
On whom you cannot therefore visit these
Affairs' ill fortune — whom you trust to guide
You safe (yes, on my soul) through these affairs!
Vic. I was about to notice, had you not
Prevented me, that since that great town kept
With its chicane D'Ormea's satchel stuffed
And D'Ormea's self sufficiently recluse,
He missed a sight, — my naval armament

When I burned Toulon. How the skiff exults
Upon the galliot's wave! — rises its height,
O'ertops it even; but the great wave bursts,
And hell-deep in the horrible profound
Buries itself the galliot: shall the skiff
Think to escape the sea's black trough in turn?
Apply this: you have been my minister
— Next me, above me possibly; — sad post,
Huge care, abundant lack of peace of mind;
Who would desiderate the eminence?
You gave your soul to get it; you'd yet give
Your soul to keep it, as I mean you shall,
D'Ormea! What if the wave ebbed with me?
Whereas it cants you to another crest;
I toss you to my son; ride out your ride!

D'O. Ah, you so much despise me?

Vic. You, D'Ormea?
Nowise: and I'll inform you why. A king
Must in his time have many ministers,
And I've been rash enough to part with mine
When I thought proper. Of the tribe, not one
(. . . . Or wait, did Pianezze? . . . ah, just the same!)
Not one of them, ere his remonstrance reached
The length of yours, but has assured me (commonly
Standing much as you stand, — or nearer, say,
The door to make his exit on his speech)
— I should repent of what I did. D'Ormea,
Be candid, you approached it when I bade you
Prepare the schedules! But you stopped in time,
You have not so assured me: how should I
Despise you then?

(*Enter* CHARLES.)

Vic. [*Changing his tone.*] Are you instructed? Do
My order, point by point! About it, sir!

D'O. You so despise me! [*Aside.*] One last stay remains —
The boy's discretion there.
[*To* CHA.] For your sake, Prince,
I pleaded, wholly in your interest,
To save you from this fate!
Cha. [*Aside.*] Must I be told
The Prince was supplicated for — by him?
Vic. [*To* D'O.] Apprise Del Borgo, Spava, and the rest,
Our son attends them; then return.
D'O. One word!
Cha. [*Aside.*] A moment's pause and they would drive me hence,
I do believe!
D'O. [*Aside.*] Let but the boy be firm!
Vic. You disobey?
Cha. [*To D'O.*] You do not disobey
Me, at least. Did you promise that or no?
D'O. Sir, I am yours: what would you? Yours am I!
Cha. When I have said what I shall say, 'tis like
Your face will ne'er again disgust me. Go!
Through you, as through a breast of glass, I see.
And for your conduct, from my youth till now,
Take my contempt! You might have spared me much,
Secured me somewhat, nor so harmed yourself:
That's over now. Go, ne'er to come again!
D'O. As son, the father — father, as the son!
My wits! My wits! [*Goes.*
Vic. [*Seated.*] And you, what meant you, pray,
Speaking thus to D'Ormea?
Cha. Let us not
Waste words upon D'Ormea! Those I spent
Have half unsettled what I came to say.
His presence vexes to my very soul.

Vic. One called to manage a kingdom, Charles, needs heart
To bear up under worse annoyances
Than seems D'Ormea — to me, at least.
Cha. [*Aside.*] Ah, good!
He keeps me to the point! Then be it so.
[*Aloud.*] Last night, sir, brought me certain papers — these —
To be reported on, — your way of late.
Is it last night's result that you demand?
Vic. For God's sake, what has night brought forth? Pronounce
The . . . what's your word? — result!
Cha. Sir, that had proved
Quite worthy of your sneer, no doubt: — a few
Lame thoughts, regard for you alone could wring,
Lame as they are, from brains like mine, believe!
As 'tis, sir, I am spared both toil and sneer.
These are the papers.
Vic. Well, sir? I suppose
You hardly burned them. Now for your result!
Cha. I never should have done great things, of course,
But . . . oh my father, had you loved me more!
Vic. Loved? [*Aside.*] Has D'Ormea played me false, I wonder?
[*Aloud.*] Why, Charles, a king's love is diffused — yourself
May overlook, perchance, your part in it.
Our monarchy is absolutest now
In Europe, or my trouble's thrown away.
I love, my mode, that subjects each and all
May have the power of loving, all and each,
Their mode: I doubt not, many have their sons
To trifle with, talk soft to, all day long:
I have that crown, this chair, D'Ormea, Charles!

Cha. 'Tis well I am a subject then, not you.
Vic. [*Aside.*] D'Ormea has told him everything. [*Aloud.*]
Aha!
I apprehend you: when all's said, you take
Your private station to be prized beyond
My own, for instance?
Cha. — Do and ever did
So take it: 'tis the method you pursue
That grieves . . .
Vic. These words! Let me express, my friend,
Your thoughts. You penetrate what I supposed
Secret. D'Ormea plies his trade betimes!
I purpose to resign my crown to you.
Cha. To me?
Vic. Now, — in that chamber.
Cha. You resign
The crown to me?
Vic. And time enough, Charles, sure?
Confess with me, at four- and-sixty years
A crown's a load. I covet quiet once
Before I die, and summoned you for that.
Cha. 'Tis I will speak: you ever hated me.
I bore it, — have insulted me, borne too —
Now you insult yourself; and I remember
What I believed you, what you really are,
And cannot bear it. What! My life has passed
Under your eye, tormented as you know, —
Your whole sagacities, one after one,
At leisure brought to play on me — to prove me
A fool, I thought and I submitted; now
You'd prove . . . what would you prove me?
Vic. This to me?
I hardly know you!
Cha. Know me? Oh indeed

You do not! Wait till I complain next time
Of my simplicity! — for here's a sage
Knows the world well, is not to be deceived,
And his experience, and his Macchiavels,
D'Ormeas, teach him — what? — that I this while
Have envied him his crown! He has not smiled,
I warrant, — has not eaten, drunk, nor slept,
For I was plotting with my Princess yonder!
Who knows what we might do or might not do?
Go now, be politic, astound the world!
That sentry in the antechamber — nay,
The varlet who disposed this precious trap
[*Pointing to the crown.*
That was to take me — ask them if they think
Their own sons envy them their posts! — Know me!
Vic. But you know me, it seems: so, learn, in brief,
My pleasure. This assembly is convened . . .
Cha. Tell me, that woman put it in your head!
You were not sole contriver of the scheme,
My father!
Vic. Now observe me, sir! I jest
Seldom — on these points, never. Here, I say,
The knights assemble to see me concede,
And you accept, Sardinia's crown.
Cha. Farewell!
'Twere vain to hope to change this: I can end it.
Not that I cease from being yours, when sunk
Into obscurity: I'll die for you,
But not annoy you with my presence. Sir,
Farewell! Farewell!
(*Enter* D'ORMEA.)
D'O. [*Aside.*] Ha, sure he's changed again —
Means not to fall into the cunning trap!
Then, Victor, I shall escape you, Victor!

Vic. [*Suddenly placing the crown upon the head of* CHARLES.] D'Ormea, your King!
[*To* CHA.] My son, obey me! Charles,
Your father, clearer-sighted than yourself,
Decides it must be so. 'Faith, this looks real!
My reasons after; reason upon reason
After: but now, obey me! Trust in me!
By this, you save Sardinia, you save me!
Why, the boy swoons! [*To D'O.*] Come this side!

D'O. [*As* CHARLES *turns from him to* VICTOR.] You persist?

Vic. Yes, I conceive the gesture's meaning. 'Faith,
He almost seems to hate you: how is that?
Be reassured, my Charles! Is't over now?
Then, Marquis, tell the new King what remains
To do! A moment's work. Del Borgo reads
The Act of Abdication out, you sign it,
Then I sign; after that, come back to me.

D'O. Sir, for the last time, pause!

Vic. Five minutes longer
I am your sovereign, Marquis. Hesitate —
And I'll so turn those minutes to account
That . . . Ay, you recollect me! [*Aside.*] Could I bring
My foolish mind to undergo the reading
That Act of Abdication!

[*As* CHARLES *motions* D'ORMEA *to precede him.*

Thanks, dear Charles!

[CHARLES *and* D'ORMEA *retire.*

Vic. A novel feature in the boy, — indeed
Just what I feared he wanted most. Quite right,
This earnest tone: your truth, now for effect!
It answers every purpose: with that look,
That voice, — I hear him: "I began no treaty,"
(He speaks to Spain,) "nor ever dreamed of this

You show me; this I from my soul regret;
But if my father signed it, bid not me
Dishonor him — who gave me all, beside:"
And, "true," says Spain, "'twere harsh to visit that
Upon the Prince." Then come the nobles trooping:
"I grieve at these exactions — I had cut
This hand off ere impose them; but shall I
Undo my father's deed?" — and they confer:
"Doubtless he was no party, after all;
Give the Prince time!"
Ay, give us time, but time!
Only, he must not, when the dark day comes,
Refer our friends to me and frustrate all.
We'll have no child's play, no desponding fits,
No Charles at each cross turn entreating Victor
To take his crown again. Guard against that!
(*Enter* D'ORMEA.)
Long live King Charles!
No — Charles's counsellor!
Well, is it over, Marquis? Did I jest?
D'O. "King Charles!" What then may you be?
Vic. Anything!
A country gentleman that, cured of bustle,
Now beats a quick retreat toward Chambery,
Would hunt and hawk and leave you noisy folk
To drive your trade without him. I'm Count Remont —
Count Tende — any little place's Count!
D'O. Then Victor, Captain against Catinat
At Staffarde, where the French beat you; and Duke
At Turin, where you beat the French; King late
Of Savoy, Piedmont, Montferrat, Sardinia,
— Now, "any little place's Count" —
Vic. Proceed!
D'O. Breaker of vows to God, who crowned you first;

Breaker of vows to man, who kept you since;
Most profligate to me who outraged God
And man to serve you, and am made pay crimes
I was but privy to, by passing thus
To your imbecile son — who, well you know,
Must — (when the people here, and nations there,
Clamor for you the main delinquent, slipped
From King to — "Count of any little place)"
Must needs surrender me, all in his reach, —
I, sir, forgive you: for I see the end —
See you on your return — (you will return) —
To him you trust, a moment . . .

Vic. Trust him? How?
My poor man, merely a prime-minister,
Make me know where my trust errs!

D'O. In his fear,
His love, his — but discover for yourself
What you are weakest, trusting in!

Vic. Aha,
D'Ormea, not a shrewder scheme than this
In your repertory? You know old Victor —
Vain, choleric, inconstant, rash — (I've heard
Talkers who little thought the King so close) —
Felicitous now, were 't not, to provoke him
To clean forget, one minute afterward,
His solemn act, and call the nobles back
And pray them give again the very power
He has abjured? — for the dear sake of what?
Vengeance on you, D'Ormea! No: such am I,
Count Tende or Count anything you please,
— Only, the same that did the things you say,
And, among other things you say not, used
Your finest fibre, meanest muscle, — you
I used, and now, since you will have it so,

Leave to your fate — mere lumber in the midst,
You and your works. Why, what on earth beside
Are you made for, you sort of ministers?
D'O. Not left, though, to my fate! Your witless son
Has more wit than to load himself with lumber:
He foils you that way, and I follow you.
Vic. Stay with my son — protect the weaker side!
D'O. Ay, to be tossed the people like a rag,
And flung by them for Spain and Austria's sport,
Abolishing the record of your part
In all this perfidy!
Vic. Prevent, beside,
My own return!
D'O. That's half prevented now!
'Twill go hard but you find a wondrous charm
In exile, to discredit me. The Alps,
Silk-mills to watch, vines asking vigilance —
Hounds open for the stag, your hawk's a-wing —
Brave days that wait the Louis of the South,
Italy's Janus!
Vic. So, the lawyer's clerk
Won't tell me that I shall repent!
D'O. You give me
Full leave to ask if you repent?
Vic. Whene'er
Sufficient time's elapsed for that, you judge!
[*Shouts inside*, "KING CHARLES!"
D'O. Do you repent?
Vic. [*After a slight pause.*] . . . I've kept them waiting? Yes!
Come in, complete the Abdication, sir! [*They go out.*
(*Enter* POLYXENA.)
Pol. A shout! The sycophants are free of Charles!
Oh, is not this like Italy? No fruit

Of his or my distempered fancy, this,
But just an ordinary fact! Beside,
Here they've set forms for such proceedings; Victor
Imprisoned his own mother: he should know,
If any, how a son's to be deprived
Of a son's right. Our duty's palpable.
Ne'er was my husband for the wily king
And the unworthy subjects: be it so!
Come you safe out of them, my Charles! Our life
Grows not the broad and dazzling life, I dreamed
Might prove your lot; for strength was shut in you
None guessed but I — strength which, untrammelled once,
Had little shamed your vaunted ancestry —
Patience and self-devotion, fortitude,
Simplicity and utter truthfulness
— All which, they shout to lose!

So, now my work
Begins — to save him from regret. Save Charles
Regret? — the noble nature! He's not made
Like these Italians: 'tis a German soul.

(CHARLES *enters crowned.*)

Oh, where's the King's heir? Gone: — the Crown-prince? Gone: —
Where's Savoy? Gone! — Sardinia? Gone! But Charles
Is left! And when my Rhine-land bowers arrive,
If he looked almost handsome yester-twilight
As his gray eyes seemed widening into black
Because I praised him, then how will he look?
Farewell, you stripped and whited mulberry-trees
Bound each to each by lazy ropes of vine!
Now I'll teach you my language: I'm not forced
To speak Italian now, Charles?
[*She sees the crown.*] What is this?
Answer me — who has done this? Answer!

Cha. He!
I am King now.
Pol. Oh worst, worst, worst of all!
Tell me! What, Victor? He has made you King?
What's he then? What's to follow this? You, King?
Cha. Have I done wrong? Yes, for you were not by!
Pol. Tell me from first to last.
Cha. Hush — a new world
Brightens before me; he is moved away
— The dark form that eclipsed it, he subsides
Into a shape supporting me like you,
And I, alone, tend upward, more and more
Tend upward: I am grown Sardinia's King.
Pol. Now stop: was not this Victor, Duke of Savoy
At ten years old?
Cha. He was.
Pol. And the Duke spent,
Since then, just four-and-fifty years in toil
To be — what?
Cha. King.
Pol. Then why unking himself?
Cha. Those years are cause enough.
Pol. The only cause?
Cha. Some new perplexities.
Pol. Which you can solve
Although he cannot?
Cha. He assures me so.
Pol. And this he means shall last — how long?
Cha. How long?
Think you I fear the perils I confront?
He's praising me before the people's face —
My people!
Pol Then he's changed — grown kind, the King?
Where can the trap be?

Cha. Heart and soul I pledge!
My father, could I guard the crown you gained,
Transmit as I received it, — all good else
Would I surrender!
Pol. Ah, it opens then
Before you, all you dreaded formerly?
You are rejoiced to be a king, my Charles?
Cha. So much to dare? The better, — much to dread?
The better. I'll adventure though alone.
Triumph or die, there's Victor still to witness
Who dies or triumphs — either way, alone!
Pol. Once, I had found my share in triumph, Charles,
Or death.
Cha. But you are I! But you I call
To take, Heaven's proxy, vows I tendered Heaven
A moment since. I will deserve the crown!
Pol. You will. [*Aside.*] No doubt it were a glorious thing
For any people, if a heart like his
Ruled over it. I would I saw the trap.
(*Enter* VICTOR.)
'Tis he must show me.
Vic. So, the mask falls off
An old man's foolish love at last. Spare thanks!
I know you, and Polyxena I know.
Here's Charles — I am his guest now — does he bid me
Be seated? And my light-haired blue-eyed child
Must not forget the old man far away
At Chambery, who dozes while she reigns.
Pol. Most grateful shall we now be, talking least
Of gratitude — indeed of anything
That hinders what yourself must need to say
To Charles.
Cha. Pray speak, sir!

Vic. 'Faith, not much to say:
Only what shows itself, you once i' the point
Of sight. You're now the King: you'll comprehend
Much you may oft have wondered at — the shifts,
Dissimulation, wiliness I showed.
For what's our post? Here's Savoy and here's Piedmont,
Here's Montferrat — a breadth here, a space there —
To o'er-sweep all these, what's one weapon worth?
I often think of how they fought in Greece
(Or Rome, which was it? You're the scholar, Charles!)
You made a front-thrust? But if your shield too
Were not adroitly planted, some shrewd knave
Reached you behind; and him foiled, straight if thong
And handle of that shield were not cast loose,
And you enabled to outstrip the wind,
Fresh foes assailed you, either side; 'scape these,
And reach your place of refuge — e'en then, odds
If the gate opened unless breath enough
Were left in you to make its lord a speech.
Oh, you will see!
Cha. No: straight on shall I go,
Truth helping; win with it or die with it.
Vic. 'Faith, Charles, you're not made Europe's fighting-man!
The barrier-guarder, if you please. You clutch
Hold and consolidate, with envious France
This side, with Austria that, the territory
I held — ay, and will hold . . . which *you* shall hold
Despite the couple! But I've surely earned
Exemption from these weary politics,
— The privilege to prattle with my son
And daughter here, though Europe wait the while.
Pol. Nay, sir, — at Chambery, away forever,
As soon you will be, 'tis farewell we bid you:

Turn these few fleeting moments to account!
'Tis just as though it were a death.

Vic. Indeed!

Pol. [*Aside.*] Is the trap there?

Cha. . Ay, call this parting — death!
The sacreder your memory becomes.
If I misrule Sardinia, how bring back
My father?

Vic. I mean . . .

Pol. [*Who watches* VICTOR *narrowly this while.*] Your father does not mean
You should be ruling for your father's sake:
It is your people must concern you wholly
Instead of him. You mean this, sir? (He drops
My hand!)

Cha. That people is now part of me.

Vic. About the people! I took certain measures
Some short time since . . . Oh, I know well, you know
But little of my measures! These affect
The nobles; we've resumed some grants, imposed
A tax or two: prepare yourself, in short,
For clamor on that score. Mark me: you yield
No jot of aught entrusted you!

Pol. No jot
You yield!

Cha. My father, when I took the oath,
Although my eye might stray in search of yours,
I heard it, understood it, promised God
What you require. Till from this eminence
He move me, here I keep, nor shall concede
The meanest of my rights.

Vic. [*Aside.*] The boy's a fool!
— Or rather, I'm a fool: for, what's wrong here?
To-day the sweets of reigning: let to-morrow

Be ready with its bitters.
(*Enter* D'ORMEA.)
There's beside
Somewhat to press upon your notice first.
Cha. Then why delay it for an instant, sir?
That Spanish claim perchance? And, now you speak,
— This morning, my opinion was mature,
Which, boy-like, I was bashful in producing
To one I ne'er am like to fear in future!
My thought is formed upon that Spanish claim.
Vic. Betimes indeed. Not now, Charles! You require
A host of papers on it.
D'O. [*Coming forward.*] Here they are.
[*To* CHA.] I, Sir, was minister and much beside
Of the late monarch; to say little, him
I served: on you I have, to say e'en less,
No claim. This case contains those papers: with them
I tender you my office.
Vic. [*Hastily.*] Keep him, Charles!
There's reason for it — many reasons: you
Distrust him, nor are so far wrong there, — but
He's mixed up in this matter — he'll desire
To quit you, for occasions known to me:
Do not accept those reasons: have him stay!
Pol. [*Aside.*] His minister thrust on us!
Cha. [*To D'O.*] Sir, believe,
In justice to myself, you do not need
E'en this commending: howsoe'er might seem
My feelings toward you, as a private man,
They quit me in the vast and untried field
Of action. Though I shall myself (as late
In your own hearing I engaged to do)
Preside o'er my Sardinia, yet your help
Is necessary. Think the past forgotten

And serve me now!
D'O. I did not offer you
My service — would that I could serve you, sir!
As for the Spanish matter . . .
Vic. But dispatch
At least the dead, in my good daughter's phrase,
Before the living! Help to house me safe
Ere with D'Ormea you set the world agape!
Here is a paper — will you overlook
What I propose reserving for my needs?
I get as far from you as possible:
Here's what I reckon my expenditure.
Cha. [*Reading.*] A miserable fifty thousand crowns!
Vic. Oh, quite enough for country gentlemen!
Beside, the exchequer happens . . . but find out
All that, yourself!
Cha. [*Still reading.*] "Count Tende" — what means this?
Vic. Me: you were but an infant when I burst
Through the defile of Tende upon France.
Had only my allies kept true to me!
No matter. Tende's, then, a name I take
Just as . . .
D'O. — The Marchioness Sebastian takes
The name of Spigno.
Cha. How, sir?
Vic. [*To D'O.*] Fool! All that
Was for my own detailing. [*To* CHA.] That anon!
Cha. [*To D'O.*] Explain what you have said, sir!
D'O. I supposed
The marriage of the King to her I named,
Profoundly kept a secret these few weeks,
Was not to be one, now he's Count.
Pol. [*Aside.*] With us
The minister — with him the mistress!

Cha. [*To* Vic.] No —
Tell me you have not taken her — that woman —
To live with, past recall!
Vic. And where's the crime . . .
Pol. [*To* Cha.] True, sir, this is a matter past recall
And past your cognizance. A day before,
And you had been compelled to note this, now: —
Why note it? The King saved his House from shame:
What the Count did, is no concern of yours.
Cha. [*After a pause.*] The Spanish claim, D'Ormea!
Vic. Why, my son,
I took some ill-advised . . . one's age, in fact,
Spoils everything: though I was overreached,
A younger brain, we'll trust, may extricate
Sardinia readily. To-morrow, D'Ormea,
Inform the King!
D'O. [*Without regarding* Victor, *and leisurely.*]
Thus stands the case with Spain:
When first the Infant Carlos claimed his proper
Succession to the throne of Tuscany . . .
Vic. I tell you, that stands over! Let that rest!
There is the policy!
Cha. [*To D'O.*] Thus must I know,
And more, — too much: the remedy?
D'O. Of course!
No glimpse of one.
Vic. No remedy at all!
It makes the remedy itself — time makes it.
D'O. [*To* Cha.] But if . . .
Vic. [*Still more hastily.*] In fine, I shall take care of that:
And, with another project that I have . . .
D'O. [*Turning on him.*] Oh, since Count Tende means to take again
King Victor's crown! —

Pol. [*Throwing herself at* VICTOR's *feet.*]
E'en now retake it, sir!
Oh, speak! We are your subjects both, once more!
Say it — a word effects it! You meant not,
Nor do mean now, to take it: but you must!
'Tis in you — in your nature — and the shame's
Not half the shame 'twould grow to afterwards!
Cha. Polyxena!
Pol. A word recalls the knights —
Say it! — What's promising and what's the past?
Say you are still King Victor!
D'O. Better say
The Count repents, in brief!
[VICTOR *rises.*
Cha. With such a crime
I have not charged you, sir!
Pol. Charles turns from me!

. . . .

(*Enter* D'ORMEA *and* VICTOR, *with Guards.*)
VIC. At last I speak; but once — that once, to you!
'Tis you I ask, not these your varletry,
Who's King of us?
Cha. [*From his seat.*] Count Tende . . .
Vic. What your spies
Assert I ponder in my soul, I say —
Here to your face, amid your guards! I choose
To take again the crown whose shadow I gave —
For still its potency surrounds the weak
White locks their felon hands have discomposed.
Or I'll not ask who's King, but simply, who
Withholds the crown I claim? Deliver it!
I have no friend in the wide world: nor France
Nor England cares for me: you see the sum
Of what I can avail. Deliver it!

Cha. Take it, my father!
And now say in turn,
Was it done well, my father — sure not well,
To try me thus! I might have seen much cause
For keeping it — too easily seen cause!
But, from that moment, e'en more woefully
My life had pined away, than pine it will.
Already you have much to answer for.
My life to pine is nothing, — her sunk eyes
Were happy once! No doubt, my people think
I am their King still . . . but I cannot strive!
Take it!

Vic. [*One hand on the crown* CHARLES *offers, the other on his neck.*] So few years give it quietly,
My son! It will drop from me. See you not?
A crown's unlike a sword to give away —
That, let a strong hand to a weak hand give!
But crowns should slip from palsied brows to heads
Young as this head: yet mine is weak enough,
E'en weaker than I knew. I seek for phrases
To vindicate my right. 'Tis of a piece!
All is alike gone by with me — who beat
Once D'Orleans in his lines — his very lines!
To have been Eugene's comrade, Louis's rival,
And now . . .

Cha. [*Putting the crown on him, to the rest.*] The King speaks, yet none kneels, I think!

Vic. I am then King! As I became a King
Despite the nations, kept myself a King,
So I die King, with Kingship dying too
Around me! I have lasted Europe's time!
What wants my story of completion? Where
Must needs the damning break show? Who mistrusts
My children here — tell they of any break

'Twixt my day's sunrise and its fiery fall?
And who were by me when I died but they?
D'Ormea there!
Cha. What means he?
Vic. Ever there!
Charles — how to save your story! Mine must go!
Say — say that you refused the crown to me!
Charles, yours shall be my story! You immured
Me, say, at Rivoli. A single year
I spend without a sight of you, then die.
That will serve every purpose — tell that tale
The world!
Cha. Mistrust me? Help!
Vic. Past help, past reach!
'Tis in the heart — you cannot reach the heart:
This broke mine, that I did believe, you, Charles,
Would have denied me and disgraced me.
Pol. Charles
Has never ceased to be your subject, sir!
He reigned at first through setting up yourself
As pattern: if he e'er seemed harsh to you,
'Twas from a too intense appreciation
Of your own character: he acted you —
N'er for an instant did I think it real,
Nor look for any other than this end.
I hold him worlds the worse on that account;
But so it was.
Cha. [*To* Pol.] I love you now indeed!
[*To* Vic.] You never knew me!
Vic. Hardly till this moment,
When I seem learning many other things
Because the time for using them is past.
It 'twere to do again! That's idly wished.
Truthfulness might prove policy as good

As guile. Is this my daughter's forehead? Yes:
I've made it fitter now to be a queen's
Than formerly: I've ploughed the deep lines there
Which keep too well a crown from slipping off.
No matter. Guile has made me King again.
Louis — 'twas in King Victor's time: — long since,
When Louis reigned and, also, Victor reigned.
How the world talks already of us two!
God of eclipse and each discolored star,
Why do I linger then?
Ha! Where lurks he?
D'Ormea! Nearer to your King! Now stand!
[*Collecting his strength as* D'ORMEA *approaches.*
You lied, D'Ormea! I do not repent. [*Dies.*

This episode has been called by Voltaire a "terrible event without consequences" in the history of Europe. That it should have had so little national or international meaning is all the more remarkable when we consider how important a part Piedmont and the Kingdom of Sardinia, formerly the Duchy of Savoy, played in Italian History.

This Duchy comes prominently into notice the latter part of the sixteenth century. At that time it included a good deal of Piedmont and part of what is now France and Switzerland. Unfortunately it was the fighting ground of France, Spain and Austria, or perhaps this was fortunate, for its Dukes were so attuned to war that they gradually, though losing their French and Swiss provinces, built up a province that became the head and front of the Kingdom of Sardinia. More important still is the fact that the people of Piedmont themselves became a nation of soldiers and when the rest of the Italian provinces grew more and more incapable of bearing arms, Piedmont led the van in the final fierce struggle for Italian Independence. Cavour and Victor Emmanuel II are the great names in Piedmontese history: without them, one may indeed wonder if Italian liberty would ever have been won. At the call of Cavour, Turin took up the Carbonari's cry for a constitution. According to Cavour there was but one possible course — war with Austria, and Piedmont felt that the time had at last come for her to uplift Italy and fight her country's battles. The time was not yet, however, though as Sedgwick points out, "In Piedmont alone was there light ahead." Victor Emmanuel was to prove a rock of defense. He had all the good qualities of his race; he was a brave soldier and of unimpeachable integrity, a better illustration of which could not be given than in his action after the defeat of Novara (1849), when pressure was brought to bear upon him to make him return to the autocratic system. "Austria," says Sedgwick, "offered him easier terms in this event, but he had been brought up with the old ideas of the royal position, still he was statesman enough to perceive that if Piedmont and the house of Savoy were to lead in the movement of Italian Independence, they must win the confidence of the liberals; and he had sworn to maintain the Constitution. He was always a man of his word, whatever policy might advise, and answered that he should be loyal to the Constitution."

In the final struggle in the North, Piedmont was the center around which the liberals rallied, but though many states wished to join themselves to Piedmont, some wanted to preserve their old historic boundaries and local government.

It was finally, upon the motion of Cavour, settled by an appeal to the will of the people, who were asked to vote not upon fusion or annexation, but upon the union of the Italian people under the constitutional government of Victor Emmanuel II. France would not give her consent unless Savoy and Nice were ceded. The King did not enjoy having to cede Savoy, the "cradle of his race," but he sunk his personal feeling, and Parma, Modena, Tuscany and the Romagna were united with the Kingdom of Sardinia under the name of the Kingdom of Italy, April 15, 1860.

There is a significant glimpse in "Pippa Passes" into this agonizing chapter of Italian History in the scene between Luigi and his mother, led up to in a striking manner by the talk of the police preceding the scene.

What Italy suffered under the Austrian yoke, and the brave struggles she made to throw it off, finally winning her freedom in 1860, as we have already seen, is history within the memory of many to-day, but how important a part the Carbonari took in the earlier phases of this struggle for freedom is sometimes overlooked and sometimes forgotten.

The secret society of the Carbonari or Charcoal-makers was organized about 1808 and first attracted attention in Naples, where the strength of the Austrians was most felt.

It will be remembered that Austrian domination preceded and followed the Napoleonic régime. At the departure of Napoleon, all the little kinglets came back to their petty thrones. The Congress of Vienna gave Venice to Austria, Genoa to Piedmont, and

Parma to Marie Louise, the Austrian wife of Napoleon, for her life. Ferdinand I of the Two Sicilies restored the old régime, swept away the autonomy of Sicily which had had a separate parliament for hundreds of years, and since 1812 a constitution also, and humbly followed every hint from Austria. The will of Austria was supreme from Naples to Venice.

Spain was responsible for setting ablaze the hidden discontent in Italy. The rebellion there had ended in their obtaining a constitution. A company of soldiers bent upon obtaining a similar constitution for Italy rebelled. They were led by two young lieutenants. Many more joined them and a general of the same mind took command. The army, refusing to fight the rebels, the King was frightened into promising to grant them all their demands, namely, a constitution, a parliament, a free press, trials according to law. But the Austrians sent an overwhelming army which made short work of these lovers of liberty. The constitution, parliament, free press, became as nought. But the Carbonari were not to be suppressed. They grew and flourished in spite of the fact that a vigilant government was always on the lookout for conspirators whom they, without ceremony, clapped into prison. Prince Canossa, head of the Naples police, founded a counter secret society which was called the "Tinkers," and which also had its secret rites and signs.

The duties of the individual Carbonaro were such that the citizens of any state might do well to cultivate their tenets. "To render to the Almighty the worship due to him; to serve the fatherland with zeal; to reverence religion and laws; to fulfil the obligations of nature and friendship; to be faithful to promises; to observe silence, discretion and charity; to cause harmony and good morals to prevail; to conquer the passions and submit the will; and to abhor the seven deadly sins. The society further was to disseminate instruction; to unite the different classes of society under the bond of love; to impress a national character on the people and to interest them in the preservation and defense of the fatherland and of religion; to destroy, by moral culture, the source of crimes, due to the general depravity of mankind; to protect the weak and to raise up the unfortunate."

It is needless to say they did not accomplish the complete regeneration of society that such tenets would lead one to expect.

Their aim was above all political and the striking down of tyrants in cold blood became a necessary part of the practice of a society that was subjected to constant and most cruel persecution. Silvio Pellico, whom Luigi's mother calls a "writer for effect," tells many grewsome stories in his book "Le Mie Prigioni" (My Prisons). He and his friend Maronelli were arrested and put in prison for ten years. Pellico tells how his confrère Maronelli was suffering with a most painful tumor on his leg. "Sometimes to make the slightest shift from one position to another cost a quarter of an hour of agony. In that deplorable condition Maronelli composed poetry, he sang and talked and did everything to deceive me, and hide from me a part of his pain. He could not digest or sleep; he grew alarmingly thin, and often went out of his head; and yet, in a few minutes gathered himself together and cheered me up. What he suffered for nine months is indescribable. Amputation was necessary; but first the surgeon had to get permission from Vienna. Maronelli uttered no cry at the operation and only said, 'You have liberated me from an enemy and I have no way to thank you.' By the window stood a tumbler with a rose in it. 'Please give me that rose,' he said to me. I handed it to him and he gave it to the old surgeon saying, 'I have nothing else to give you in testimony of my gratitude.' The surgeon took the rose and burst into tears. Such was the character of the men who plotted for the freedom of Italy."

Carbonarism was really a tentative Republic amid an autocracy which it intended to abolish, and the forms of its government were Republican, but there was also mixed up with their organization an immense deal of symbolism, much after the manner of the order of Free Masons, from whom they indeed borrowed some of their rites. Mythical stories arose of its origin. Black, red, and blue were their colors, to each of which were attached symbolic meanings. Black signified first charcoal, and then faith; red was fire and charity; blue was smoke and hope.

In the scene from "Pippa Passes," which we give, is brought vividly before the reader the intense and reckless patriotism of the young Carbonaro, Luigi, and, in Luigi's Mother, the conservative element, fearful of the dangers of a revolution — an element which kept back the progress of liberty for many weary years.

III. EVENING

Inside the Turret on the Hill above Asolo. Luigi *and his* Mother *entering.*

Mother. If there blew wind, you'd hear a long sigh, easing
The utmost heaviness of music's heart.
Luigi. Here in the archway?
Mother. Oh no, no — in farther,
Where the echo is made, on the ridge.
Luigi. Here surely, then.
How plain the tap of my heel as I leaped up!
Hark — "Lucius Junius!" The very ghost of a voice
Whose body is caught and kept by . . . what are those?
Mere withered wallflowers, waving overhead?
They seem an elvish group with thin bleached hair
That lean out of their topmost fortress — look
And listen, mountain men, to what we say,
Hand under chin of each grave earthy face.
Up and show faces all of you! — "All of you!"
That's the king dwarf with the scarlet comb; old Franz,
Come down and meet your fate? Hark — "Meet your fate!"
Mother. Let him not meet it, my Luigi — do not
Go to his City! Putting crime aside,
Half of these ills of Italy are feigned:
Your Pellicos and writers for effect,
Write for effect.
Luigi. Hush! Say A writes, and B.
Mother. These A's and B's write for effect, I say.
Then, evil is in its nature loud, while good
Is silent; you hear each petty injury,
None of his virtues; he is old beside,
Quiet and kind, and densely stupid. Why
Do A and B not kill him themselves?

Luigi. They teach
Others to kill him — me — and, if I fail,
Others to succeed; now, if A tried and failed,
I could not teach that: mine's the lesser task.
Mother, they visit night by night . . .
Mother. — You, Luigi?
Ah, will you let me tell you what you are?
Luigi. Why not? Oh, the one thing you fear to hint,
You may assure yourself I say and say
Ever to myself! At times — nay, even as now
We sit — I think my mind is touched, suspect
All is not sound: but is not knowing that,
What constitutes one sane or otherwise?
I know I am thus — so, all is right again.
I laugh at myself as through the town I walk,
And see men merry as if no Italy
Were suffering; then I ponder — "I am rich,
Young, healthy; why should this fact trouble me,
More than it troubles these?" But it does trouble.
No, trouble's a bad word: for as I walk
There's springing and melody and giddiness,
And old quaint turns and passages of my youth,
Dreams long forgotten, little in themselves,
Return to me — whatever may amuse me:
And earth seems in a truce with me, and heaven
Accords with me, all things suspend their strife,
The very cicala laughs "There goes he, and there!
Feast him, the time is short; he is on his way
For the world's sake: feast him this once, our friend!"
And in return for all this, I can trip
Cheerfully up the scaffold-steps. I go
This evening, mother!
Mother. But mistrust yourself —
Mistrust the judgment you pronounce on him!

Luigi. Oh, there I feel — am sure that I am right!
Mother. Mistrust your judgment then, of the mere means
To this wild enterprise: say, you are right, —
How should one in your state e'er bring to pass
What would require a cool head, a cool heart,
And a calm hand? You never will escape.
Luigi. Escape? To even wish that, would spoil all.
The dying is best part of it. Too much
Have I enjoyed these fifteen years of mine,
To leave myself excuse for longer life:
Was not life pressed down, running o'er with joy,
That I might finish with it ere my fellows
Who, sparelier feasted, make a longer stay?
I was put at the board-head, helped to all
At first; I rise up happy and content.
God must be glad one loves his world so much.
I can give news of earth to all the dead
Who ask me: — last year's sunsets, and great stars
Which had a right to come first and see ebb
The crimson wave that drifts the sun away —
Those crescent moons with notched and burning rims
That strengthened into sharp fire, and there stood,
Impatient of the azure — and that day
In March, a double rainbow stopped the storm —
May's warm slow yellow moonlit summer nights —
Gone are they, but I have them in my soul!
Mother. (He will not go!)
Luigi. You smile at me? 'Tis true, —
Voluptuousness, grotesqueness, ghastliness,
Environ my devotedness as quaintly
As round about some antique altar wreathe
The rose festoons, goats' horns, and oxen's skulls.
Mother. See now: you reach the city, you must cross
His threshold — how?

Luigi. Oh, that's if we conspired!
Then would come pains in plenty, as you guess —
But guess not how the qualities most fit
For such an office, qualities I have,
Would little stead me, otherwise employed,
Yet prove of rarest merit only here.
Every one knows for what his excellence
Will serve, but no one ever will consider
For what his worst defect might serve: and yet
Have you not seen me range our coppice yonder
In search of a distorted ash? — I find
The wry spoilt branch a natural perfect bow.
Fancy the thrice-sage, thrice-precautioned man
Arriving at the palace on my errand!
No, no! I have a handsome dress packed up —
White satin here, to set off my black hair;
In I shall march — for you may watch your life out
Behind thick walls, make friends there to betray you;
More than one man spoils everything. March straight —
Only, no clumsy knife to fumble for.
Take the great gate, and walk (not saunter) on
Through guards and guards — I have rehearsed it all
Inside the turret here a hundred times.
Don't ask the way of whom you meet, observe!
But where they cluster thickliest is the door
Of doors; they'll let you pass — they'll never blab
Each to the other, he knows not the favorite,
Whence he is bound and what's his business now.
Walk in — straight up to him; you have no knife:
Be prompt, how should he scream? Then, out with you!
Italy, Italy, my Italy!
You're free, you're free! Oh mother, I could dream
They got about me — Andrea from his exile,
Pier from his dungeon, Gualtier from his grave!

Mother. Well, you shall go. Yet seems this patriotism
The easiest virtue for a selfish man
To acquire: he loves himself — and next, the world —
If he must love beyond, — but naught between:
As a short-sighted man sees naught midway
His body and the sun above. But you
Are my adored Luigi, ever obedient
To my least wish, and running o'er with love:
I could not call you cruel or unkind.
Once more, your ground for killing him! — then go!

Luigi. Now do you try me, or make sport of me?
How first the Austrians got these provinces . . .
(If that is all, I'll satisfy you soon)
— Never by conquest but by cunning, for
That treaty whereby . . .

Mother. Well?

Luigi. (Sure, he's arrived,
The tell-tale cuckoo: spring's his confidant,
And he lets out her April purposes!)
Or . . . better go at once to modern time.
He has . . . they have . . . in fact, I understand
But can't restate the matter; that's my boast:
Others could reason it out to you, and prove
Things they have made me feel.

Mother. Why go to-night?
Morn's for adventure. Jupiter is now
A morning-star. I cannot hear you, Luigi!

Luigi. "I am the bright and morning-star," saith God —
And, "to such an one I give the morning-star."
The gift of the morning-star! Have I God's gift
Of the morning-star?

Mother. Chiara will love to see
That Jupiter an evening-star next June.

Luigi. True, mother. Well for those who live through June!
Great noontides, thunder-storms, all glaring pomps
That triumph at the heels of June the god
Leading his revel through our leafy world.
Yes, Chiara will be here.
Mother. In June: remember,
Yourself appointed that month for her coming.
Luigi. Was that low noise the echo?
Mother. The night-wind.
She must be grown — with her blue eyes upturned
As if life were one long and sweet surprise:
In June she comes.
Luigi. We were to see together
The Titian at Treviso. There, again!
[*From without is heard the voice of* PIPPA, *singing* —

A king lived long ago,
In the morning of the world,
When earth was nigher heaven than now;
And the king's locks curled,
Disparting o'er a forehead full
As the milk-white space 'twixt horn and horn
Of some sacrificial bull —
Only calm as a babe new-born:
For he was got to a sleepy mood,
So safe from all decrepitude,
Age with its bane, so sure gone by,
(*The gods so loved him while he dreamed*)
That, having lived thus long, there seemed
No need the king should ever die.

Luigi. No need that sort of king should ever die!

Among the rocks his city was:
Before his palace, in the sun,

He sat to see his people pass,
And judge them every one
From its threshold of smooth stone.
They haled him many a valley-thief
Caught in the sheep-pens, robber-chief
Swarthy and shameless, beggar-cheat,
Spy-prowler, or rough pirate found
On the sea-sand left aground;
And sometimes clung about his feet,
With bleeding lip and burning cheek,
A woman, bitterest wrong to speak
Of one with sullen thickset brows;
And sometimes from the prison-house
The angry priests a pale wretch brought,
Who through some chink had pushed and pressed
On knees and elbows, belly and breast,
Worm-like into the temple, — caught
He was by the very god,
Who ever in the darkness strode
Backward and forward, keeping watch
O'er his brazen bowls, such rogues to catch!
These, all and every one,
The king judged, sitting in the sun.

Luigi. That king should still judge sitting in the sun!

His councillors, on left and right,
Looked anxious up, — but no surprise
Disturbed the king's old smiling eyes
Where the very blue had turned to white.
'Tis said, a Python scared one day
The breathless city, till he came,
With forky tongue and eyes on flame,
Where the old king sat to judge alway;

But when he saw the sweepy hair
Girt with a crown of berries rare
Which the god will hardly give to wear
To the maiden who singeth, dancing bare
In the altar-smoke by the pine-torch lights,
At his wondrous forest rites,—
Seeing this, he did not dare
Approach that threshold in the sun,
Assault the old king smiling there.
Such grace had kings when the world begun!

[PIPPA *passes.*

Luigi. And such grace have they, now that the world ends!
The Python at the city, on the throne,
And brave men, God would crown for slaying him,
Lurk in by-corners lest they fall his prey.
Are crowns yet to be won in this late time,
Which weakness makes me hesitate to reach?
'Tis God's voice calls: how could I stay? Farewell!

Browning gives another picture of this period in his poem "The Italian in England." The speaker evidently belonged to the Carbonari in the early days, before the revolution was successful, and has taken refuge in England to escape Austrian persecution. He gives an account of a typical experience that had befallen him. It reveals how the lukewarm attitude of the Italians themselves, and their backsliding into the pay of Austria kept back the progress of Italian independence; and how true patriots could feel, as expressed in his hatred of the distinguished Austrian diplomatist, Metternich, and above all how they could act, the supreme illustration of this being shown in the help the beautiful Italian girl gave him. The poem tells its own story far better than any description of it can do, and completes in a brilliant manner the series of historical pictures that Browning has given us, touching almost every great problem in Italian History.

THE ITALIAN IN ENGLAND

That second time they hunted me
From hill to plain, from shore to sea,
And Austria, hounding far and wide
Her blood-hounds through the country-side,
Breathèd hot and instant on my trace, —
I made six days a hiding-place
Of that dry green old aqueduct
Where I and Charles, when boys, have plucked
The fire-flies from the roof above,
Bright creeping through the moss they love:
— How long it seems since Charles was lost!
Six days the soldiers crossed and crossed
The country in my very sight:
And when that peril ceased at night,
The sky broke out in red dismay
With signal fires; well, there I lay
Close covered o'er in my recess,
Up to the neck in ferns and cress,
Thinking on Metternich our friend,
And Charles's miserable end,

And much beside, two days; the third,
Hunger o'ercame me when I heard
The peasants from the village go
To work among the maize; you know,
With us in Lombardy, they bring
Provisions packed on mules, a string
With little bells that cheer their task,
And casks, and boughs on every cask
To keep the sun's heat from the wine;
These I let pass in jingling line,
And, close on them, dear noisy crew,
The peasants from the village, too;
For at the very rear would troop
Their wives and sisters in a group
To help, I know. When these had passed,
I threw my glove to strike the last,
Taking the chance: she did not start,
Much less cry out, but stooped apart,
One instant rapidly glanced round,
And saw me beckon from the ground.
A wild bush grows and hides my crypt;
She picked my glove up while she stripped
A branch off, then rejoined the rest
With that; my glove lay in her breast.
Then I drew breath: they disappeared:
It was for Italy I feared.

An hour, and she returned alone
Exactly where my glove was thrown.
Meanwhile came many thoughts; on me
Rested the hopes of Italy.
I had devised a certain tale
Which, when 'twas told her, could not fail
Persuade a peasant of its truth;

I meant to call a freak of youth
This hiding, and give hopes of pay,
And no temptation to betray.
But when I saw that woman's face,
Its calm simplicity of grace,
Our Italy's own attitude
In which she walked thus far, and stood,
Planting each naked foot so firm,
To crush the snake and spare the worm —
At first sight of her eyes, I said,
"I am that man upon whose head
They fix the price, because I hate
The Austrians over us: the State
Will give you gold — oh, gold so much! —
If you betray me to their clutch,
And be your death, for aught I know,
If once they find you saved their foe.
Now, you must bring me food and drink,
And also paper, pen and ink,
And carry safe what I shall write
To Padua, which you'll reach at night
Before the duomo shuts; go in,
And wait till Tenebræ begin;
Walk to the third confessional,
Between the pillar and the wall,
And kneeling whisper, *Whence comes peace?*
Say it a second time, then cease;
And if the voice inside returns,
From Christ and Freedom; what concerns
The cause of Peace? — for answer, slip
My letter where you placed your lip;
Then come back happy we have done
Our mother service — I, the son,
As you the daughter of our land!"

Three mornings more, she took her stand
In the same place, with the same eyes:
I was no surer of sunrise
Than of her coming. We conferred
Of her own prospects, and I heard
She had a lover — stout and tall,
She said — then let her eyelids fall,
"He could do much" — as if some doubt
Entered her heart, — then, passing out,
"She could not speak for others, who
Had other thoughts; herself she knew:"
And so she brought me drink and food.
After four days, the scouts pursued
Another path; at last arrived
The help my Paduan friends contrived
To furnish me: she brought the news.
For the first time I could not choose
But kiss her hand, and lay my own
Upon her head — "This faith was shown
To Italy, our mother; she
Uses my hand and blesses thee."
She followed down to the sea-shore;
I left and never saw her more.

How very long since I have thought
Concerning — much less wished for — aught
Beside the good of Italy,
For which I live and mean to die!
I never was in love; and since
Charles proved false, what shall now convince
My inmost heart I have a friend?
However, if I pleased to spend
Real wishes on myself — say, three —
I know at least what one should be.

I would grasp Metternich until
I felt his red wet throat distil
In blood through these two hands. And next,
— Nor much for that am I perplexed —
Charles, perjured traitor, for his part,
Should die slow of a broken heart
Under his new employers. Last
— Ah, there, what should I wish? For fast
Do I grow old and out of strength.
If I resolved to seek at length
My father's house again, how scared
They all would look, and unprepared!
My brothers live in Austria's pay
— Disowned me long ago, men say;
And all my early mates who used
To praise me so — perhaps induced
More than one early step of mine —
Are turning wise: while some opine
"Freedome grows license," some suspect
"Haste breeds delay," and recollect
They always said, such premature
Beginnings never could endure!
So, with a sullen "All's for best,"
The land seems settling to its rest.
I think then, I should wish to stand
This evening in that dear, lost land,
Over the sea the thousand miles,
And know if yet that woman smiles
With the calm smile; some little farm
She lives in there, no doubt: what harm
If I sat on the door-side bench,
And, while her spindle made a trench
Fantastically in the dust,
Inquired of all her fortunes — just

Her children's ages and their names,
And what may be the husband's aims
For each of them. I'd talk this out,
And sit there, for an hour about,
Then kiss her hand once more, and lay
Mine on her head, and go my way.

So much for idle wishing — how
It steals the time! To business now.

III

THE ITALIAN SCHOLAR

"So let us say — not 'Since we know, we love,'
But rather 'Since we love, we know enough.'"

— *A Pillar at Sebzevar.*

ALTHOUGH there are but two of Browning's poems that touch directly the purely scholarly aspects of Italian culture in the Renaissance, these two open up for our inspection two or three of the most interesting tendencies that manifested themselves during the period, namely, the influence of scientific knowledge and the influence of the Revival of ancient Greek learning, with all that it brought in its train of philosophical studies and language studies.

In "Pietro of Abano," science and the philosophical side of Greek learning figure, and in "The Grammarian's Funeral" the enthusiasm for language study — particularly that of Greek is shown.

Science, especially medical science, was

making great strides in the hands of the Arabians, who had the beginnings of their learning from the Jews and Nestorians, when Constantine the Great, influenced by the Church, declared the Church the enemy of worldly learning. The antagonism thus set up between the church and science produced some very curious results. The church took upon itself to see to the physical as well as the spiritual well-being of the people, and in consequence hospitals and benevolent organizations were founded and endowed with land and money, but instead of the care of the sick being in the hands of regular physicians with such education as they had at the time, it was in those of unskilled ecclesiastics. The outcome was a resort to miracle cures, and for succeeding ages there was a gradually increasing credulity and exercise of imposture until at length there was almost universal reliance on the quackeries of miracle cure, shrine cure, relic cure. Crowds repaired to the shrines of saints to be cured.

But the most curious aspect of this division of religion and science was the fact that at the same time that religion was developing credulity in miracles, science was going in the direction of sorcery. This pseudo science was "the glimmering lamp," as Draper says, "which sustained knowledge when it was all but ready to die out." He goes on, "By the Arabians it was handed down to us. The grotesque forms of some of those who took charge of it are not without interest. They exhibit a strange mixture of the Neoplatonist, the Pantheist, the Mohammedan, the Christian. In such untoward times it was perhaps needful that the strongest passions of men should be excited and science stimulated by inquiries for methods of turning lead into gold, or of prolonging life indefinitely. We have now to deal with the philosopher's stone, the elixir *vitæ*, the powder of projection, magical mirrors, perpetual lamps, the transmutation of metals. In smoky caverns under ground where the great work is stealthily carried on, the alchemist and his familiar are busy with their alembics, cucurbites, and pelicans, maintaining their fires for so many years that salamanders are asserted to be born in them. Experimental science was thus restored."

There were various channels by which this Arabian knowledge reached Italy. The Crusaders brought back the knowledge of the East, but more important was the establishment of the Saracens in Spain. Science was cultivated assiduously among them, and from there, their learning spread into Southern France, and into Sicily. Frederick II was especially friendly to the Saracens, and Arab learning flourished in his court in Sicily. Among the distinguished savants surrounding him were the two sons of Averrhoes of Cordova. Their father was one of the great lights of erudition at that period. Among other things he was learned in astronomy and is said to have been the first to have observed a transit of Mercury across the sun. He was also a commentator upon the works of Plato and Aristotle. He was furthermore a total disbeliever in all revelation.

"Pietro of Abano" may be taken as a type of this medieval learning. Pietro lived from 1249 to 1315, just at the time when Italy's intellectual aspiration was gaining in power. He was called Petrus Aponensis, Aponon being the name of the famous medicinal springs of Abano, near Padua (*a*, without, and *ponos*, pain), near which Peter was born. According to all accounts he was profoundly learned in science and magic. He had studied at Paris, at Constantinople and in the Orient and was said to keep the seven spirits of philosophy, alchemy, astrology, physic, poetry and music in seven crystal vases tamed to his will.

It is needless to say that a man of this caliber was persecuted by the Church. He was accused of being a heretic and an atheist by the Inquisition, but escaped his fate of burning by his own able defense of himself. Accused again later, he died before he was convicted, but his body was condemned to be burned, and had it not been for the devotion of a friend the sentence would have been carried out. The friend, however, hid the body, and it was burned only in effigy.

He did not, however, wait as long as other illustrious men for recognition. The Duke of Urbino had his statue put up among other statues of distinguished men in Padua, and the Senate honored it by placing it upon the gate of the Senate-house. Still other honors were accorded him, for in 1560 a tablet with a Latin epitaph was put up in his memory in the Church of St. Augustine. The Rev. John Sharpe, who wrote about this poem in The London Browning Society Papers, found an early inscription in the wall of the vestibule of the Sacristy of the Church of the Eremitani to this effect: "Petri Aponi (Cineres) Ob. an. 1315: æt. 66."

Browning brings into connection with this historic personage, versed in the lore derived from the Saracens, a Greek without a name, who is anxious to become as learned as Pietro in magic lore. In exchange for his learning, the Greek offers Pietro the love he is supposed to lack. In reply to his demands, Pietro gives him a magic powder. This causes him in an instant of time, between the beginning and ending of Pietro's pronouncing the word "Benedicity," to live through all the successive stages of the career he would like to win by means of Pietro's magic: a man of wealth, a statesman, a churchman. As he advances by means of the magic powder, instead of giving Pietro the love promised, he treats him with more and more scorn and finally tries to drive him from his presence, thus showing what a pretense his ambition to rule men for their good had been.

This legend, as is usually the case with such stories, occurs in various forms in the Middle Ages, but what we are more concerned with now is the glimpse of the Greek character and the relation of the Greeks to Italian culture which it gives us.

At this time the Greeks, according to one of their own countrymen, Gemistos Plethon, were a thoroughly degenerate people. The first appearance of Gemistos in Italy was at a council held in Florence of the Latin Church and the Greek Church, looking toward some sort of union between them. At this council it was natural that the Greeks should attract much attention, as the fervor for Greek studies had already taken hold of the Florentine mind. But on the whole these Greeks were not quite what the Florentines expected of the descendants of Homer and Plato. "While honoring them," says Symonds, "as the last scions of the noblest nation of the past, as the authentic teachers of Hellenic learning and the Masters of the Attic tongue, they despised their empty vanity, their facile apostasy, their trivial pedantry, their personal absurdities." Their erudition finally resolved itself into the meager accomplishment of being able to speak their mother tongue, an "emasculated" Greek. There was, however, a noble exception among these visiting Greeks. Gemistos had all the lore that the hungry Florentines craved. "From the treasures of a memory stored with Platonic, Pythagorean and Alexandrian mysticism, he poured forth copious streams of erudition. The ears of his audience were open; their intellects were far from critical. They accepted the gold and dross of his discourse alike as purest metal. Hanging upon the lips of the eloquent, grave, beautiful old man, who knew so much that they desired to learn, they called him Socrates and Plato in their ecstacy."

This delightful old fellow, of whom Symonds draws such a charming picture, had a philosophy that reminds us strongly of the wily Greek in this poem, and an opinion of his own countrymen's character that chimes in well with Browning's portrayal of the Greek. He lived in the Peloponnesus, upon the site of the ancient Sparta, for the greater part of his life. He drew a terrible picture of the anarchy and immorality of the decadent Hellenic race, and being a learned man and a philosopher he concocted a scheme of life and religion which was to regenerate not only his race but the world. The soul of Plato was believed by his disciples to be re-incarnate in him, and his followers called him "the mystagogue of sublime and celestial dogmas." His scheme included metaphysics, a new religion, an elaborate psychology, a theory of ethics and a theory of political administration. It is impossible here to go into its recondite ramifications, in which the old Greek gods and goddesses and human qualities seem to masquerade in each other's likenesses. It has been described as a "Sort of Neoplatonism — a mystical fusion of Greek mythology and Greek logic." The work in which he set forth his ideas was called "The Laws," the name itself being reminiscent of Plato's "Laws."

Such a plan of ruling men for their good might have emanated from Browning's Greek if he had been clever enough, and it is more than likely that our poet when he speaks in the poem of Plato's Tractate had in mind this latter day mystical Neoplatonism and felt much as Symonds does about it when he exclaims, "There is something ludicrous as well as sad in the spectacle of this sophist, nourishing the vain fancy that he might coin a complete religious system, which would supersede Christianity and restore vigor to the decayed body of the Greek empire."

For a sudden and rapid rise from obscurity to the Papal throne one does not need to go to legend, for history supplies the remarkable instance of Pope Nicholas V who, however, was true to his word that if ever he obtained wealth he would devote it to books and buildings. He flourished in the hey-day of the revival of learning. Born at Pisa in 1398, he was taken while yet an infant to Sarzana, whither his parents were exiled. Though very poor this young Tommaso Parenturelli managed to attend the University of Bologna, where he studied theology and the seven liberal arts. Next we hear of him totally destitute, seeking work in Florence, where he was engaged first as house tutor to the children of Rinaldo degli Albizzi and afterwards to those of Palla degli Strozzi. With the money obtained here he returned to Bologna and took his degree of Doctor of Theology at the age of twenty-two. Soon he acquires a patron in Niccolo degli Albergati, Archbishop of Bologna, who appoints him controller of his household. Albergati was one of the Cardinals of Eugenius IV, and, when the papal court went to Florence, he went also, and took Tommaso with him. It was not long before he became known to Cosimo de' Medici, and so grew to be a constant attendant at the gatherings of the learned.

How he appeared at this time is graphically described by Vespasiano. "It was the custom for many men of learning to congregate every morning and evening at the side of the Palazzo where they entered into discussions and disputes on various subjects. As soon then as Maestro Tommaso had attended the Cardinal to the Palazzo, he joined them, mounted on a mule, with two servants on foot; and generally he was attired in blue and his servants in long dresses of a darker color. In the place I have named he was always to be found conversing and disputing, since he was a most impassioned debater."

At this time he was always buying books, even borrowing money to secure them.

In 1443 Albergati died and soon after Eugenius promoted Tommaso to the see of Bologna; within a few months he was made Cardinal and in 1447 he was elected Pope of Rome. His love for books resulted in his founding the Vatican library, and his erudition in his being a munificent patron of learning. So the true story of Pope Nicholas V is not sullied by the selfishness displayed by the Greek, but it shows the stuff out of which such a story might grow.

Though at the end of the poem Browning speaks of lilting in lazy fashion this legend of Padua, yet we cannot help feeling that in treating his subject he has been conscious of all these diverse elements that went to the making of the intellectually awakened Italy, into which was coming by various channels the learning of the Arab and the learning of the Greek, both of which had their battles to fight sooner or later with the Church.

PIETRO OF ABANO

Petrus Aponensis — there was a magician!
When that strange adventure happened, which I mean to tell my hearers,
Nearly had he tried all trades — beside physician,
Architect, astronomer, astrologer, — or worse:
How else, as the old books warrant, was he able,
All at once, through all the world, to prove the promptest of appearers
Where was prince to cure, tower to build as high as Babel,
Star to name or sky-sign read, — yet pouch, for pains, a curse?

— Curse: for when a vagrant, — foot-sore, travel-tattered,
Now a young man, now an old man, Turk or Arab, Jew or Gypsy, —
Proffered folk in passing — Oh, for pay, what mattered? —
"I'll be doctor. I'll play builder, star I'll name — sign read!"
Soon as prince was cured, tower built, and fate predicted,
"Who may you be?" came the question; when he answered "*Petrus ipse,*"
"Just as we divined!" cried folk — "A wretch convicted
Long ago of dealing with the devil — you indeed!"

So, they cursed him roundly, all his labor's payment,
Motioned him — the convalescent prince would — to vacate the presence:
Babylonians plucked his beard and tore his raiment,
Drove him from that tower he built: while, had he peered at stars,
Town howled "Stone the quack who styles our Dog-star — Sirius!"
Country yelled "Aroint the churl who prophesies we take no pleasance

Under vine and fig-tree, since the year's delirious,
Bears no crop of any kind, — all through the planet Mars!"

Straightway would the whilom youngster grow a grisard,
Or, as case might hap, the hoary eld drop off and show a stripling.
Town and country groaned — indebted to a wizard!
"Curse — nay, kick and cuff him — fit requital of his pains!
Gratitude in word or deed were wasted truly!
Rather make the Church amends by crying out on, cramping, crippling
One who, on pretence of serving man, serves duly
Man's arch foe: not ours, be sure, but Satan's — his the gains!"

Peter grinned and bore it, and such disgraceful usage:
Somehow, cuffs and kicks and curses seem ordained his like to suffer:
Prophet's pay with Christians, now as in the Jew's age,
Still is — stoning: so, he meekly took his wage and went,
— Safe again was found ensconced in those old quarters,
Padua's blackest blindest by-street, — none the worse, nay, somewhat tougher:
"Calculating," quoth he, "soon I join the martyrs,
Since, who magnify my lore on burning me are bent."

Therefore, on a certain evening, to his alley
Peter slunk, all bruised and broken, sore in body, sick in spirit,
Just escaped from Cairo where he launched a galley
Needing neither sails nor oars nor help of wind or tide
— Needing but the fume of fire to set a-flying
Wheels like mad which whirled you quick — North, South, where'er you pleased require it, —

That is — would have done so had not priests come prying,
Broke his engine up and bastinadoed him beside.

As he reached his lodgings, stopped there unmolested,
(Neighbors feared him, urchins fled him, few were bold enough to follow)
While his fumbling fingers tried the lock and tested
Once again the queer key's virtue, oped the sullen door, —
Some one plucked his sleeve, cried, "Master, pray your pardon!
Grant a word to me who patient wait you in your archway's hollow!
Hard on you men's hearts are: be not your heart hard on
Me who kiss your garment's hem, O Lord of magic lore!

"Mage — say I, who no less, scorning tittle-tattle,
To the vulgar give no credence when they prate of Peter's magic,
Deem his art brews tempest, hurts the crops and cattle,
Hinders fowls from laying eggs and worms from spinning silk,
Rides upon a he-goat, mounts at need a broomstick:
While the price he pays for this (so turns to comic what was tragic)
Is — he may not drink — dreads like the Day of Doom's tick —
One poor drop of sustenance ordained mere men — that's milk!

"Tell such tales to Padua! Think me no such dullard!
Not from these benighted parts did I derive my breath and being!
I am from a land whose cloudless skies are colored
Livelier, suns orb largelier, airs seem incense, — while, on earth —

What, instead of grass, our fingers and our thumbs cull,
Proves true moly! sounds and sights there help the body's hearing, seeing,
Till the soul grows godlike: brief, — you front no numskull
Shaming by ineptitude the Greece that gave him birth!

"Mark within my eye its iris mystic-lettered —
That's my name! and note my ear — its swan-shaped cavity, my emblem!
Mine's the swan-like nature born to fly unfettered
Over land and sea in search of knowledge — food for song.
Art denied the vulgar! Geese grow fat on barley,
Swans require ethereal provend, undesirous to resemble 'em —
Soar to seek Apollo — favored with a parley
Such as, Master, you grant me — who will not hold you long.

"Leave to learn to sing — for that your swan petitions:
Master, who possess the secret, say not nay to such a suitor!
All I ask is — bless mine, purest of ambitions!
Grant me leave to make my kind wise, free, and happy! How?
Just by making me — as you are mine — their model!
Geese have goose-thoughts: make a swan their teacher first, then coadjutor, —
Let him introduce swan-notions to each noddle, —
Geese will soon grow swans, and men become what I am now!

"That's the only magic — had but fools discernment,
Could they probe and pass into the solid through the soft and seeming!
Teach me such true magic — now, and no adjournment!
Teach your art of making fools subserve the man of mind!

Magic is the power we men of mind should practice,
Draw fools to become our drudges — docile henceforth, never dreaming —
While they do our hests for fancied gain — the fact is
What they toil and moil to get proves falsehood: truth's behind!

"See now! you conceive some fabric — say, a mansion
Meet for monarch's pride and pleasure: this is truth — a thought has fired you,
Made you fain to give some cramped concept expansion,
Put your faculty to proof, fulfil your nature's task,
First you fascinate the monarch's self: he fancies
He it was devised the scheme you execute as he inspired you:
He in turn set slaving insignificances
Toiling, moiling till your structure stands there — all you ask!

"Soon the monarch's known for what he was — a ninny:
Soon the rabble-rout leave labor, take their work-day wage and vanish:
Soon the late puffed bladder, pricked, shows lank and skinny —
'Who was its inflator?' ask we, 'whose the giant lungs?'
Petri en pulmones! What though men prove ingrates?
Let them — so they stop at crucifixion — buffet, ban and banish!
Peter's power's apparent: human praise — its din grates
Harsh as blame on ear unused to aught save angels' tongues.

"Ay, there have been always, since our world existed,
Mages who possessed the secret — needed but to stand still, fix eye
On the foolish mortal: straight was he enlisted
Soldier, scholar, servant, slave — no matter for the style!

Only through illusion; ever what seemed profit —
Love or lucre — justified obedience to the *Ipse dixi:*
Work done — palace reared from pavement up to soffit —
Was it strange if builders smelt out cheating all the while?

"Let them pelt and pound, bruise, bray you in a mortar!
What's the odds to you who seek reward of quite another nature?
You've enrolled your name where sages of your sort are,
— Michael of Constantinople, Hans of Halberstadt!
Nay and were you nameless, still you've your conviction
You it was and only you — what signifies the nomenclature?—
Ruled the world in fact, though how you ruled be fiction
Fit for fools: true wisdom's magic you — if e'er man — had t'!

"But perhaps you ask me, 'Since each ignoramus
While he profits by such magic persecutes the benefactor,
What should I expect but — once I render famous
You as Michael, Hans, and Peter — just one ingrate more?
If the vulgar prove thus, whatsoe'er the pelf be,
Pouched through my beneficence — and doom me dungeoned, chained, or racked, or
Fairly burned outright — how grateful will yourself be
When, his secret gained, you match your — master just before?'

"That's where I await you! Please, revert a little!
What do folk report about you if not this — which, though chimeric,
Still, as figurative, suits you to a tittle —
That, — although the elements obey your nod and wink,
Fades or flowers the herb you chance to smile or sigh at,
While your frown bids earth quake palled by obscuration atmospheric, —

Brief, although through nature naught resists your *fiat*,
There's yet one poor substance mocks you — milk you may not drink!

"Figurative language! Take my explanation!
Fame with fear, and hate with homage, these your art procures in plenty.
All's but daily dry bread: what makes moist the ration?
Love, the milk that sweetens man his meal — alas, you lack:
I am he who, since he fears you not, can love you.
Love is born of heart not mind, *de corde natus haud de mente;*
Touch my heart and love's yours, sure as shines above you
Sun by day and star by night though earth should go to wrack!

"Stage by stage you lift me — kiss by kiss I hallow
Whose but your dear hand my helper, punctual as at each new impulse
I approach my aim? Shell chipped, the eaglet callow
Needs a parent's pinion-push to quit the eyrie's edge:
But once fairly launched forth, denizen of ether,
While each effort sunward bids the blood more freely through each limb pulse,
Sure the parent feels, as gay they soar together,
Fully are all pains repaid when love redeems its pledge!"

Then did Peter's tristful visage lighten somewhat,
Vent a watery smile as though inveterate mistrust were thawing.
"Well, who knows?" he slow broke silence. "Mortals — come what
Come there may — are still the dupes of hope there's luck in store.
Many scholars seek me, promise mounts and marvels:

Here stand I to witness how they step 'twixt me and clapper-
clawing!
Dry bread, — that I've gained me: truly I should starve else:
But of milk, no drop was mine! Well, shuffle cards once
more!"

At the word of promise thus implied, our stranger —
What can he but cast his arms, in rapture of embrace, round
Peter?
"Hold! I choke!" the mage grunts. "Shall I in the manger
Any longer play the dog? Approach, my calf, and feed!
Bene . . . won't you wait for grace?" But sudden incense
Wool-white, serpent-solid, curled up — perfume growing
sweet and sweeter
Till it reached the young man's nose and seemed to win sense
Soul and all from out his brain through nostril: yes, indeed!

Presently the young man rubbed his eyes. "Where am I?
Too much bother over books! Some reverie has proved
amusing.
What did Peter prate of? 'Faith, my brow is clammy!
How my head throbs, how my heart thumps! Can it be I
swooned?
Oh, I spoke my speech out — cribbed from Plato's tractate,
Dosed him with 'the Fair and Good,' swore — Dog of Egypt
— I was choosing
Plato's way to serve men! What's the hour? Exact eight!
Home now, and to-morrow never mind how Plato mooned!

"Peter has the secret! Fair and Good are products
(So he said) of Foul and Evil: one must bring to pass the other.
Just as poisons grow drugs, steal through sundry odd ducts
Doctors name and ultimately issue safe and changed.
You'd abolish poisons, treat disease with dainties

Such as suit the sound and sane? With all such kickshaws
vain you pother!
Arsenic's the stuff puts force into the faint eyes,
Opium sets the brain to rights — by cark and care deranged.

"What, he's safe within door? — would escape — no question —
Thanks, since thanks and more I owe, and mean to pay in
time befitting.
What most presses now is — after night's digestion,
Peter, of thy precepts! — promptest practice of the same.
Let me see! The wise man, first of all, scorns riches:
But to scorn them must obtain them: none believes in his
permitting
Gold to lie ungathered: who picks up, then pitches
Gold away — philosophizes: none disputes his claim.

"So with worldly honors: 'tis by abdicating,
Incontestably he proves he could have kept the crown discarded.
Sulla cuts a figure, leaving off dictating:
Simpletons laud private life? 'The grapes are sour,' laugh
we.
So, again — but why continue? All's tumultuous
Here: my head's a-whirl with knowledge. Speedily shall be
rewarded
He who taught me! Greeks prove ingrates? So insult you
us?
When your teaching bears its first-fruits, Peter — wait and
see!"

As the word, the deed proved; ere a brief year's passage,
Fop — that fool he made the jokes on — now he made the
jokes for, *gratis:*

Hunks — that hoarder, long left lonely in his crass age —
Found now one appreciative deferential friend:
Powder-paint-and-patch, Hag Jezebel — recovered,
Strange to say, the power to please, got courtship till she cried *Jam satis!*
Fop be-flattered, Hunks be-friended, Hag be-lovered —
Nobody o'erlooked, save God — he soon attained his end.

As he lounged at ease one morning in his villa,
(Hag's the dowry) estimated (Hunks' bequest) his coin in coffer,
Mused on how a fool's good word (Fop's word) could fill a
Social circle with his praise, promote him man of mark, —
All at once — "An old friend fain would see your Highness!"
There stood Peter, skeleton and scarecrow, plain writ *Phi-lo-so-pher*
In the woe-worn face — for yellowness and dryness,
Parchment — with a pair of eyes — one hope their feeble spark.

"Did I counsel rightly? Have you, in accordance,
Prospered greatly, dear my pupil? Sure, at just the stage I find you,
When your hand may draw me forth from the mad war-dance
Savages are leading round your master — down, not dead.
Padua wants to burn me: balk them, let me linger
Life out — rueful though its remnant — hid in some safe hold behind you!
Prostrate here I lie: quick, help with but a finger
Lest I house in safety's self — a tombstone o'er my head!

"Lodging, bite and sup, with — now and then — a copper
—Alms for any poorer still, if such there be, — is all my asking.

Take me for your bedesman, — nay, if you think proper,
Menial merely, — such my perfect passion for repose!
Yes, from out your plenty Peter craves a pittance
— Leave to thaw his frozen hands before the fire whereat
you're basking!
Double though your debt were, grant this boon — remittance
He proclaims of obligation: 'tis himself that owes!"

"Venerated Master — can it be, such treatment
Learning meets with, magic fails to guard you from, by all
appearance?
Strange! for, as you entered, — what the famous feat meant,
I was full of, — why you reared that fabric, Padua's boast.
Nowise for man's pride, man's pleasure, did you slyly
Raise it, but man's seat of rule whereby the world should
soon have clearance
(Happy world) from such a rout as now so vilely
Handles you — and hampers me, for which I grieve the most.

"Since if it got wind you now were my familiar,
How could I protect you — nay, defend myself against the
rabble?
Wait until the mob, now masters, willy-nilly are
Servants as they should be: then has gratitude full play!
Surely this experience shows how unbefitting
'Tis that minds like mine should rot in ease and plenty.
Geese may gabble,
Gorge, and keep the ground: but swans are soon for quitting
Earthly fare — as fain would I, your swan, if taught the way.

"Teach me, then, to rule men, have them at my pleasure!
Solely for their good, of course, — impart a secret worth
rewarding.
Since the proper life's-prize! Tantalus's treasure

Aught beside proves, vanishes, and leaves no trace at all.
Wait awhile, nor press for payment prematurely!
Over-haste defrauds you. Thanks! since, — even while I speak, — discarding
Sloth and vain delights, I learn how — swiftly, surely —
Magic sways the sceptre, wears the crown and wields the ball!

"Gone again — what, is he? 'Faith, he's soon disposed of!
Peter's precepts work already, put within my lump their leaven!
Ay, we needs must don glove would we pluck the rose — doff
Silken garment would we climb the tree and take its fruit.
Why sharp thorn, rough rind? To keep unviolated
Either prize! We garland us, we mount from earth to feast in heaven,
Just because exist what once we estimated
Hindrances which, better taught, as helps we now compute.

"Foolishly I turned disgusted from my fellows!
Pits of ignorance — to fill, and heaps of prejudices — to level —
Multitudes in motley, whites and blacks and yellows —
What a hopeless task it seemed to discipline the host!
Now I see my error. Vices act like virtues
— Not alone because they guard — sharp thorns — the rose we first dishevel,
Not because they scrape, scratch — rough rind — through the dirt-shoes
Bare feet cling to bole with, while the half-mooned boot we boast.

"No, my aim is nobler, more disinterested!
Man shall keep what seemed to thwart him, since it proves his true assistance,

Leads to ascertaining which head is the best head,
Would he crown his body, rule its members — lawless else.
Ignorant the horse stares, by deficient vision
Takes a man to be a monster, lets him mount, then, twice the distance
Horse could trot unridden, gallops — dream Elysian! —
Dreaming that his dwarfish guide's a giant, — jockeys tell 's."

Brief, so worked the spell, he promptly had a riddance:
Heart and brain no longer felt the pricks which passed for conscience-scruples:
Free henceforth his feet, — *Per Bacco*, how they did dance
Merrily through lets and checks that stopped the way before!
Politics the prize now, — such adroit adviser,
Opportune suggester, with the tact that triples and quadruples
Merit in each measure, — never did the Kaiser
Boast as subject such a statesman, friend, and something more!

As he, up and down, one noonday, paced his closet
— Council o'er, each spark (his hint) blown flame, by colleagues' breath applauded,
Strokes of statecraft hailed with "*Salomo si nôsset!*"
(His the nostrum) — every throw for luck come double-six, —
As he, pacing, hugged himself in satisfaction,
Thump, — the door went. "What, the Kaiser? By none else were I defrauded
Thus of well-earned solace. Since 'tis fate's exaction, —
Enter, Liege my lord! Ha, Peter, you here? *Teneor vix!*"

"Ah, Sir, none the less, contain you, nor wax irate!
You so lofty, I so lowly, — vast the space which yawns between us!
Still, methinks, you — more than ever — at a high rate

Needs must prize poor Peter's secret since it lifts you thus.
Grant me now the boon whereat before you boggled!
Ten long years your march has moved — one triumph —
— (though *e*'s short) — *hactĕnus*,
While I down and down disastrously have joggled
Till I pitch against Death's door, the true *Nec Ultra Plus.*

"Years ago — some ten 'tis — since I sought for shelter,
Craved in your whole house a closet, out of all your means
a comfort.
Now you soar above these: as is gold to spelter
So is power — you urged with reason — paramount to
wealth.
Power you boast in plenty: let it grant me refuge!
House-room now is out of question: find for me some strong-
hold — some fort —
Privacy wherein, immured, shall this blind deaf huge
Monster of a mob let stay the soul I'd save by stealth!

"Ay, for all too much with magic have I tampered!
— Lost the world, and gained, I fear, a certain place I'm to
describe loth!
Still, if prayer and fasting tame the pride long pampered,
Mercy may be mine: amendment never comes too late.
How can I amend beset by curses, kickers?
Pluck this brand from out the burning! Once away, I take
my Bible-oath,
Never more — so long as life's weak lamp-flame flickers —
No, not once I'll tease you, but in silence bear my fate!"

"Gently, good my Genius, Oracle unerring!
Strange now! can you guess on what — as in you peeped —
it was I pondered?
You and I are both of one mind in preferring

Power to wealth, but — here's the point — what sort of power, I ask?
Ruling men is vulgar, easy, and ignoble:
Rid yourself of conscience, quick you have at beck and call the fond herd.
But who wields the crozier, down may fling the crow-bill:
That's the power I covet now; soul's sway o'er souls — my task!

"'Well but,' you object, 'you have it, who by glamour
Dress up lies to look like truths, mask folly in the garb of reason:
Your soul acts on theirs, sure, when the people clamor,
Hold their peace, now fight now fondle, — ear-wigged through the brains.'
Possibly! but still the operation 's mundane,
Grosser than a taste demands which — craving manna — kecks at peason —
Power o'er men by wants material: why should one deign
Rule by sordid hopes and fears — a grunt for all one's pains?

"No, if men must praise me, let them praise to purpose!
Would we move the world, not earth but heaven must be our fulcrum — *pou sto!*
Thus I seek to move it: Master, why intérpose —
Balk my climbing close on what's the ladder's topmost round?
Statecraft 'tis I step from: when by priestcraft hoisted
Up to where my foot may touch the highest rung which fate allows toe,
Then indeed ask favor. On you shall be foisted
No excuse: I'll pay my debt, each penny of the pound!

"Ho, my knaves without there! Lead this worthy downstairs!

No farewell, good Paul — nay, Peter .. What's your name
remembered rightly?
Come, he's humble: out another would have flounced — airs
Suitors often give themselves when our sort bow them forth.
Did I touch his rags? He surely kept his distance:
Yet, there somehow passed to me from him — where'er the
virtue might lie —
Something that inspires my soul — Oh, by assistance
Doubtlessly of Peter! — still, he's worth just what he's worth!

"'Tis my own soul soars now: soaring — how? By crawling!
I'll to Rome, before Rome's feet the temporal-supreme lay
prostrate!
'Hands' (I'll say) 'proficient once in pulling, hauling
This and that way men as I was minded — feet now clasp!'
Ay, the Kaiser's self has wrung them in his fervor!
Now — they only sue to slave for Rome, nor at one doit the
cost rate.
Rome's adopted child — no bone, no muscle, nerve or
Sinew of me but I'll strain, thoughout my life I gasp!"

As he stood one evening proudly — (he had traversed
Rome on horseback — peerless pageant! — claimed the
Lateran as new Pope) —
Thinking "All's attained now! Pontiff! Who could have erst
Dreamed of my advance so far when, some ten years ago,
I embraced devotion, grew from priest to bishop,
Gained the Purple, bribed the Conclave, got the Two-thirds,
saw my coop ope,
Came out — what Rome hails me! O were there a wish-shop,
Not one wish more would I purchase — Lord of all below!

"Ha! — who dares intrude now — puts aside the arras?
What, old Peter, here again, at such a time, in such a presence?

Satan sends this plague back merely to embarrass
Me who enter on my office — little needing you!
'Faith, I'm touched myself by age, but you look Tithon!
Were it vain to seek of you the sole prize left — rejuvenescence?
Well, since flesh is grass which time must lay his scythe on,
Say your say, and so depart and make no more ado!"

Peter faltered — coughing first by way of prologue —
"Holiness, your help comes late: a death at ninety little matters.
Padua, build poor Peter's pyre now, on log roll log,
Burn away — I've lived my day! Yet here's the sting in death —
I've an author's pride: I want my Book's survival:
See, I've hid it in my breast to warm me 'mid the rags and tatters!
Save it — tell next age your Master had no rival!
Scholar's debt discharged in full, be 'Thanks' my latest breath!"

"Faugh, the frowsy bundle — scribbling harum-scarum
Scattered o'er a dozen sheepskins! What's the name of this farrago?
Ha — '*Conciliator Differentiarum*' —
Man and book may burn together, cause the world no loss!
Stop — what else? A tractate — eh, '*De Speciebus*
Ceremonialis Ma-gi-ae?' I dream sure! Hence, away, go,
Wizard, — quick avoid me! Vain you clasp my knee, buss
Hand that bears the Fisher's ring or foot that boasts the Cross!

"Help! The old magician clings like an octopus!
Ah, you rise now — fuming, fretting, frowning, if I read your features!

Frown, who cares? We're Pope — once Pope, you can't
unpope us!
Good — you muster up a smile: that's better! Still so brisk?
All at once grown youthful? But the case is plain! Ass —
Here I dally with the fiend, yet know the Word — compels
all creatures
Earthly, heavenly, hellish. *Apage, Sathanas*
Dicam verbum Salomonis —" "*dicite!*" When — whisk! —

What was changed? The stranger gave his eyes a rubbing:
There smiled Peter's face turned back a moment at him o'er
the shoulder,
As the black door shut, bang! "So he 'scapes a drubbing!"
(Quoth a boy who, unespied, had stopped to hear the talk.)
"That's the way to thank these wizards when they bid men
Benedicite! What ails you? You, a man, and yet no bolder?
Foreign Sir, you look but foolish!" "*Idmen, idmen!*"
Groaned the Greek. "O Peter, cheese at last I know from
chalk!"

Peter lived his life out, menaced yet no martyr,
Knew himself the mighty man he was — such knowledge all
his guerdon,
Left the world a big book — people but in part err
When they style a true *Scientiae Com-pen-di-um:*
"*Admirationem incutit*" they sourly
Smile, as fast they shut the folio which myself was somehow
spurred on
Once to ope: but love — life's milk which daily, hourly,
Blockheads lap — O Peter, still thy taste of love's to come!

Greek, was your ambition likewise doomed to failure?
True, I find no record you wore purple, walked with axe and
fasces,
Played some antipope's part: still, friend, don't turn tail, you're
Certain, with but these two gifts, to gain earth's prize in time!

Cleverness uncurbed by conscience — if you ransacked
Peter's book you'd find no potent spell like these to rule the
masses;
Nor should want example, had I not to transact
Other business. Go your ways, you'll thrive! So ends my rhyme.

When these parts Tiberius — not yet Cæsar — travelled,
Passing Padua, he consulted Padua's Oracle of Geryon
(God three-headed, thrice wise) just to get unravelled
Certain tangles of his future. "Fling at Abano
Golden dice," it answered; "dropt within the fount there,
Note what sum the pips present!" And still we see each die,
the very one,
Turn up, through the crystal, — read the whole account there
Where 'tis told by Suetonius, — each its highest throw

Scarce the sportive fancy-dice I fling show "Venus:"
Still — for love of that dear land which I so oft in dreams
revisit —
I have — oh, not sung! but lilted (as — between us —
Grows my lazy custom) this its legend. What the lilt?

The Grammarian belongs to a later stage of development in Italian culture. Browning dates the poem "Shortly after the Revival of Learning," so we may consider that this learned man belongs to the rising or flood tide of humanism, before the appearance of those degenerate tendencies that self-seeking later brought upon it. The talks by Gemistos Plethon in Florence, already mentioned, are by some given as the date of the beginning of the Revival of Learning.

He certainly exerted a tremendous influence through Cosimo de' Medici, whom he convinced of the importance of the study of Plato, and who thereupon founded the famous Florentine Academy. Cosimo also appointed young Marsilio Ficino to the important office of translating and explaining the Platonic writings. This Academy exerted a profound influence over the thought not only of Italy but of Germany, and so persistent was the influence of Gemistos that, as Symonds remarks, "Platonic studies in Italy never recovered from the impress of Neoplatonic mysticism which proceeded from his mind."

But it must not be forgotten that there was already a Greek professorship in Florence, held by Manuel Chrysoloras, a Byzantine of noble birth. He came first to Venice on an important church mission, was visited there by the Florentines, Roberto di Rossi and Giacomo d'Angelo Scarparia. The latter went back to Byzantium with him, and Rossi, returning to Florence, enlarged so upon the erudite qualities of the learned Greek that the Signory sent him an invitation to fill the Greek chair in the university, which he accepted in 1396. Thus it was that Greeks came to Italy and Italians went to Constantinople to learn Greek. As Sedgwick puts it "The humanists played a part analogous to that which men of science play to-day. They devoted themselves heart and soul to the classics, as men of science do to nature. For some time they had had access to the Latin past through Italy, and now they also found their way to the far greater classic world of Greece. The one uninterrupted communication with that world was through Constantinople, which, like a long, ill-lighted and ill-repaired corridor, led back to the great pleasure domes of Plato and Homer, and all the wonderland of Greek literature and thought."

Although in the fourteenth century great and general enthusiasm for classical antiquity burst forth, it was not until the fifteenth that new discoveries of manuscripts were made, and the systematic creation of libraries begun by means of copies and the rapid multiplication of translations from the Greek. Burckhard declares that if it had not been for the "enthusiasm of a few collectors of the age, who shrank from no effort or privation in their researches, we should certainly possess only a small part of the literature, especially that of the Greeks, which is now in our hands." Many are the stories told of fortunes spent and time devoted to the collection of manuscripts. Pope Nicholas V, whom we have already mentioned, when only a simple monk, ran deeply into debt through buying manuscripts or having them copied, and when he became Pope he gave enormous sums for translations of Polybius, Strabo, and others.

A Florentine, Niccoto Niccoli, spent his whole fortune in buying books and at last when his money gave out, the Medici allowed him to draw upon them to any amount.

Following upon the collection of manuscripts came the study of them, which was carried on to some extent in the Universities, but more especially in monasteries and by private individuals singly or in groups. The Latin schools, too, which existed in every town of any importance, attained under distinguished humanists great perfection of organization and became instruments of higher education. But, on the whole, individual enterprise seems to have accomplished the greatest results.

Burckhard tells at length of two humanist teachers who remind us much of Browning's Grammarian in their utter devotion. "At the court of Giovan Francesco Gonzaga at Mantua appeared the illustrious Vittorino da Feltre — one of those men who devote their whole life to an object for which their natural gifts constitute a special vocation. He wrote almost nothing and finally destroyed the few poems of his youth which he had long kept by him. He studied with unwearied industry; he never sought after titles, which, like all outward distinctions, he scorned; and he lived on terms of the closest friendship with teachers, companions, and pupils, whose good-will he knew how to preserve. He excelled in bodily no less than in mental exercises, was an admirable rider, dancer, and fencer, wore the same clothes in winter as in summer, walked in nothing but sandals even during the severest frost, and lived so that until his old age he was never ill. He so restrained his passions, his natural inclination to sensuality and anger, that he remained chaste his whole life through and hardly ever hurt any one by a hard word.

"He directed the education of the sons and daughters of the princely house, and one of the latter became under his care a woman of learning. When his reputation extended far and wide over Italy, and numbers of great and wealthy families came from far and wide, even from Germany in search of his instructions, Gonzaga was not only willing that they should be received, but seems to have held it an honor for Mantua to be the chosen school of the aristocratic world. Here for the first time gymnastics and all noble bodily exercises were treated along with scientific instruction as indispensable to a liberal education. Besides these pupils came others, whose instruction Vittorino probably held to be his highest earthly aim, the gifted poor, often as many as seventy together, whom he supported in his house and educated along with the other high-born youths who here learned to live under the same roof with untitled genius. The greater the crowd of pupils who flocked to Mantua the more teachers were needed to impart the instruction which aimed at giving each pupil that sort of learning which he was most fitted to receive. Gonzaga paid him a yearly salary of two hundred and forty gold florins, built him besides a splendid house, "La Giocosa," in which the master lived with his scholars and contributed to the expenses caused by the poorer pupils. What was still further needed Vittorino begged from princes and wealthy people, who did not always, it is true, give a ready ear to his entreaties, and forced him by their hard-heartedness to run into debt. Yet in the end he found himself in comfortable circumstances, owned a small property in town, and an estate in the country where he stayed with his pupils during the holidays, and possessed a famous collection of books which he gladly lent or gave away, though he was not a little angry when they were taken without leave. In the early morning he read religious books, then scourged himself and went to church; his pupils were also compelled to go to church, like him to confess once a month, and to observe fast days most strictly. His pupils respected him, but trembled before his glance. When they did anything wrong, they were punished immediately after the offense. He was honored by all his contemporaries no less than by his pupils and people took the journey to Mantua merely to see him."

Another equally interesting scholar of the

time was Guarino of Verona. In 1429 he was called to Ferrara to educate Lionello, the son of Niccolo d'Este.

"He had many other pupils besides Lionello from various parts of the country, and, besides, supported wholly or in part a select class of poor scholars in his own house. He laid more stress on pure scholarship than Vittorino. Far into the night he heard lessons or indulged in instructive conversation. Yet with all this he found time to write translations from the Greek and voluminous original works.

"Like Vittorino's his house was the home of a strict religion and morality."

Italy was full of scholars of similar attainments to these. They were not only teachers and translators and professors in Universities, but they held important positions in the Church and State, but by the time the sixteenth century arrives a sad change in the attitude of society toward them has to be recorded. "The whole class fell into deep and general disgrace," writes Burckhard. "To the two chief accusations against them — that of malicious self-conceit, and that of abominable profligacy — a third charge of irreligion was now loudly added by the rising powers of the Counter-reformation."

The humanists themselves were loudest in defaming one another.

Burckhard's summing up explains this downfall as fully, perhaps, as it can be at this distance of time. "Three facts," he says "explain and perhaps diminish their guilt: the overflowing excess of favor and fortune when the luck was on their side; the uncertainty of the future in which luxury or misery depended on the caprice of a patron or the malice of an enemy, and finally the misleading influence of antiquity. This undermined their morality without giving them its own instead; and in religious matters, since they could never think of accepting the positive belief in the old gods, it affected them only on the negative and sceptical side. Just because they conceived of antiquity dogmatically — that is, took it for the model of all thought and action — its influence was here pernicious. But that an age existed which idolized the ancient world and its products with an exclusive devotion, was not the fault of individuals. It was the work of an historical providence, and all the culture of the ages which have followed and of the ages to come rests upon the fact that it was so, and that all the ends of life but this one were then deliberately put aside."

In "The Grammarian's Funeral," Browning has preserved for us the breath and finer spirit of this scholarly aspect of the Renaissance. We may imagine the pupils of Vittorino or Guarino burying their master in the same lofty spirit. Figuratively speaking their memories are enshrined upon the heights of humanism in its most aspiring manifestations, and similarly the poem is, as it were, the supreme blossom of art growing out of the complex elements provided by the historians of the learning of the time.

A GRAMMARIAN'S FUNERAL

SHORTLY AFTER THE REVIVAL OF LEARNING IN EUROPE

Let us begin and carry up this corpse,
    Singing together.
Leave we the common crofts, the vulgar thorpes
    Each in its tether
Sleeping safe on the bosom of the plain,
    Cared-for till cock-crow:
Look out if yonder be not day again
    Rimming the rock-row!
That's the appropriate country; there, man's thought,
    Rarer, intenser,
Self-gathered for an outbreak, as it ought,
    Chafes in the censer.
Leave we the unlettered plain its herd and crop;
    Seek we sepulture
On a tall mountain, citied to the top,
    Crowded with culture!

All the peaks soar, but one the rest excels;
Clouds overcome it;
No! yonder sparkle is the citadel's
Circling its summit.
Thither our path lies; wind we up the heights;
Wait ye the warning?
Our low life was the level's and the night's;
He's for the morning.
Step to a tune, square chests, erect each head,
'Ware the beholders!
This is our master, famous, calm and dead,
Borne on our shoulders.

Sleep, crop and herd! sleep, darkling thorpe and croft.
Safe from the weather!
He, whom we convoy to his grave aloft,
Singing together,
He was a man born with thy face and throat,
Lyric Apollo!
Long he lived nameless: how should Spring take note
Winter would follow?
Till lo! the little touch, and youth was gone,
Cramped and diminished,
Moaned he, "New measures, other feet anon!
My dance is finished"?
No, that's the world's way: (keep the mountain-side,
Make for the city!)
He knew the signal, and stepped on with pride
Over men's pity;
Left play for work, and grappled with the world
Bent on escaping:
"What's in the scroll," quoth he, "thou keepest furled?
Show me their shaping,

Theirs who most studied man, the bard and sage, —
    Give!" — So, he gowned him,
Straight got my heart that book to its last page:
    Learned, we found him.
Yea, but we found him bald too, eyes like lead,
    Accents uncertain:
"Time to taste life," another would have said,
    "Up with a curtain!"
This man said rather, "Actual life comes next?
    Patience a moment!
Grant I have mastered learning's crabbed text,
    Still there's the comment.
Let me know all! Prate not of most or least,
    Painful or easy!
Even to the crumbs I'd fain eat up the feast,
    Ay, nor feel queasy."
Oh, such a life as he resolved to live,
    When he had learned it,
When he had gathered all books had to give!
    Sooner, he spurned it.
Image the whole, then execute the parts —
    Fancy the fabric
Quite, ere you build, ere steel strike fire from quartz,
    Ere mortar dab brick!

(Here's the town-gate reached: there's the market-place
    Gaping before us.)
Yea, this in him was the peculiar grace
    (Hearten our chorus!)
That before living he'd learn how to live —
    No end to learning:
Earn the means first — God surely will contrive
    Use for our earning.

Others mistrust and say, "But time escapes:
  Live now or never!"
He said, "What's time? Leave Now for dogs and apes!
  Man has Forever."
Back to his book then: deeper drooped his head:
  Calculus racked him:
Leaden before, his eyes grew dross of lead:
  Tussis attacked him.
"Now, master, take a little rest!" — not he!
  (Caution redoubled,
Step two abreast, the way winds narrowly!)
  Not a whit troubled,
Back to his studies, fresher than at first,
  Fierce as a dragon
He (soul-hydroptic with a sacred thirst)
  Sucked at the flagon.
Oh, if we draw a circle premature,
  Heedless of far gain,
Greedy for quick returns of profit, sure
  Bad is our bargain!
Was it not great? did not he throw on God,
  (He loves the burthen) —
God's task to make the heavenly period
  Perfect the earthen?
Did not he magnify the mind, show clear
  Just what it all meant?
He would not discount life, as fools do here,
  Paid by instalment.
He ventured neck or nothing — heaven's success
  Found, or earth's failure:
"Wilt thou trust death or not?" He answered "Yes!
  Hence with life's pale lure!"
That low man seeks a little thing to do,
  Sees it and does it:

This high man, with a great thing to pursue,
    Dies ere he knows it.
That low man goes on adding one to one,
    His hundred's soon hit:
This high man, aiming at a million,
    Misses an unit.
That, has the world here — should he need the next,
    Let the world mind him!
This, throws himself on God, and unperplexed
    Seeking shall find him.
So, with the throttling hands of death at strife,
    Ground he at grammar;
Still, through the rattle, parts of speech were rife:
    While he could stammer
He settled *Hoti's* business — let it be! —
    Properly based *Oun* —
Gave us the doctrine of the enclitic *De*,
    Dead from the waist down.
Well, here's the platform, here's the proper place;
    Hail to your purlieus,
All ye highfliers of the feathered race,
    Swallows and curlews!
Here's the top-peak; the multitude below
    Live, for they can, there:
This man decided not to Live but Know —
    Bury this man there?
Here — here's his place, where meteors shoot, clouds form,
    Lightnings are loosened,
Stars come and go! Let joy break with the storm,
    Peace let the dew send!
Lofty designs must close in like effects:
    Loftily lying,
Leave him — still loftier than the world suspects,
    Living and dying.

IV

THE ARTIST AND HIS ART

"Each Art a-strain
Would stay the apparition, — nor in vain:
The Poet's word-mesh, Painter's sure and swift
Color-and-line-throw — proud the prize they lift!
Thus felt Man and thus looked Man, — passions caught
I' the midway swim of sea, — not much, if aught,
Of nether-brooding loves, hates, hopes, and fears,
Enwombed past Art's disclosure."

— *Charles Avison.*

BROWNING'S interest in Italian art, in his poetry at any rate, centered itself principally upon the painters of the earlier Renaissance and upon those who inaugurated the later and greater Renaissance in art. With the exception of Andrea del Sarto, who belongs in the period of the culmination of Italian art, though not among its greatest exemplars, he has celebrated none of those whom the world has acclaimed the supreme masters. In fact he very distinctly states his determination not to do so in his poem, "Old Pictures in Florence": —

"For oh, this world and the wrong it does;
They are safe in heaven with their backs to it,
The Michaels and Rafaels, you hum and buzz
Round the works of, you of the little wit!

. . . .

"Much they reck of your praise and you!
But the wronged great souls — can they be quit
Of a world where their work is all to do,
Where you style them you of the little wit,
Old Master This and Early the Other,
Not dreaming that Old and New are fellows:
A younger succeeds to an elder brother,
Da Vincis derive in good time from Dellos."

What he declares that he loves is the season

"Of Art's spring birth so dim and dewy;
My sculptor is Nicolo the Pisan
My painter — who but Cimabue?
Nor even was man of them all indeed,
From these to Ghiberti and Ghirlandajo,
Could say that he missed my critic meed."

When one reads the extravagant praises bestowed upon these early painters and sculptors in Vasari's "Lives of the Painters," and the echoes from these that appear in later works upon art, it would hardly seem as if Cimabue or Giotto or Nicolo Pisano needed Browning's defense. But it is well to remember in this connection that one meets plenty of laymen who do not especially

Florence, Old and New: Old Gate and Triumphal Arch.

admire Giotto's Campanile, though John Addington Symonds calls it "that lily among Campanili," and who are bored beyond measure by the dingy, ancient pictures to be found in the chapels and cloisters of Florence, cracked with age and melancholy by reason of the white-washings they have had, and from which they can never quite recover. Furthermore, Symonds, who has done more than any one else to set the key-note of criticism, makes a decided distinction between the artists of the earlier Renaissance and those who inaugurated the later Renaissance — the "Pre-Raphaelites." For the first he has enthusiasm almost as unbounded as Vasari, but his attitude toward the latter is often unsympathetic, as any one may see who cares to compare what he has to say about Ghirlandajo and Botticelli with what the Editors of Vasari's "Lives," the Blashfields and A. A. Hopkins say about these same painters. Symonds "hummed and buzzed" around the Michaels and Rafaels, though one could hardly say he did it with "little wit." Among the jewels of criticism in his studies of the Italian Renaissance there is perhaps not a more brilliant one than his summing up of the qualities of the four great masters, Leonardo da Vinci, Raphael,

Michael Angelo, and Correggio. He hummed and buzzed to some purpose here.

"To these four men, each in his own degree and according to his own peculiar quality of mind, the fulness of the Renaissance in its power and freedom was revealed. They entered the inner shrine, where dwelt the spirit of their age, and bore to the world without the message each of them had heard. In their work posterity still may read the meaning of that epoch, differently rendered according to the difference of gift of each consummate artist, but comprehended in its unity by study of the four together. Leonardo is the wizard or diviner; to him the Renaissance offers her mystery and lends her magic. Raphael is the Phœbean singer; to him the Renaissance reveals her joy and dowers him with her gifts of melody. Correggio is the Ariel or Faun, the lover and light-giver; he has surprised laughter upon the face of the universe, and he paints this laughter in ever-varying movement. Michael Angelo is the prophet and Sibylline seer; to him the Renaissance discloses the travail of her spirit; him she endues with power; he wrests her secret, voyaging like an ideal Columbus, the vast abyss of thought alone."

Browning's attitude on the other hand,

as expressed in this poem is very much like that of the English Brotherhood of Pre-Raphaelites, who formulated their doctrines in 1849, only six years before this poem was written. We are told that Hunt, Millais, and Rossetti reached their final resolve through the study of Lasinio's engravings of the frescos in the Campo Santo at Pisa. "These revealed to the young students an art not satisfied with itself, but reaching after higher things and earnestly seeking to interpret nature and human life. To be of the same spirit as the painters who preceded Raphael, using art as a means to noblest ends, and not merely to emulate the accomplishment of Raphael, as if art had said its last word when he died, was the ambition that the engravings awakened in the three young artists as they studied them. They were not blind to the genius of Raphael, nor did they deny that art had accomplished great things after his time; but, in Holman Hunt's own words, 'It appeared to them that afterwards art was so frequently tainted with the canker of corruption that it was only in the earlier work they could find with certainty absolute health. Up to a definite point the tree was healthy: above it disease began, side by side with life there appeared death.'" By way of showing his preference for imperfect, aspiring art Browning draws a contrast between Greek art and the early Italian art.

"If you knew their work you would deal your dole."
May I take upon me to instruct you?
When Greek Art ran and reached the goal,
Thus much had the world to boast *in fructu* —
The Truth of Man, as by God first spoken,
Which the actual generations garble,
Was re-uttered, and Soul (which Limbs betoken)
And Limbs (Soul informs) made new in marble.

"So, you saw yourself as you wished you were,
As you might have been, as you cannot be;
Earth here, rebuked by Olympus there:
And grew content in your poor degree
With your little power, by those statues' godhead,
And your little scope, by their eyes' full sway,
And your little grace, by their grace embodied,
And your little date, by their forms that stay.

"You would fain be kinglier, say, than I am?
Even so, you will not sit like Theseus.
You would prove a model? The Son of Priam
Has yet the advantage in arms' and knees' use.
You're wroth — can you slay your snake like Apollo?
You're grieved — still Niobe's the grander!
You live — there's the Racers' frieze to follow:
You die — there's the dying Alexander.

"So, testing your weakness by their strength,
Your meager charms by their rounded beauty,

Measured by Art in your breadth and length,
You learned — to submit is a mortal's duty.
— When I say 'you' 'tis the common soul,
The collective, I mean: the race of Man
That receives life in parts to live in a whole,
And grow here according to God's clear plan.

"Growth came when, looking your last on them all,
You turned your eyes inwardly one fine day
And cried with a start — What if we so small
Be greater and grander the while than they?
Are they perfect of lineament, perfect of stature?
In both, of such lower types are we
Precisely because of our wider nature;
For time, theirs — ours, for eternity.

"To-day's brief passion limits their range;
It seethes with the morrow for us and more.
They are perfect — how else? they shall never change:
We are faulty — why not? we have time in store.
The Artificer's hand is not arrested
With us; we are rough-hewn, nowise polished:
They stand for our copy, and, once invested
With all they can teach, we shall see them abolished.

"'Tis a life-long toil till our lump be leaven —
The better! What's come to perfection perishes.
Things learned on earth, we shall practise in heaven:
Works done least rapidly, Art most cherishes.
Thyself shalt afford the example, Giotto!
Thy one work, not to decrease or diminish,
Done at a stroke, was just (was it not?) 'O!'
Thy great Campanile is still to finish.

"Is it true that we are now, and shall be hereafter,
But what and where depend on life's minute?
Hails heavenly cheer or infernal laughter
Our first step out of the gulf or in it?
Shall Man, such step within his endeavor,
Man's face, have no more play and action
Than joy which is crystallized forever,
Or grief, an eternal petrifaction?

"On which I conclude, that the early painters,
To cries of 'Greek Art and what more wish you?' —
Replied, 'To become now self-acquainters,
And paint man man, whatever the issue!
Make new hopes shine through the flesh they fray,
New fears aggrandize the rags and tatters:
To bring the invisible full into play!
Let the visible go to the dogs — what matters?'

"Give these, I exhort you, their guerdon and glory
For daring so much, before they well did it.
The first of the new, in our race's story,
Beats the last of the old; 'tis no idle quiddit.
The worthies began a revolution,
Which if on earth you intend to acknowledge,
Why, honor them now! (ends my allocution)
Nor confer your degree when the folk leave college."

The poem resolves itself into a genuine bit of criticism with which one may or may not agree. Probably the wisest attitude is to like each phase of art for its own special quality. To offset Symonds' praise of the Masters we may take to our hearts Pater's exquisite appreciation of the Italian sculptors of the earlier half of the fifteenth century. He says they are "more than mere forerunners of the great masters of its close, and often reach perfection within the narrow limits which they chose to impose on their work. Their sculpture shares with the paintings of Botticelli and the churches of Brunelleschi that profound expressiveness, that intimate impress of an indwelling soul, which is the peculiar fascination of the art of Italy in that century. Their works have been much neglected and often almost hidden away amid the frippery. of modern decoration, and we come with some surprise to the places where their fire still smoulders. One longs to penetrate into the lives of the men who have given expression to so much power and sweetness, but it is part of the reserve, the austere dignity and simplicity of their existence, that their lives are for the most part lost or told but briefly: from their lives as from their works all tumult of sound and color has passed away."

This poem of Browning's, however, is much more than a criticism of Italian art; we get from it real glimpses of Florence and its pictures flooded with the light of the poet's own feeling — a half serious, half sportive mood in which he berates the ghosts of these early artists whom he has always praised, because they do not help him to unearth some precious bit of which he might become the happy owner. Even Giotto has treated him badly and let some one else discover a certain rare little tablet.

Let us try now and see with the poet's eyes what he saw

"The morn when first it thunders in March,
  The eel in the pond gives a leap they say:
As I leaned and looked over the aloed arch
  Of the villa-gate this warm March day,
No flash snapped, no dumb thunder rolled
  In the valley beneath where, white and wide
And washed by the morning water-gold,
  Florence lay out on the mountain-side.

"River and bridge and street and square
  Lay mine, as much at my beck and call,
Through the live translucent bath of air,
  As the sights in a magic crystal ball.
And of all I saw and of all I praised
  The most to praise and the best to see
Was the startling bell-tower Giotto raised:
  But why did it more than startle me?

"Giotto, how, with that soul of yours,
  Could you play me false who loved you so?
Some slights if a certain heart endures
  Yet it feels. I would have you fellows know!
I' faith, I perceive not why I should care

To break a silence that suits them best,
But the thing grows somewhat hard to bear,
When I find a Giotto join the rest!"

Any praise of Giotto will find an echo in the heart of most critics if not in that of all laymen. Cimabue, whom later on in the poem, Browning as we have already seen, calls "his painter," was the pioneer and did very remarkable work as such.

What he meant to the Florentines of his day is well illustrated by the story Vasari tells of his painting of the Virgin for the church of Santa Maria Novella. It was so much admired, they never having seen anything better, that it was carried in solemn procession with the sound of trumpets and other festal demonstrations from the house of Cimabue to the church, he himself being highly rewarded and honored for it. No doubt the poet often looked at this picture where it still hangs in a dark transept of Santa Maria Novella, and he doubtless saw what some see to-day, an attempt at expression which warmed the cockles of his heart. The spark of life has been struck, the figures have movement, as some one has facetiously said "Noah and his family, indeed, in the story of the Ark move almost with violence," but considering these unmistakable signs of life, it is easy to overlook Cimabue's archaisms,—such as the crinkled, pointed draperies, characteristic of Byzantine art.

Everybody concedes, however, that Giotto was quite another matter. He outstripped his teacher Cimabue, by such strides that he took art a hundred years forwards along the lines of composition, dramatic feeling and invention. Browning instinctively recognizes this greatness, and doesn't mind the fact that Giotto's faces resemble one another, that they have elongated eyes, short, straight, rather snub noses and very full chins. And neither did Symonds mind this, for he is enthusiastic about both Giotto and his pupils. "It is no exaggeration," he says, "to claim that Giotto and his scholars, within the space of little more than half a century, painted out upon the walls of the Churches and public places of Italy every great conception of the Middle Ages."

The Campanile which the poet sees from his villa adjoins the Duomo already spoken of in connection with "Luria."

Like the Duomo, more than one artist worked upon it, though the design was originally Giotto's and was to have had a spire fifty braccia high to crown the tower. Unfortunately Giotto died after only three

Giotto.

THE CAMPANILE.

years' work upon it, when it had reached a very small portion of its height. The work is said to have been continued by Taddeo Gaddi, his godson, and his pupil and disciple for twenty-five years. He was succeeded by Francesco Talenti, who it is supposed may have modified and enriched the design. In form and decoration it was quite different from anything that had preceded it, and in the opinion of many combines every element of beauty possible in such a work. It covers a square of about forty-five feet and towers up two hundred and seventy-five feet. It has no openings except the doorway on the east side for more than a third of the way up. This lower third is divided into two stages with a slight projection at the top of each stage. Above these are two stages of equal height and exactly similar design. There are two two-light windows in each face, beautiful in their graceful proportions and delicate ornamentation, with gabled arches and traceried balconies. To crown all is the belfry in a single stage much greater in height, and with a broad three-light opening in each face through which looks the blue Italian sky like a fair face more fair through the meshes of a veil. The wall is everywhere encrusted with panelings of white and green marble, similar but richer than that of the cathedral, and with floral sculpture in the friezes. Figure sculpture adorns the lowest range of paneling in the first stage of the base, the designs believed to be by Giotto, and partly executed by him, partly by Andrea Pisano, Lucca della Robia and others. Also, in the upper stage of the base the lower range of paneling is ornamented with a series of standing figures in small, pointed arched niches, by Donatello, and others.

Browning makes the incompleteness of this tower serve his argument of the superior interest attaching to the less "perfect" things of art.

"'Tis a life-long toil till our lump be leaven —
 The better! What's come to perfection perishes.
Things learned on earth we shall practice in heaven:
 Works done least rapidly, Art most cherishes.
Thyself shalt afford the example Giotto!
 Thy one work, not to decrease or diminish,
Done at a stroke, was just (was it not) 'O!'[1]
 Thy great Campanile is yet to finish."

[1] Referring to the well-known anecdote of the envoy of Benedict IX who, when visiting Giotto, asked for a drawing to carry as a proof of his skill to the Pope. Giotto taking a sheet of paper and a brush-full of red paint and resting his elbow on his hip to form a sort of compass, with one turn of his hand drew a circle so perfect that it was a marvel to behold, whence the proverb "Rounder than the O of Giotto."

The poet later on is guilty of a slight inconsistency in regard to the bell-tower, for after admiring it because it is not finished, he has an enthusiastic vision of the attaining of Italian political independence and its celebration by the finishing of the spire.

"When the hour grows ripe, and a certain dotard
  Is pitched, no parcel that needs invoicing,
To the worse side of the Mont Saint Gothard,
  We shall begin by way of rejoicing;
None of that shooting the sky (blank cartridge),
  Nor a civic guard, all plumes and lacquer,
Hunting Radetzky's soul like a partridge
  Over Morello with squib and cracker.

"This time we'll shoot better game and bag 'em hot —
  No mere display at the stone of Dante,
But a kind of sober Witanagamot
  (Ex: 'Casa Guidi,' *quod videas ante*)
Shall ponder, once Freedom restored to Florence,
  How Art may return that departed with her.
Go, hated house, go each trace of the Loraine's,
  And bring us the days of Orgagna hither!

"How we shall prologize, how we shall perorate,
  Utter fit things upon art and history,
Feel truth at blood-heat and falsehood at zero rate,
  Make of the want of the age no mystery;
Contrast the fructuous and sterile eras,
  Show — Monarchy ever its uncouth cub licks
Out of the bear's shape into Chimæra's,
  While Pure Art's birth is still the republic's.

"Then one shall propose in a speech (curt Tuscan —
 Expurgate and sober, with scarcely an 'issimo,')
To end now our half-told tale of Cambuscan,
 And turn the bell-tower's *alt* to *altissimo:*
And fine as the beak of a young beccaccia
 The Campanile, the Duomo's fit ally,
Shall soar up in gold full fifty braccia,
 Completing Florence, as Florence Italy.

"Shall I be alive that morning the scaffold
 Is broken away, and the long pent fire,
Like the golden hope of the world, unbaffled
 Springs from its sleep, and up goes the spire
While 'God and the People' plain for its motto,
 Thence the new tricolor flaps at the sky?
At least to foresee that glory of Giotto
 And Florence together, the first am I."

In still another mood of the poem, however, he presents a possible solution of these two moods.

"There's a fancy some lean to and others hate —
 That, when this life is ended, begins
New work for the soul in another state,
 Where it strives and gets weary, loses and wins:
Where the strong and the weak, this world's congeries,
 Repeat in large what they practised in small,
Through life after life in unlimited series;
 Only the scale's to be changed, that's all.

"Yet I hardly know. When a soul has seen
 By the means of Evil that Good is best,
And, through earth and its noise, what is heaven's serene, —

Giotto.

SCULPTURE FROM CAMPANILE REPRESENTING AGRICULTURE.

When our faith in the same has stood the test —
Why, the child grown man, you burn the rod,
The uses of labor are surely done;
There remaineth a rest for the people of God:
And I have had troubles enough for one."

This is tantamount to saying that the quality of imperfection appeals to the human mind as long as it is itself in a state of imperfection, but once having passed on to another phase of existence, with a soul fully developed by the lessons learned through life's imperfections, then delight and joy and peace will be the portion of the soul attuned to perfection. It will be such a state of exaltation as that described by Shelley in the climax of "Prometheus Unbound."

Thus his musings over the early painters lead the poet into political prophecy and philosophical ruminations, both of which, in spite of his praise of imperfection, bring the conclusion that perfection is best.

Neither could the fame of Nicolo the Pisan be materially enhanced by Browning's calling him "his sculptor." Vasari's enthusiasm for him is unbounded, so much so in fact, that he attributes to this sculptor numerous buildings which the ruthless editors of later days say there is no proof that he designed.

His inspiration came direct from ancient

Greek sculpture, if Vasari is to be believed; thus he brought in one of the important elements of the Renaissance, the return to ancient models, Giotto and Cimabue having inaugurated the "return to nature."

"Among the many spoils of marbles," Vasari relates, "brought by the armaments of Pisa to their city, were several antique sarcophagi, now in the Campo Santo of that town. One of these, on which the Chase of Meleager and the Calydonian boar was cut with great truth and beauty, surpassed all the others; the nude as well as draped figures, being perfect in design, and executed with great skill. This sarcophagus, having been placed for its beauty by the Pisans in that façade of the Cathedral which is opposite to San Rocco, and beside the principal door of that front, was used as a tomb for the mother of the Countess Matilda. Nicolo was attracted by the excellence of this work, in which he greatly delighted, and which he studied diligently, with the many other valuable sculptures of the relics around him, imitating the admirable manner of these works with so much success that no long time had elapsed before he was esteemed the best sculptor of his time."

Nicolo's work for Florence was not extensive; about all that the poet could have called to mind as surely his is the church of Santa Trinita; but doubtless his thoughts wandered to other famous works of his, like the Pulpits, at Pisa and Sienna, and the Arca di San Domenico at Bologna.

His date is really precedent to that of Giotto, so that he may truly be considered to have struck the death-blow to the stiff Byzantine art that flourished before. His influence was felt not only in Italy but as some scholars have shown it even penetrated into the remote forests of Germany.

Ghiberti is famous among other things for having won the commission for the doors for the church of San Giovanni in Florence. All the artists in Italy were invited to compete by submitting an example of their skill to the Guild of the merchants and the Signoria of Florence. Let Vasari again tell the story by virtue of his nearness to the times. "A great concourse of artists assembled in Florence. Each of these artists received a sum of money, and it was commanded that within a year each should produce a story in bronze as a specimen of his powers, all to be of the same size which was that of one of the compartments of the first door. The subject was chosen by the consuls, and was the sacrifice of Isaac by his father Abraham, that being selected as presenting sufficient opportunity for the artists to display their mastery over the difficulties of their art, this story comprising landscape with human figures, nude and clothed, as well as those of animals; the foremost of these figures were to be in full relief, the second in half-relief, and the third in low relief. The candidates for this work were Filippo di Ser Brunellesco, Donato, and Lorenzo di Bartoluccio, who were Florentines, with Jacopo della Quercia of Sienna: Nicolo d'Arezzo, his disciple; Francesco di Valdambrina, and Simone da Colle, called Simon of the bronzes.[1] All these masters made promise before the consuls that they would deliver each his specimen completed at the prescribed time, and all set themselves to work with the utmost care and study, putting forth all their strength, and calling all their knowledge to aid, in the hope of surpassing one another. They kept their labors meanwhile entirely secret, one from the other, that they might not copy each others plans. Lorenzo, alone, who had Bartoluccio to guide him, which last suffered him to shrink before no amount of labor, but compelled him to make various models before

[1] It has been since found that there were other competing artists.

he resolved on adopting any one of them, Lorenzo only, I say, permitted all the citizens to see his work, inviting them or any stranger who might be passing and had acquaintance with the art, to say what they thought on the subject; and these various opinions were so useful to the artist, that he produced a model which was admirably executed and without any defect whatever. He then made the ultimate preparations, cast the work in bronze, and found it succeed to admiration. When Lorenzo, assisted by Bartoluccio, his father, completed and polished the whole with such love and patience, that no work could be executed with more care, or finished with greater delicacy." As a result of all this "The story executed by Lorenzo only, which is still to be seen in the Hall of Audience, belonging to the Guild of the Merchants, was perfect in all its parts. The whole work was admirably designed and very finely composed: the figures, graceful, elegant and in beautiful attitudes and all was finished with so much care and so much perfection, that the work seemed not to have been cast and polished with instruments of iron, but to have been blown by the breath."

Again to Ghiberti is accorded a chorus of praise by modern critics. Among these no more powerful note is sounded than that by Symonds who says that "he came into the world to create a new and inimitable style of hybrid beauty. Though so passionate an admirer of the Greeks that he reckoned time by Olympiads, he remained, nevertheless, unaffectedly natural and in a true sense Christian. Ghiberti's people of the bronze gates are so long and delicate and graceful, with a certain character of exquisiteness that they appear to belong to a Praxitelian rather than to a Phidian epoch — to a second rather than to a first phase of evolution. They are marvelously precocious, pressing forward in advance of their time. They are pictorial rather than sculptural, but are so beautiful and so different from the works of other men that Ghiberti will always remain to us as one of the four or five most individual sculptors of the Renaissance, and as one of the supreme masters of pictorial composition affording a precedent even to Raphael."

Besides this masterpiece Florence has several tombs designed by him, among them that of Ludovico degli Obizzi, Captain of the Florentine army, in Santa Croce, and most important the tomb of S. Zanobius, bishop and patron saint of Florence, in the Duomo.

Ghirlandajo, to whom Browning again refers by his family name Bigordi, properly belongs to the Pre-Raphaelite period, and is regarded by Symonds as the most complete representative of the coming splendor of the full Renaissance. He was a naturalist of a robust order, furnishing a fine contrast to another of the distinguished Pre-Raphaelites, Sandro Botticelli, with his subtle idealism and delicate ornamentation.

The most sympathetic criticism of his work to be found is in the notes to the Blashfield and Hopkins' edition of Vasari's Lives, for Symonds, while acknowledging his greatness, is too much dazzled by the effulgence of the "great masters," near at hand, to see him, it seems to us, in his true proportions. The same may be said of Symond's attitude toward Botticelli.

"In his work there is none of the mannerism of Botticelli, only a trace of the classicism of Filippino and not a sign of the exaggerated movement of Signorelli. His figures do not mince nor swagger, they take the pose of well-bred people sitting for their portraits, and stand naturally and quietly on either side of his compositions, looking out at the spectator or at each other, not paying much attention to the drama or the miracle in which

Ghirlandajo, himself takes but little interest. Costume and background are treated in the same sober spirit. Goldsmith as he was, he did not fill his pictures with dainty details like Botticelli, who devised strange settings for jewels and patterns for brocades and curiously intricate headgear: costume and background are accessories, and are subordinated to the general effect. He does not lack invention, and can introduce charming episodes when he pleases, but the contemporary Florentines, standing with hand on hip or folded arms, are apt to form the strongest portion of the composition. His drawing is very firm and frank, and he was the best all-round draughtsman that had appeared up to his time; the color in his frescos tends to bricky reds and ochers, in his *tempera* to strong and brilliant tones, which are occasionally even gaudy. He shows his subtlety in characterization, in differentiation of feature, in seizing the personality of each model, in sympathetic comprehension of widely differing types of men."

Frescos by Ghirlandajo abound in Florence in the churches of Santa Maria Novella, Santa Trinita and the Ognissanti, some of them in a good state of preservation and some of them much faded. His finest frescos are perhaps those illustrating the history of St. Francis in Santa Trinita, though the scenes from the lives of the Virgin and St. John the Baptist in Santa Maria Novella are extremely interesting because they contain many portraits of members of distinguished Florentine families.

In the following stanzas, the poet mentions a number of painters at whose pictures in Florence we must take glimpses with him. Some of the artists he evidently feels are too near greatness for him to trouble their ghosts with his importunities to lend him a helping hand to find stray specimens of their work.

"Their ghosts still stand, as I said before,
  Watching each fresco flaked and rasped,
Blocked up, knocked out, or whitewashed o'er:
  — No getting again what the church has grasped!
The works on the wall must take their chance;
  'Works never conceded to England's thick clime!'
(I hope they prefer their inheritance
  Of a bucketful of Italian quick-lime.)

"When they go at length, with such a shaking
  Of heads o'er the old delusion, sadly
Each master his way through the black streets taking,
  Where many a lost work breathes though badly —
Why don't they bethink them of who has merited?
  Why not reveal, while their pictures dree

Such doom, how a captive might be out-ferreted?
  Why is it they never remember me?

"Not that I expect the great Bigordi,
  Nor Sandro to hear me, chivalric, bellicose;
Nor the wronged Lippino; and not a word I
  Say of a scrap of Fra Angelico's:
But are you too fine, Taddeo Gaddi,
  To grant me a taste of your intonaco,
Some Jerome that seeks the heaven with a sad eye?
  Not a churlish saint, Lorenzo Monaco?

"Could not the ghost with the close red cap,
  My Pollajolo, the twice a craftsman,
Save me the sample, give me the hap,
  Of a muscular Christ that shows the draughtsman?
No virgin by him the somewhat petty
  Of finical touch and tempera crumbly —
Could not Alesso Baldovinetti
  Contribute so much, I ask him humbly?

"Margheritone of Arezzo,
  With the grave-clothes garb and swadling barret
(Why purse up mouth and beak in a pet so,
  You bald old saturnine poll-clawed parrot?)
Not a poor glimmering Crucifixion,
  Where in the foreground kneels the donor?
If such remain, as is my conviction,
  The hoarding it does you but little honor.

There are many of Botticelli's most famous pictures in the galleries in Florence, for example, the wonderful "Coronation of the

Virgin" in the Academy of Fine Arts, the "Birth of Venus," and "Primevera," in the Ufizzi, or there is the fresco of St. Augustine in the Ognissanti. Any or all of these the poet might have had in mind, and it is not surprising that he felt some timidity at approaching the ghost of any one so widely discussed as Botticelli. It is quite true as some one has said that he is the most easily understood of any of the early painters to-day; we might add that only a critic of the era of Maeterlinck could fully appreciate his qualities. Symonds does not, but the Vasari editors have summed up his characteristics in an outburst of appreciation which all lovers of Botticelli must approve.

"No one has created so intensely personal a type: the very name of Botticelli calls up to one's mental vision the long, thin face; the querulous mouth with its over ripe lips; the prominent chin sometimes a little to one side; the nose, thin at the root and full, often almost swollen at the nostrils; the heavy tresses of ocher-colored hair, with the frequent touches of gilding; the lank limbs and the delicately undulating outline of the lithe body, under its fantastically embroidered or semi-transparent vesture. This strange type charms us by its introspective quality, its mournful ardor, its fragility, even by its morbidness, and it so charmed the painter that he reproduced it continually and saw it or certain distinctive features of it in every human creature that he painted. Like all the artists of his time his paganism was somewhat timid and ascetic, his Christianity somewhat paganized and eclectic, but to this fusion of the waning ideals common to all the workers of his age, he added something of his own — a fantastic elfin quality as impossible to define as it is to resist. His Madonnas, his goddesses, his saints have a touch of the sprite or the Undine in them. Saint Augustine in his study is a Doctor Faustus who has known forbidden love; his fantastic people of the 'Primevera' have danced in the mystic ring. We feel in his painted folk and his attitude toward them a subtle discord that is at once poignant and alluring, the crowned Madonna dreams somewhat dejectedly in the midst of her glories, and seems rather the mother of Seven Sorrows than a triumphant Queen; the Venus, sailing over the flower-strewn sea is no radiant goddess, but an anæmic, nervous, medieval prude longing for her mantle; the graces who accompany the bride in the Lemni frescos are highly strung, self-conscious girls, who have grown up in the shadow of the cloister, but to them all Botticelli has lent the same subtle, suggestive charm."

Filippino, too, inspires awe in the poet as he well may with his extraordinary frescos in the Santa Maria Novella, which depict many sacred legends with amazing if somewhat exaggerated dramatic power; or there are the impressive examples of his work in his earlier manner in the Brancacci chapel of the Carmine; the martyrdom of St. Peter and St. Paul, and St. Paul before the Proconsul — pictures that rival Masaccio's wonderful frescos in the same chapel. Speaking of Filippino's place in art, the Vasari editors say of him, "He remains the third of the great Florentine trio of Middle Renaissance painters; but while Ghirlandajo and Botticelli were always intensely personal and always developed along the same lines, Filippino seems to be three different men at three different times: first the painter of St. Bernard, equaling Botticelli in grace and surpassing him in a certain fervor of feeling, secondly, the painter of the Brancacci frescos, imitating Masaccio, passing beyond him in scientific acquirement, but falling far behind his grand style and last of all, the painter of the cycle of St. Thomas, leaving behind him his quattro cento charm, still retaining some of his quattro cento awkwardness, but attaining dramatic composition and becoming a precursor of Raphael."

It seems a little curious that while Browning was calling up so many of these old artists, that he should have omitted to mention Masaccio, who is by general consent considered one of the greatest — the link indeed between Giotto and Raphael. Lafenestre, the art critic, says of him that "he determines anew the destiny of painting by setting it again, but this time strengthened by a perfected technique in the broad straight path which Giotto had opened. In technique he added to art a fuller comprehension of perspective, especially of aerial perspective, the differences in the planes of figures in the same composition. Simplicity and style were both his to such an extent that the Chapel of the Brancacci became a school room to the masters of the fifteenth century. His color was agreeable, gray and atmospheric, his drawing direct and simple."

Another critic adds to this "He was at once an idealist and a realist, having the merit, not of being the only one to study familiar reality, but of understanding better than any of his predecessors the conditions in virtue of which reality becomes worthy of art."

We may get over the difficulty by imagining that Masaccio was one of those painters between Ghiberti and Ghirlandajo who had not "missed" his "critic meed."

The poet also stands in some awe of Fra Angelico, who is a figure dwelling apart in the art of the time. Intensely religious by nature, he thought it a sin to paint the nude human figure, consequently his pictures are full of beings always decorously draped, and with almost naively angelical countenances. There is, however, such great charm in his work and such a wonderful spiritual uplift that, with few exceptions, he is the beloved of the critics as well as of the people of his own times and the people of to-day. His place in the evolution of art is so difficult to define that Symonds says of him, he is like a placid and beautiful lake off from the shore of the great river of art that flows from Giotto to Raphael. There are many, indeed most of his pictures are in the galleries in Florence, for the poet to take his fill of. We choose for illustration of his style, not a fresco, but an easel picture, which is regarded by some as his finest work. Lord Lindsay says of this picture in his "Christian Art."

"The Madonna crossing her arms meekly on her bosom and bending in humble awe to receive the crown of heaven, is very lovely, — the Saviour is perhaps a shade less excellent: the angels are admirable and many of the assistant saints full of grace and dignity, but the characteristic of the picture is the flood of radiance and glory diffused over it, the brightest colors — gold, azure, pink, red, yellow, pure, and unmixed, yet harmonizing and blending, like a rich burst of wind-music, in a manner incommunicable in recital — distinct and yet soft, as if the whole scene were mirrored in the sea of glass that burns before the throne."

The remaining painters whom Browning dares to ask for something are of a distinctly inferior order of genius. Taddeo Gaddi is chiefly famous as the favorite pupil of Giotto, whom he imitates but does not equal in any way, and, furthermore, time has destroyed his frescos and diminished his title to fame by showing him not to be the architect of the Ponta Vecchio, the Ponta Santa Trinita, and not to have helped in the Campanile.

The Poet, himself, very well describes the qualities of Pollajolo. The two brothers — Antonio and Pietro, belonged to the extremely realistic type, and as such had their place in

Fra Angelico.

CORONATION OF THE VIRGIN.

the development of art. Critics have decided they were neither of them great artists. But, in the words of one of these, "The brothers, especially Antonio, were important contributors to the Renaissance movement in the direction of anatomical study." Antonio is accused by Perkins of absence of imagination and affectation of originality, by Symonds of almost brutal energy and bizarre realism. Müntz declares that in his pictures of St. Sebastian, every one of the qualities which make up the Renaissance harmony, rhythm, beauty is outrageously violated. Finally, Lafenestre says he is "frank even to brutality, vigorous even to ferocity, yet his strange art impresses by its virility."

Antonio like many of the artists of the time was a trained goldsmith, and with him the training developed a taste for anatomy, while in an artist of Botticelli's temperament it developed a taste for delicate ornamentation. In the former instance it resulted in a predeliction for exaggerated and coarse forms; such artists were interested chiefly in construction. Over-developed muscles, strained tendons and violent action, recorded with brutal truth were therefore the distinguishing characteristics of their art.

Pictures by these and also the remaining

minor lights were probably examined by Browning in Florence, though his memory here may have dwelt upon two in his own possession which he describes in these stanzas.

Of these minor lights, perhaps the most interest attaches to Margheritone, because he was among the first to show some departure from the Byzantine manner. Crucifix painting was his especial work. His sour expression refers to mixed disdain and despair aroused in him by Giotto's innovations, which made him take to his death-bed in vexation.

One other painter of true distinction is mentioned in the poem, Orcagna.

"This time we'll shoot better game and bag 'em hot —
No mere display at the stone of Dante,
But a kind of sober Witanagemot
(Ex.: 'Casa Guidi,' *quod videas ante*)
Shall ponder, once Freedom restored to Florence,
How Art may return that departed with her.
Go, hated house, go each trace of the Loraine's
And bring us the days of Orgagna hither!"

There are wonderful frescos of his in the Santa Maria Novella, among them the Inferno and Paradise suggested by Dante. The beauty and variety in the expressions of his faces is so noticeable a feature of his work that one wonders why Symonds says it can only be discovered after long study. He became more impressed with their beauty after examining some tracings, taken chiefly by the Right Hon. A. H. Layard, of these and other frescos of the early masters. He declares that by the selection of simple form in outline is demonstrated "not only the grand composition of these religious paintings, but also the incomparable loveliness of their types. How great they were as draughtsmen, how imaginative was the beauty of their conception, can be best appreciated by thus artificially separating their design from their coloring. The semblance of archaism disappears, and leaves a vision of pure beauty, delicate and spiritual."

On the whole it will be seen, that the souls of these early painters have been far from wronged so terribly as Browning implies. All the greatest art students and critics have given them a meed of praise far more enthusiastic than any note of praise struck in the poem. Yet the poet's mood is understandable. He was overwhelmed by the appearance of neglect, the whitewashings, the removals, the paintings over, the fadings out that many of these early pictures have suffered, not at the hands of the art-lovers of later days, but at the hands of the unappreciative who were either too near or too blind or too bigoted to realize their value.

While this poem may stand for the point of view of a modern man looking back at the early art, in the remaining poems the reader is introduced to the painters themselves, and made to see in a remarkable manner the peculiar individuality of each artist described.

The poet has chosen to portray three types in this way.—Fra Lippo Lippi, who stands for the break into realism and secularism, marking one phase of the developing Renaissance; "Andrea del Sarto," who stands for the calm after the flood-tide of development had been reached; and "Pictor Ignotus," who perhaps stands for a mood which means the outflow of the tide, the decay of the creative impulse through the development of too great self-consciousness.

In "Fra Lippo Lippi," the poet has portrayed one scene in his life, and through the talk of the painter has revealed what manner of man he was according to Vasari's account of him.

This painter-poet was born in Florence, 1406, in a by-street, called Ardiglione, behind the convent of the Carmelites. His mother died shortly after his birth and his father two years later so that he was left in the care of his father's sister, Mona Lapaccia. She managed to look out for him until his eighth year, when she placed him with the Carmelites.

He proved a very poor scholar as far as learning was concerned, but showed such a remarkable talent for drawing that the prior very sensibly decided to give him every opportunity to learn. —What else could be done with a little chap who in place of studying never did anything but daub his books and those of the other boys with caricatures? The poet enlivens this fact by making Fra Lippo add arms and legs to the notes in his music books.—

He went daily into the chapel of the Carmine, which had recently been painted with very beautiful frescos by Masaccio, and there he continually practised along with the other youths who were always studying them, so that when still a child he did some really marvelous work. He soon came to paint pictures after the style of Masaccio so well that many affirmed that the spirit of Masaccio had entered into him. At seventeen he decided to leave the convent and become a painter, through not ceasing to be a friar.

There is a story to the effect that he was once taken captive by a Moorish galley and carried off to Barbary, but was freed by his master upon his drawing a wonderful portrait of the Moor, with a piece of charcoal which he took from the fire. He had the good fortune to secure the friendship and patronage of Cosimo de' Medici. A story told in connection with his painting for Cosimo is made the central event of the poem.

"It is said that Fra Lippo Lippi was much addicted to the pleasures of sense, insomuch that he would give all he possessed to secure the gratification of whatever inclination might at the moment be predominant, but if he could by no means accomplish his wishes, he would then depict the object which had attracted his attention. It was known that, while occupied in the pursuit of his pleasures, the works undertaken by him received little or none of his attention; for which reason Cosimo de' Medici wishing him to execute a work in his own palace, shut him up that he might not waste his time in running about, but having endured this confinement for two days, he then made ropes with the sheets of his bed, which he cut to pieces for that purpose, and so having let himself down from the window, escaped, and for several days gave himself up to his amusements. When Cosimo found that the painter had disappeared he caused him to be sought, and Fra Lippo at last returned to work, but from that time forth Cosimo gave him liberty to go in and out at his pleasure, repenting greatly of having shut him up, when he considered the danger that Lippo had run by his folly in descending from the window; and ever afterwards laboring to keep him to his work by kindness only, he was by this means much more promptly and effectually served by the painter and was wont to say that excellencies of rare genius were as forms of light and not beasts of burden."

The Coronation of the Virgin, described at the end of the poem, was according to Vasari, the picture which made Lippo Lippi known to Cosimo de' Medici, but it has been shown on other authority that this picture was executed long after Cosimo first knew Lippo Lippi, so Browning is justified in imagining it a kind of a penance picture for the escapade described. It has been said that the woman with the children in the foreground in this picture is either Spinetta or Lucrezia Buti, but at the time they were both small children.

One of these, Lucrezia, was the beautiful girl with whom Lippo fell in love at the Convent of Santa Margherita in Prato. He asked the nuns to allow him to use her for the model of the Virgin in the picture he was painting for them for the high altar. They consented and the result was that he carried her off from the convent. The nuns felt deeply disgraced and the father was outraged, but Lucrezia could not be prevailed upon to return. She became the mother of the famous painter Filippino Lippi, and it is said that Lippo and Lucrezia were afterwards granted a dispensation of marriage from the Pope. It is evidently to her that Lippo refers as "a sweet angelic slip of a thing" in the poem.

All these events are woven into the poem, and life-likeness is given to the scene by its dramatic form and the introduction of the guard and of the girls singing the fascinating little flower songs, — the Stornelli, — which the Italians at that time used to improvise with the greatest ease. The criticism which Browning puts into the mouths of the monks, who objected to his eminently human portraitures of sacred subjects does not seem to be justified by Vasari's accounts of the way in which his work was received. Symonds, among modern critics, comes the nearest to voicing their objections when he says, "Bound down to sacred subjects, he was too apt to

Fra Lippo Lippi.

Coronation of the Virgin.

make angels out of street urchins and to paint the portraits of peasant-loves for Virgins. His delicate sense of natural beauty gave peculiar charm to this false treatment of religious themes. Nothing, for example, can be more attractive than the rows of angels bearing lilies in his 'Coronation of the Virgin;' and yet, when we regard them closely, we find that they have no celestial quality of form or feature."

It is this very fact of an intense quality of human sympathy that commends him to others and makes him a most important factor in the development of art.

– Lafenestre speaks of the warm expansion of sympathy with which he brought the human type into art, in exchange for the conventional type which had been called divine, making Madonna a real mother of a real baby, and giving to sacred personages, without scruple and without coarseness, the features of living men and women. In the midst of a grave severe school he sounds a joyous note, which is the first utterance of modern painting. –

"He often sacrifices precision to vivacity and variety, caring more about expression than pure form and falling frequently into a mannerism shown in his flattened and widened skulls and broad faces, but conquering his audience of the fifteenth as of the nineteenth century by his unaffected sincerity and his joyous realism. As he had humanized Madonna he domesticated art, reducing the altar piece to the genre picture."

How well the poet has shown his qualities as an artist in conjunction with his qualities as a man the poem itself can best illustrate:

FRA LIPPO LIPPI

I am poor brother Lippo, by your leave!
You need not clap your torches to my face.
Zooks, what's to blame? you think you see a monk!
What, 'tis past midnight, and you go the rounds,
And here you catch me at an alley's end
Where sportive ladies leave their doors ajar?
The Carmine's my cloister: hunt it up,
Do, — harry out, if you must show your zeal,
Whatever rat, there, haps on his wrong hole,
And nip each softling of a wee white mouse,
Weke, weke, that's crept to keep him company,
Aha, you know your betters! Then, you'll take
Your hand away that's fiddling on my throat,
And please to know me likewise. Who am I?
Why, one, sir, who is lodging with a friend
Three streets off — he's a certain . . . how d' ye call?
Master — a . . . Cosimo of the Medici,
I' the house that caps the corner. Boh! you were best!
Remember and tell me, the day you're hanged,
How you affected such a gullet's-gripe!
But you, sir, it concerns you that your knaves

Pick up a manner nor discredit you:
Zooks, are we pilchards, that they sweep the streets
And count fair prize what comes into their net?
He's Judas to a tittle, that man is!
Just such a face! Why, sir, you make amends.
Lord, I'm not angry! Bid your hangdogs go
Drink out this quarter-florin to the health
Of the munificent House that harbors me
(And many more beside, lads! more beside!)
And all's come square again. I'd like his face —
His, elbowing on his comrade in the door
With the pike and lantern, — for the slave that holds
John Baptist's head a-dangle by the hair
With one hand ("Look you, now," as who should say)
And his weapon in the other, yet unwiped!
It's not your chance to have a bit of chalk,
A wood-coal or the like? or you should see!
Yes, I'm the painter, since you style me so.
What, brother Lippo's doings, up and down,
You know them and they take you? like enough!
I saw the proper twinkle in your eye —
'Tell you, I liked your looks at very first.
Let's sit and set things straight now, hip to haunch.
Here's spring come, and the nights one makes up bands
To roam the town and sing out carnival,
And I've been three weeks shut within my mew,
A-painting for the great man, saints and saints
And saints again. I could not paint all night —
Ouf! I leaned out of window for fresh air.
There came a hurry of feet and little feet,
A sweep of lute-strings, laughs, and whifts of song, —
Flower o' the broom,
Take away love, and our earth is a tomb!
Flower o' the quince,

I let Lisa go, and what good in life since?
Flower o' the thyme — and so on. Round they went.
Scarce had they turned the corner when a titter
Like the skipping of rabbits by moonlight, — three slim shapes,
And a face that looked up . . . zooks, sir, flesh and blood,
That's all I'm made of! Into shreds it went,
Curtain and counterpane and coverlet,
All the bed-furniture — a dozen knots,
There was a ladder! Down I let myself,
Hands and feet, scrambling somehow, and so dropped,
And after them. I came up with the fun
Hard by Saint Laurence, hail fellow, well met, —
Flower o' the rose,
If I've been merry, what matter who knows?
And so as I was stealing back again
To get to bed and have a bit of sleep
Ere I rise up to-morrow and go work
On Jerome knocking at his poor old breast
With his great round stone to subdue the flesh,
You snap me of the sudden. Ah, I see!
Though your eye twinkles still, you shake your head —
Mine's shaved — a monk, you say — the sting's in that!
If Master Cosimo announced himself,
Mum's the word naturally; but a monk!
Come, what am I a beast for? tell us, now!
I was a baby when my mother died
And father died and left me in the street.
I starved there, God knows how, a year or two
On fig-skins, melon-parings, rinds and shucks,
Refuse and rubbish. One fine frosty day,
My stomach being empty as your hat,
The wind doubled me up and down I went.
Old Aunt Lapaccia trussed me with one hand,

(Its fellow was a stinger as I knew)
And so along the wall, over the bridge,
By the straight cut to the convent. Six words there,
While I stood munching my first bread that month:
"So, boy, you're minded," quoth the good fat father,
Wiping his own mouth, 'twas refection-time, —
"To quit this very miserable world?
Will you renounce" . . . "the mouthful of bread?" thought I;
By no means! Brief, they made a monk of me;
I did renounce the world, its pride and greed,
Palace, farm, villa, shop, and banking-house,
Trash, such as these poor devils of Medici
Have given their hearts to — all at eight years old.
Well, sir, I found in time, you may be sure,
'Twas not for nothing — the good bellyful,
The warm serge and the rope that goes all round,
And day-long blessed idleness beside!
"Let's see what the urchin's fit for" — that came next.
Not overmuch their way, I must confess.
Such a to-do! They tried me with their books;
Lord, they'd have taught me Latin in pure waste!
Flower o' the clove,
All the Latin I construe is "amo," I love!
But, mind you, when a boy starves in the streets
Eight years together, as my fortune was,
Watching folk's faces to know who will fling
The bit of half-stripped grape-bunch he desires,
And who will curse or kick him for his pains, —
Which gentleman processional and fine,
Holding a candle to the Sacrament,
Will wink and let him lift a plate and catch
The droppings of the wax to sell again,
Or holla for the Eight and have him whipped, —
How say I? — nay, which dog bites, which lets drop

His bone from the heap of offal in the street, —
Why, soul and sense of him grow sharp alike,
He learns the look of things, and none the less
For admonition from the hunger-pinch.
I had a store of such remarks, be sure,
Which, after I found leisure, turned to use.
I drew men's faces on my copy-books,
Scrawled them within the antiphonary's marge,
Joined legs and arms to the long music-notes,
Found eyes and nose and chin for A's and B's,
And made a string of pictures of the world
Betwixt the ins and outs of verb and noun,
On the wall, the bench, the door. The monks looked black.
"Nay," quoth the Prior, "turn him out, d'ye say?
In no wise. Lose a crow and catch a lark.
What if at last we get our man of parts,
We Carmelites, like those Camaldolese
And Preaching Friars, to do our church up fine
And put the front on it that ought to be!"
And hereupon he bade me daub away.
Thank you! my head being crammed, the walls a blank,
Never was such prompt disemburdening
First, every sort of monk, the black and white,
I drew them, fat and lean: then, folk at church,
From good old gossips waiting to confess
Their cribs of barrel-droppings, candle-ends, —
To the breathless fellow at the altar-foot,
Fresh from his murder, safe and sitting there
With the little children round him in a row
Of admiration, half for his beard and half
For that white anger of his victim's son
Shaking a fist at him with one fierce arm,
Signing himself with the other because of Christ
(Whose sad face on the cross sees only this

After the passion of a thousand years)
Till some poor girl, her apron o'er her head,
(Which the intense eyes looked through) came at eve
On tiptoe, said a word, dropped in a loaf,
Her pair of earrings and a bunch of flowers
(The brute took growling), prayed, and so was gone.
I painted all, then cried "'Tis ask and have;
Choose, for more's ready!" — laid the ladder flat,
And showed my covered bit of cloister-wall.
The monks closed in a circle and praised loud
Till checked, taught what to see and not to see,
Being simple bodies, — "That's the very man!
Look at the boy who stoops to pat the dog!
That woman's like the Prior's niece who comes
To care about his asthma: it's the life!"
But there my triumph's straw-fire flared and funked;
Their betters took their turn to see and say:
The Prior and the learned pulled a face
And stopped all that in no time. "How? what's here?
Quite from the mark of painting, bless us all!
Faces, arms, legs, and bodies like the true
As much as pea and pea! it's devil's-game!
Your business is not to catch men with show,
With homage to the perishable clay,
But lift them over it, ignore it all,
Make them forget there's such a thing as flesh.
Your business is to paint the souls of men —
Man's soul, and it's a fire, smoke . . . no, it's not . . .
It's vapor done up like a new-born babe —
(In that shape when you die it leaves your mouth)
It's . . . well, what matters talking, it's the soul!
Give us no more of body than shows soul!
Here's Giotto, with his Saint a-praising God,
That sets us praising, — why not stop with him?

Why put all thoughts of praise out of our head
With wonder at lines, colors, and what not?
Paint the soul, never mind the legs and arms!
Rub all out, try at it a second time.
Oh, that white smallish female with the breasts,
She's just my niece . . . Herodias, I would say, —
Who went and danced and got men's heads cut off!
Have it all out!" Now, is this sense, I ask?
A fine way to paint soul, by painting body
So ill, the eye can't stop there, must go further
And can't fare worse! Thus, yellow does for white
When what you put for yellow's simply black,
And any sort of meaning looks intense
When all beside itself means and looks naught.
Why can't a painter lift each foot in turn,
Left foot and right foot, go a double step,
Make his flesh liker and his soul more like,
Both in their order? Take the prettiest face,
The Prior's niece . . . patron-saint — is it so pretty
You can't discover if it means hope, fear,
Sorrow or joy? won't beauty go with these?
Suppose I've made her eyes all right and blue,
Can't I take breath and try to add life's flash,
And then add soul and heighten them three-fold?
Or say there's beauty with no soul at all —
(I never saw it — put the case the same —)
If you get simple beauty and naught else,
You get about the best thing God invents:
That's somewhat: and you'll find the soul you have missed,
Within yourself, when you return him thanks.
"Rub all out!" Well, well, there's my life, in short,
And so the thing has gone on ever since.
I'm grown a man no doubt, I've broken bounds:
You should not take a fellow eight years old

And make him swear to never kiss the girls.
I'm my own master, paint now as I please —
Having a friend, you see, in the Corner-house!
Lord, it's fast holding by the rings in front —
Those great rings serve more purposes than just
To plant a flag in, or tie up a horse!
And yet the old schooling sticks, the old grave eyes
Are peeping o'er my shoulder as I work,
The heads shake still — "It's art's decline, my son!
You're not of the true painters, great and old;
Brother Angelico's the man, you'll find;
Brother Lorenzo stands his single peer:
Fag on at flesh, you'll never make the third!"
Flower o' the pine,
You keep your mistr . . . manners, and I'll stick to mine!
I'm not the third, then: bless us, they must know!
Don't you think they're the likeliest to know,
They with their Latin? So, I swallow my rage,
Clench my teeth, suck my lips in tight, and paint
To please them — sometimes do and sometimes don't;
For, doing most, there's pretty sure to come
A turn, some warm eve finds me at my saints —
A laugh, a cry, the business of the world —
(*Flower o' the peach,*
Death for us all, and his own life for each!)
And my whole soul revolves, the cup runs over,
The world and life's too big to pass for a dream,
And I do these wild things in sheer despite,
And play the fooleries you catch me at,
In pure rage! The old mill-horse, out at grass
After hard years, throws up his stiff heels so,
Although the miller does not preach to him
The only good of grass is to make chaff.
What would men have? Do they like grass or no —

May they or may n't they? all I want's the thing
Settled forever one way. As it is,
You tell too many lies and hurt yourself:
You don't like what you only like too much,
You do like what, if given you at your word,
You find abundantly detestable.
For me, I think I speak as I was taught;
I always see the garden and God there
A-making man's wife: and, my lesson learned,
The value and significance of flesh,
I can't unlearn ten minutes afterwards.

You understand me: I'm a beast, I know.
But see, now — why, I see as certainly
As that the morning-star's about to shine,
What will hap some day. We've a youngster here
Comes to our convent, studies what I do,
Slouches and stares and lets no atom drop:
His name is Gùidi — he'll not mind the monks —
They call him Hulking Tom, he lets them talk —
He picks my practice up — he'll paint apace,
I hope so — though I never live so long,
I know what's sure to follow. You be judge!
You speak no Latin more than I, belike;
However, you're my man, you've seen the world
— The beauty and the wonder and the power,
The shapes of things, their colors, lights and shades,
Changes, surprises, — and God made it all!
— For what? Do you feel thankful, ay or no,
For this fair town's face, yonder river's line,
The mountain round it and the sky above,
Much more the figures of man, woman, child,
These are the frame to? What's it all about?
To be passed over, despised? or dwelt upon,

Wondered at? oh, this last of course! — you say.
But why not do as well as say, — paint these
Just as they are, careless what comes of it?
God's works — paint anyone, and count it crime
To let a truth slip. Don't object, "His works
Are here already; nature is complete:
Suppose you reproduce her — (which you can't)
There's no advantage! You must beat her, then."
For, don't you mark? we're made so that we love
First when we see them painted, things we have passed
Perhaps a hundred times nor cared to see;
And so they are better, painted — better to us,
Which is the same thing. Art was given for that;
God uses us to help each other so,
Lending our minds out. Have you noticed, now,
Your cullion's hanging face? A bit of chalk,
And trust me but you should, though! How much more,
If I drew higher things with the same truth!
That were to take the Prior's pulpit-place,
Interpret God to all of you! Oh, oh,
It makes me mad to see what men shall do
And we in our graves! This world's no blot for us,
Nor blank; it means intensely and means good:
To find its meaning is my meat and drink.
"Ay, but you don't so instigate to prayer!"
Strikes in the Prior: "When your meaning's plain
It does not say to folk — remember matins,
Or, mind you fast next Friday!" Why, for this
What need of art at all? A skull and bones,
Two bits of stick nailed crosswise, or what's best,
A bell to chime the hour with, does as well.
I painted a Saint Laurence six months since
At Prato, splashed the fresco in fine style:
"How looks my painting, now the scaffold's down?"

I ask a brother: "Hugely," he returns —
"Already not one phiz of your three slaves
Who turn the Deacon off his toasted side,
But's scratched and prodded to our heart's content,
The pious people have so eased their own
With coming to say prayers there in a rage:
We get on fast to see the bricks beneath.
Expect another job this time next year,
For pity and religion grow i' the crowd —
Your painting serves its purpose!" Hang the fools!

— That is — you'll not mistake an idle word.
Spoke in a huff by a poor monk, God wot,
Tasting the air this spicy night which turns
The unaccustomed head like Chianti wine!
Oh, the church knows! don't misreport me, now!
It's natural a poor monk out of bounds
Should have his apt word to excuse himself:
And hearken how I plot to make amends.
I have bethought me, I shall paint a piece
. . . There's for you! Give me six months, then go, see
Something in Sant' Ambrogio's! Bless the nuns!
They want a cast o' my office. I shall paint
God in the midst, Madonna and her babe,
Ringed by a bowery, flowery angel-brood,
Lilies and vestments and white faces, sweet
As puff on puff of grated orris-root
When ladies crowd to church at midsummer.
And then i' the front, of course a saint or two —
Saint John, because he saves the Florentines,
Saint Ambrose, who puts down in black and white
The convent's friends and gives them a long day,
And Job, I must have him there past mistake,
The man of Uz (and Us without the z,

Painters who need his patience). Well, all these
Secured at their devotion, up shall come
Out of a corner when you least expect,
As one by a dark stair into a great light,
Music and talking, who but Lippo! I! —
Mazed, motionless and moonstruck — I'm the man!
Back I shrink — what is this I see and hear?
I, caught up with my monk's-things by mistake,
My old serge gown and rope that goes all round,
I, in this presence, this pure company!
Where's a hole, where's a corner for escape?
Then steps a sweet angelic slip of a thing
Forward, puts out a soft palm — "Not so fast!"
— Addresses the celestial presence, "nay —
He made you and devised you, after all,
Though he's none of you! Could Saint John there draw —
His camel-hair make up a painting-brush?
We come to brother Lippo for all that,
Iste perfecit opus!" So, all smile —
I shuffle sideways with my blushing face
Under the cover of a hundred wings
Thrown like a spread of kirtles when you're gay
And play hot cockles, all the doors being shut,
Till, wholly unexpected, in there pops
The hothead husband! Thus I scuttle off
To some safe bench behind, not letting go
The palm of her, the little lily thing
That spoke the good word for me in the nick,
Like the Prior's niece . . . Saint Lucy, I would say.
And so all's saved for me, and for the church
A pretty picture gained. Go, six months hence!
Your hand, sir, and good-bye: no lights, no lights!
The street's hushed, and I know my own way back,
Don't fear me! There's the gray beginning. Zooks!

Vasari describes Andrea del Sarto, whose, pupil he was, as "One in whom art and nature combined to show all that may be done in painting, when design, coloring and invention unite in one and the same person." His story in brief as gathered from Vasari's life is as follows:

"He was born in Florence in 1488, his father being a tailor, for which cause he was always called Andrea del Sarto, meaning 'the Tailor's Andrew.' At seven he was taken from school and placed with a goldsmith, where he showed more aptitude for using the pencil than the chisel. He soon attracted the attention of a Florentine painter, Gian Barile, who taught him painting. He progressed so rapidly, to Gian's delight, that the latter spoke to Piero di Cosimo, then considered one of the best masters in Florence. Piero was equally delighted with his progress and became very fond of him. From this he passed to a friendship with the young artist, Franciabigio. They lived together and executed many works in company.

"Later his friendship with the young sculptor, Jacopo Sansovino, seems to have done much for his development, for we are told that the conversations of these young artists were, for the most part, respecting the difficulties of their art; wherefore, there was no reason to be surprised that both of them should ultimately attain to great excellence. Page after page in Vasari is taken up with describing the numerous and beautiful works with which Andrea adorned Florence."

The next important step in his life was his marriage. The relation between Sarto and his wife forms so integral a part of the atmosphere of the poem that we give it just as Vasari did in the first edition of his Lives:

"At that time there was a most beautiful girl in the 'via di San Gallo,' who was married to a cap-maker, and who, though born of a poor and vicious father, carried about her as much pride and haughtiness as beauty and fascination. She delighted in trapping the hearts of men, and among others ensnared the unlucky Andrea, whose immoderate love for her soon caused him to neglect the studies demanded by his art and in great measure to discontinue the assistance which he had given to his parents.

"Now it happened that a sudden and grievous illness seized the husband of this woman, who rose no more from his bed, but died thereof. Without taking counsel of his friends, therefore, without regard to the dignity of his art or the consideration due to his genius and to the eminence he had attained with so much labor; without a word, in short, to any of his kindred, Andrea took this Lucrezia di Baccio del Fede, such was the name of the woman, to be his wife; her beauty appearing to him to merit thus much at his hands, and his love for her having more influence over him than the glory and honor towards which he had begun to make such hopeful advances. But when this news became known in Florence, the respect and affection which his friends had previously borne to Andrea changed to contempt and disgust, since it appeared to them that the darkness of this disgrace had obscured for a time all the glory and renown obtained by his talents.

"But he destroyed his own peace as well as estranged his friends by this act, seeing that he soon became jealous and found that he had besides fallen into the hands of an artful woman, who made him do as she pleased in all things. He abandoned his own poor father and mother, for example, and adopted the father and sisters of his wife in their stead; insomuch that all who knew the facts mourned over him and he soon began to be as much avoided as he had been previously sought after. His disciples still re-

Portrait of Andrea del Sarto, by Himself.

mained with him, it is true, in the hope of learning something useful, yet there was not one of them, great or small that was not maltreated by his wife, both by evil words and despiteful actions: none could escape her blows, but although Andrea lived in the midst of all that torment, he yet accounted it a high pleasure."

The darkness of this story is somewhat lightened by the fact that Del Sarto in his will, made a few years before his death, speaks of her with great affection and makes ample provision for her. Though still handsome she remained a widow, and while selling Andrea's other pictures, she retained his portrait of himself. It is further related that more than thirty years after Del Sarto's death, when the young Jacopo Chimenti da Empoli was making some studies from the frescos in the portico of the Annunziata, an old woman on her way to Mass stopped and spoke to him; after some talk about his work and the paintings, she told him that she was the model for several of the figures in them. It was Lucrezia, who had outlived the great school of Florence and who still came to pray in the church where her husband was buried. She died in 1570.

The other damaging event of his life

grew out of his relation with the King of France.

The King of France had been delighted with two pictures painted for him by Andrea del Sarto, and hearing that Andrea might be prevailed upon to visit France, invited him and had him provided with everything needful for the expenses of the journey.

Having in due time arrived at the French Court he was received by the monarch very amicably and with many favors, even the first day of his arrival was marked to Andrea by proofs of that magnanimous sovereign's liberality and courtesy, since he at once received not only a present of money, but the added gift of very rich and honorable vestments. He painted many pictures, gave great satisfaction to the whole court and received a considerable annual income from the King.

"One day he received a letter, after having received many others from Lucrezia his wife, whom he had left disconsolate for his departure, although she wanted for nothing. She wrote with bitter complaints to Andrea, declaring that she never ceased to weep and was in perpetual affliction at his absence. He, therefore, asked the King's permission to return to Florence, but said that when he had arranged his affairs in that city he would return without fail to his majesty: he added that when he came back his wife should accompany him to the end that he might remain in France the more quietly, and that he would bring with him pictures and sculptures of great value. The King, confiding in these promises, gave him money for the purchase of those pictures and sculptures, Andrea taking an oath on the gospels to return within the space of a few months, and that done he departed to his native city.

"He arrived safely in Florence enjoying the society of his beautiful wife and that of her friends, with the sight of his native city during several months, but when the period specified by the King and that at which he ought to have returned had come and passed, he found himself at the end, not only of his own money, but what with building, indulging himself in various pleasures and doing no work, of that belonging to the French King also, the whole of which he had consumed. He was nevertheless determined to return to France, but the prayers and tears of his wife had more power than his own necessities, or the faith which he had pledged to the King: he remained, therefore, in Florence and the King was so angered thereby that for a long time he would not look at any

Florentine pictures, and declared that if ever he laid hands on him he would do him more harm than he had ever done him good. He remained in Florence as we have said and from a highly eminent position he sank to the very lowest, procuring a livelihood and passing his time as he best might."

Browning not only uses these events in his poem, but he allows Vasari's opinion of Del Sarto to color the portrayal of his character. We can say of the man in the poem exactly the same things that Vasari says of the actual man:

"Had this master possessed a somewhat bolder and more elevated mind, had he been as much distinguished for higher qualifications as he was for genius and depth of judgment in the art he practised, he would, beyond all doubt, have been without an equal. But there was a certain timidity of mind, a sort of diffidence and want of force in his nature, which rendered it impossible that those evidences of ardor and animation which are proper to the more exalted character, should ever appear in him; nor did he at any time display one particle of that elevation which, could it have been added to the advantages wherewith he was endowed, would have rendered him a truly divine painter. His figures are entirely free from errors and

THE ANNUNCIATION.

Andrea del Sarto.

perfect in all their proportions and are for the most part simple and chaste."

Later criticism is in much the same key as that of Vasari's. He is admitted to deserve the name given him by the Italians of "the faultless painter," because as Symonds says "in all the technical requirements of art, in drawing, composition, handling of fresco and oils, disposition of draperies, and feeling for light and shadow, he was above criticism." Furthermore Symonds gives expression to what every one must feel in looking at his pictures, the beauty of his coloring.—"His silver-gray harmonies and liquid blendings of lines cool, yet lustrous, have a charm peculiar to himself alone. We find the like nowhere else in Italy." And yet, and yet, he echoes the old feeling that Andrea del Sarto cannot take rank among the greatest Renaissance painters. "What he lacked was precisely the most precious gift — inspiration, depth of emotion, energy of thought."

Browning has made known the personality, and awakened our sympathy for this brilliant failure among the great painters of Italy in a masterly manner, which as in the case of "Fra Lippo Lippi," and the remaining art monologues, can be appreciated only by reading the poems themselves.

ANDREA DEL SARTO

(CALLED "THE FAULTLESS PAINTER")

But do not let us quarrel any more,
No, my Lucrezia; bear with me for once:
Sit down and all shall happen as you wish.
You turn your face, but does it bring your heart?
I'll work then for your friend's friend, never fear,
Treat his own subject after his own way,
Fix his own time, accept too his own price,
And shut the money into this small hand
When next it takes mine. Will it? tenderly?
Oh, I'll content him, — but to-morrow, Love!
I often am much wearier than you think,
This evening more than usual, and it seems
As if — forgive now — should you let me sit
Here by the window with your hand in mine
And look a half-hour forth on Fiesole,
Both of one mind, as married people use,
Quietly, quietly the evening through,
I might get up to-morrow to my work
Cheerful and fresh as ever. Let us try.
To-morrow, how you shall be glad for this!
Your soft hand is a woman of itself,
And mine the man's bared breast she curls inside.
Don't count the time lost, neither; you must serve
For each of the five pictures we require:
It saves a model. So! keep looking so —
My serpentining beauty, rounds on rounds!
— How could you ever prick those perfect ears,
Even to put the pearl there! oh, so sweet —
My face, my moon, my everybody's moon,
Which everybody looks on and calls his,
And, I suppose, is looked on by in turn,

While she looks — no one's: very dear, no less.
You smile? why there's my picture ready made,
There's what we painters call our harmony!
A common grayness silvers everything, —
All in a twilight, you and I alike
— You, at the point of your first pride in me
(That's gone you know), — but I, at every point;
My youth, my hope, my art, being all toned down
To yonder sober pleasant Fiesole.
There's the bell clinking from the chapel-top;
That length of convent-wall across the way
Holds the trees safer, huddled more inside;
The last monk leaves the garden; days decrease,
And autumn grows, autumn in everything.
Eh? the whole seems to fall into a shape
As if I saw alike my work and self
And all that I was born to be and do,
A twilight-piece. Love, we are in God's hand.
How strange now, looks the life he makes us lead;
So free we seem, so fettered fast we are!
I feel he laid the fetter: let it lie!
This chamber for example — turn your head —
All that's behind us! You don't understand
Nor care to understand about my art,
But you can hear at least when people speak:
And that cartoon, the second from the door
— It is the thing, Love! so such things should be —
Behold Madonna! — I am bold to say.
I can do with my pencil what I know,
What I see, what at bottom of my heart
I wish for, if I ever wish so deep —
Do easily, too — when I say, perfectly,
I do not boast, perhaps: yourself are judge,
Who listened to the Legate's talk last week,

And just as much they used to say in France.
At any rate 'tis easy, all of it!
No sketches first, no studies, that's long past:
I do what many dream of all their lives,
— Dream? strive to do, and agonize to do,
And fail in doing. I could count twenty such
On twice your fingers, and not leave this town,
Who strive — you don't know how the others strive
To paint a little thing like that you smeared
Carelessly passing with your robes afloat, —
Yet do much less, so much less, Someone says,
(I know his name, no matter) — so much less!
Well, less is more, Lucrezia: I am judged.
There burns a truer light of God in them,
In their vexed beating stuffed and stopped-up brain,
Heart, or whate'er else, than goes on to prompt
This low-pulsed forthright craftsman's hand of mine.
Their works drop groundward, but themselves, I know,
Reach many a time a heaven that's shut to me,
Enter and take their place there sure enough,
Though they come back and cannot tell the world.
My works are nearer heaven, but I sit here.
The sudden blood of these men! at a word —
Praise them, it boils, or blame them, it boils too.
I, painting from myself and to myself,
Know what I do, am unmoved by men's blame
Or their praise either. Somebody remarks
Morello's outline there is wrongly traced,
His hue mistaken; what of that? or else,
Rightly traced and well ordered; what of that?
Speak as they please, what does the mountain care?
Ah, but a man's reach should exceed his grasp,
Or what's a heaven for? All is silver-gray
Placid and perfect with my art: the worse!

I know both what I want and what might gain,
And yet how profitless to know, to sigh
"Had I been two, another and myself,
Our head would have o'erlooked the world!" No doubt.
Yonder's a work now, of that famous youth
The Urbinate who died five years ago.
('Tis copied, George Vasari sent it me.)
Well, I can fancy how he did it all,
Pouring his soul, with kings and popes to see,
Reaching, that heaven might so replenish him,
Above and through his art — for it gives way;
That arm is wrongly put — and there again —
A fault to pardon in the drawing's lines,
Its body, so to speak: its soul is right,
He means right — that, a child may understand.
Still, what an arm! and I could alter it:
But all the play, the insight and the stretch —
Out of me, out of me! And wherefore out?
Had you enjoined them on me, given me soul,
We might have risen to Rafael, I and you!
Nay, Love, you did give all I asked, I think —
More than I merit, yes, by many times.
But had you — oh, with the same perfect brow,
And perfect eyes, and more than perfect mouth,
And the low voice my soul hears, as a bird
The fowler's pipe, and follows to the snare —
Had you, with these the same, but brought a mind!
Some women do so. Had the mouth there urged
"God and the glory! never care for gain.
The present by the future, what is that?
Live for fame, side by side with Agnolo!
Rafael is waiting: up to God, all three!"
I might have done it for you. So it seems:
Perhaps not. All is as God overrules.

Beside, incentives come from the soul's self;
The rest avail not. Why do I need you?
What wife had Rafael, or has Agnolo?
In this world, who can do a thing, will not;
And who would do it, cannot, I perceive:
Yet the will's somewhat — somewhat, too, the power —
And thus we half-men struggle. At the end,
God, I conclude, compensates, punishes.
'Tis safer for me, if the award be strict,
That I am something underrated here,
Poor this long while, despised, to speak the truth.
I dared not, do you know, leave home all day,
For fear of chancing on the Paris lords.
The best is when they pass and look aside;
But they speak sometimes; I must bear it all.
Well may they speak! That Francis, that first time,
And that long festal year at Fontainebleau!
I surely then could sometimes leave the ground,
Put on the glory, Rafael's daily wear,
In that humane great monarch's golden look, —
One finger in his beard or twisted curl
Over his mouth's good mark that made the smile,
One arm about my shoulder, round my neck,
The jingle of his gold chain in my ear,
I painting proudly with his breath on me,
All his court round him, seeing with his eyes,
Such frank French eyes, and such a fire of souls
Profuse, my hand kept plying by those hearts, —
And, best of all, this, this, this face beyond,
This in the background, waiting on my work,
To crown the issue with a last reward!
A good time, was it not, my kingly days?
And had you not grown restless . . . but I know —
'Tis done and past; 'twas right, my instinct said;

Too live the life grew, golden and not gray,
And I'm the weak-eyed bat no sun should tempt
Out of the grange whose four walls make his world.
How could it end in any other way?
You called me, and I came home to your heart.
The triumph was — to reach and stay there; since
I reached it ere the triumph, what is lost?
Let my hands frame your face in your hair's gold,
You beautiful Lucrezia that are mine!
"Rafael did this, Andrea painted that;
The Roman's is the better when you pray,
But still the other's Virgin was his wife" —
Men will excuse me. I am glad to judge
Both pictures in your presence; clearer grows
My better fortune, I resolve to think.
For, do you know, Lucrezia, as God lives,
Said one day Agnolo, his very self,
To Rafael . . . I have known it all these years . . .
(When the young man was flaming out his thoughts
Upon a palace-wall for Rome to see,
Too lifted up in heart because of it)
"Friend, there's a certain sorry little scrub
Goes up and down our Florence, none cares how,
Who, were he set to plan and execute
As you are, pricked on by your popes and kings,
Would bring the sweat into that brow of yours!"
To Rafael's! — And indeed the arm is wrong.
I hardly dare . . . yet, only you to see,
Give the chalk here — quick, thus the line should go!
Ay, but the soul! he's Rafael! rub it out!
Still, all I care for, if he spoke the truth,
(What he? why, who but Michel Agnolo?
Do you forget already words like those?)
If really there was such a chance, so lost, —

Is, whether you're — not grateful — but more pleased.
Well, let me think so. And you smile indeed!
This hour has been an hour! Another smile?
If you would sit thus by me every night
I should work better, do you comprehend?
I mean that I should earn more, give you more.
See, it is settled dusk now; there's a star;
Morello's gone, the watch-lights show the wall,
The cue-owls speak the name we call them by.
Come from the window, love, — come in, at last,
Inside the melancholy little house
We built to be so gay with. God is just.
King Francis may forgive me: oft at nights
When I look up from painting, eyes tired out,
The walls become illumined, brick from brick
Distinct, instead of mortar, fierce bright gold,
That gold of his I did cement them with!
Let us but love each other. Must you go?
That Cousin here again? he waits outside?
Must see you — you, and not with me? Those loans?
More gaming debts to pay? you smiled for that?
Well, let smiles buy me! have you more to spend?
While hand and eye and something of a heart
Are left me, work's my ware, and what's it worth?
I'll pay my fancy. Only let me sit
The gray remainder of the evening out,
Idle, you call it, and muse perfectly
How could I paint, were I but back in France,
One picture, just one more — the Virgin's face,
Not yours this time! I want you at my side
To hear them — that is, Michel Agnolo —
Judge all I do and tell you of its worth.
Will you? To-morrow, satisfy your friend.
I take the subjects for his corridor,

Finish the portrait out of hand — there, there,
And throw him in another thing or two
If he demurs; the whole should prove enough
To pay for this same Cousin's freak. Beside,
What's better and what's all I care about,
Get you the thirteen scudi for the ruff!
Love, does that please you? Ah, but what does he,
The Cousin! what does he to please you more?

I am grown peaceful as old age to-night.
I regret little, I would change still less.
Since there my past life lies, why alter it?
The very wrong to Francis! — it is true
I took his coin, was tempted and complied,
And built this house and sinned, and all is said.
My father and my mother died of want.
Well, had I riches of my own? you see
How one gets rich! Let each one bear his lot.
They were born poor, lived poor, and poor they died:
And I have labored somewhat in my time
And not been paid profusely. Some good son
Paint my two hundred pictures — let him try!
No doubt, there's something strikes a balance. Yes,
You loved me quite enough, it seems to-night.
This must suffice me here. What would one have?
In heaven, perhaps, new chances, one more chance —
Four great walls in the New Jerusalem,
Meted on each side by the angel's reed,
For Leonard, Rafael, Agnolo and me
To cover — the three first without a wife,
While I have mine! So — still they overcome
Because there's still Lucrezia, — as I choose.

Again the Cousin's whistle! Go, my Love.

Pictor Ignotus reveals the feelings of a sensitive spirit, failing for quite other reasons than Andrea del Sarto. While such a being might think the reasons for his not painting pictures like the youth so much praised were because of his dislike to merchandize his art, or because he did not wish to have them sullied by blundering criticism, the truth is that the feeling itself is a sign of the self-consciousness which leads to imitation rather than to real creative force. We may imagine this painter belonging to the crowd of painters who filled up the latter part of the sixteenth century and marked the decline of the great age of Italian art.

PICTOR IGNOTUS

FLORENCE, 15—

I COULD have painted pictures like that youth's
  Ye praise so. How my soul springs up! No bar
Stayed me — ah, thought which saddens while it soothes!
  — Never did fate forbid me, star by star,
To outburst on your night with all my gift
  Of fires from God: nor would my flesh have shrunk
From seconding my soul, with eyes uplift
  And wide to heaven, or, straight like thunder, sunk
To the centre, of an instant; or around
  Turned calmly and inquisitive, to scan
The license and the limit, space and bound,
  Allowed to truth made visible in man.

And, like that youth ye praise so, all I saw,
  Over the canvas could my hand have flung,
Each face obedient to its passion's law,
  Each passion clear proclaimed without a tongue;
Whether Hope rose at once in all the blood,
  A-tiptoe for the blessing of embrace,
Or Rapture drooped the eyes, as when her brood
  Pull down the nesting dove's heart to its place;
Or Confidence lit swift the forehead up,
  And locked the mouth fast, like a castle braved, —
O human faces, hath it spilt, my cup?
  What did ye give me that I have not saved?
Nor will I say I have not dreamed (how well!)
  Of going — I, in each new picture, — forth,
As, making new hearts beat and bosoms swell,
  To Pope or Kaiser, East, West, South, or North,
Bound for the calmly satisfied great State,
  Or glad aspiring little burgh, it went,
Flowers cast upon the car which bore the freight,
  Through old streets named afresh from the event,
Till it reached home, where learned age should greet
  My face, and youth, the star not yet distinct
Above his hair, lie learning at my feet! —
  Oh, thus to live, I and my picture, linked
With love about, and praise, till life should end,
  And then not go to heaven, but linger here,
Here on my earth, earth's every man my friend —
  The thought grew frightful, 'twas so wildly dear!
But a voice changed it. Glimpses of such sights
  Have scared me, like the revels through a door
Of some strange house of idols at its rites!
  This world seemed not the world it was before:
Mixed with my loving trusting ones, there trooped
  . . . Who summoned those cold faces that begun

To press on me and judge me? Though I stooped
  Shrinking, as from the soldiery a nun,
They drew me forth, and spite of me . . . enough!
  These buy and sell our pictures, take and give,
Count them for garniture and household-stuff,
  And where they live needs must our pictures live
And see their faces, listen to their prate,
  Partakers of their daily pettiness,
Discussed of, — "This I love, or this I hate,
  This likes me more, and this affects me less!"
Wherefore I chose my portion. If at whiles
  My heart sinks, as monotonous I paint
These endless cloisters and eternal aisles
  With the same series, Virgin, Babe and Saint,
With the same cold calm beautiful regard, —
  At least no merchant traffics in my heart;
The sanctuary's gloom at least shall ward
  Vain tongues from where my pictures stand apart;
Only prayer breaks the silence of the shrine
  While, blackening in the daily candle-smoke,
They moulder on the damp wall's travertine,
  'Mid echoes the light footsteps never woke.
So, die my pictures! surely, gently die!
  O youth, men praise so, — holds their praise its worth?
Blown harshly, keeps the trump its golden cry?
  Tastes sweet the water with such specks of earth?

One more poem of Browning's gives a glimpse of Renaissance art, "The Bishop orders his tomb at St. Praxed's." This may be read in connection with "Pictor Ignotus" as revealing another phase of the decadence of art, when gross worldliness, luxury and hypocrisy had become the distinguishing marks of the clergy and were manifested in the art which they encouraged for their own glorification. The Bishop and his tomb are both imaginary, but they none the less reveal with absolute fidelity the hypocrisy of the clergy, not to say their absolute wickedness, and the vulgar art that appealed to their degenerate taste.

THE BISHOP ORDERS HIS TOMB AT SAINT PRAXED'S CHURCH

ROME, 15—

Vanity, saith the preacher, vanity!
Draw round my bed: is Anselm keeping back?
Nephews — sons mine . . . ah God, I know not!
  Well —
She, men, would have to be your mother once,
Old Gandolf envied me, so fair she was!
What's done is done, and she is dead beside,
Dead long ago, and I am Bishop since,
And as she died so must we die ourselves,
And thence ye may perceive the world's a dream.
Life, how and what is it? As here I lie
In this state-chamber, dying by degrees,
Hours and long hours in the dead night, I ask
"Do I live, am I dead?" Peace, peace seems all.
Saint Praxed's ever was the church for peace;
And so, about this tomb of mine. I fought
With tooth and nail to save my niche, ye know:
— Old Gandolf cozened me, despite my care;

Shrewd was that snatch from out the corner South
He graced his carrion with, God curse the same!
Yet still my niche is not so cramped but thence
One sees the pulpit o' the epistle-side,
And somewhat of the choir, those silent seats,
And up into the aery dome where live
The angels, and a sunbeam's sure to lurk:
And I shall fill my slab of basalt there,
And 'neath my tabernacle take my rest,
With those nine columns round me, two and two,
The odd one at my feet where Anselm stands:
Peach-blossom marble all, the rare, the ripe
As fresh-poured red wine of a mighty pulse.
— Old Gandolf with his paltry onion-stone,
Put me where I may look at him! True peach,
Rosy and flawless: how I earned the prize!
Draw close: that conflagration of my church
— What then? So much was saved if aught were missed!
My sons, ye would not be my death? Go dig
The white-grape vineyard where the oil-press stood,
Drop water gently till the surface sink,
And if ye find . . . Ah God, I know not, I! . . .
Bedded in store of rotten fig-leaves soft,
And corded up in a tight olive-frail,
Some lump, ah God, of *lapis lazuli*,
Big as a Jew's head cut off at the nape,
Blue as a vein o'er the Madonna's breast . . .
Sons, all have I bequeathed you, villas, all,
That brave Frascati villa with its bath,
So, let the blue lump poise between my knees,
Like God the Father's globe on both his hands
Ye worship in the Jesu Church so gay,
For Gandolf shall not choose but see and burst!
Swift as a weaver's shuttle fleet our years:

Man goeth to the grave and where is he?
Did I say basalt for my slab, sons? Black —
'Twas ever antique-black I meant! How else
Shall ye contrast my frieze to come beneath?
The bas-relief in bronze ye promised me,
Those Pans and Nymphs ye wot of, and perchance
Some tripod, thyrsus, with a vase or so,
The Saviour at his sermon on the Mount,
Saint Praxed in a glory, and one Pan
Ready to twitch the Nymph's last garment off,
And Moses with the tables . . . but I know
Ye mark me not! What do they whisper thee,
Child of my bowels, Anselm? Ah, ye hope
To revel down my villas while I gasp
Bricked o'er with beggar's mouldy travertine
Which Gandolf from his tomb-top chuckles at!
Nay, boys, ye love me — all of jasper, then!
'Tis jasper ye stand pledged to, lest I grieve
My bath must needs be left behind, alas!
One block, pure green as a pistachio-nut,
There's plenty jasper somewhere in the world —
And have I not St. Praxed's ear to pray
Horses for ye, and brown Greek manuscripts,
And mistresses with great smooth marbly limbs?
— That's if ye carve my epitaph aright,
Choice Latin, picked phrase, Tully's every word,
No gaudy ware like Gandolf's second line —
Tully, my masters? Ulpian serves his need!
And then how I shall lie through centuries,
And hear the blessed mutter of the Mass,
And see God made and eaten all day long,
And feel the steady candle-flame, and taste
Good strong thick stupefying incense-smoke!
For as I lie here, hours of the dead night,

Dying in state and by such slow degrees,
I fold my arms as if they clasped a crook,
And stretch my feet forth straight as stone can point,
And let the bedclothes, for a mort cloth, drop
Into great laps and folds of sculptor's-work:
And as yon tapers dwindle, and strange thoughts
Grow, with a certain humming in my ears,
About the life before I lived this life,
And this life too, popes, cardinals and priests,
Saint Praxed at his sermon on the mount,
Your tall pale mother with her talking eyes,
And new-found agate urns as fresh as day,
And marble's language, Latin, pure, discreet,
— Aha, ELUCESCEBAT quoth our friend?
No Tully, said I, Ulpian at the best!
Evil and brief hath been my pilgrimage.
All *lapis*, all, sons! Else I give the Pope
My villas! Will ye ever eat my heart?
Ever your eyes were as a lizard's quick,
They glitter like your mother's for my soul,
Or ye would heighten my impoverished frieze,
Piece out its starved design, and fill my vase
With grapes, and add a vizor and a Term,
And to the tripod ye would tie a lynx
That in his struggle throws the thyrsus down,
To comfort me on my entablature
Wherever I am to lie till I must ask
"Do I live, am I dead?" There, leave me, there!
For ye have stabbed me with ingratitude
To death — ye wish it — God, ye wish it! Stone —
Gritstone, a-crumble! Clammy squares which sweat
As if the corpse they keep were oozing through —
And no more *lapis* to delight the world!
Well go! I bless ye. Fewer tapers there,

But in a row: and, going, turn your backs
— Ay, like departing altar-ministrants,
And leave me in my church the church for peace,
That I may watch at leisure if he leers —
Old Gandolf, at me, from his onion-stone,
As still he envied me, so fair she was!

Though it does not come within our present scope to dwell upon the marvelous genius shown by the poet in these portrayals of diverse types of Renaissance artists, one word must be said, namely, that we cannot help feeling some sense of regret that he refrained from illuminating for the world with his poetic vision the souls of men like Michael Angelo and Raphael. Perhaps he felt before them as he did before Shakespeare, "To such name's sounding, what succeeds Fitly as silence."

Besides the dramatic power of these monologues by means of which these artists seem to live and breathe before us, they have genuine value as criticism, and, be it said, criticism of the highest order, not merely appreciation, but that penetrating insight into the nature of the man and the conditions surrounding him that go to make the qualities by which his art must perforce be distinguished.

To close with a remark of Symonds who

has been our chief guide through the mazes of this world of the painter's imagination, —

"It is one of the sad features of this subject, that each section has to end in lamentation. Servitude in the sphere of politics; literary feebleness in scholarship; decadence in art — to shun these conclusions is impossible. He who has undertaken to describe the parabola of a projectile cannot be satisfied with tracing its gradual rise and determining its culmination. He must follow its spent force, and watch it slowly sink with ever dwindling impetus to the earth."

V

PICTURES OF SOCIAL LIFE

"The year's at the spring
And day's at the morn;
Morning's at seven;
The hill-side's dew-pearled;
The lark's on the wing;
The snail's on the thorn:
God's in his heaven —
All's right with the world!"

THE poems in which Browning gives some idea of the social conditions in Italy have dates ranging from the sixteenth century to near the end of the eighteenth. Four of them, "My Last Duchess," "Cenciaja," "In a Gondola" and "The Ring and the Book," have to do with murders, while all show appalling conditions of social decay. These glimpses of the time are only too true to the actual facts as they may be gleaned from contemporary records.

"My Last Duchess" is not dated, but it is quite significant that the scene of the poem is Ferrara, for the story of Lucrezia de' Medici furnishes a strikingly similar incident. She was the daughter of Cosimo de' Medici and became the Duchess of Ferrara, and falling under suspicion of infidelity was possibly removed by poison in 1561. This would be quite enough of a hint for the poet to build his poem upon. The poem, it is true, was first entitled more vaguely "Italy," yet this episode of Medici family history could hardly have failed to serve the poet as the initiative idea of the poem.

The Duke of Ferrara is pictured arranging for a new match with an ambassador from another Count. In the course of the conversation, he shows the ambassador a portrait of his last Duchess, whose general kindliness of nature was cause enough in this Duke's eyes for jealousy and for punishment by death. He is a typical art-connoisseur of the time, and evidently takes an emotionally artistic delight in the possession of the portrait of his beautiful murdered wife.

It is a gem among Browning's poems for its incisive, swift and perfect portraiture of the Duke and his wife and its suggestion of the social conditions of the time in the scene setting — and all in the space of fifty-six lines:

MY LAST DUCHESS

FERRARA

THAT'S my last Duchess painted on the wall,
Looking as if she were alive. I call

That piece a wonder now: Frà Pandolf's hands
Worked busily a day, and there she stands.
Will 't please you sit and look at her? I said
"Frà Pandolf" by design, for never read
Strangers like you that pictured countenance,
The depth and passion of its earnest glance,
But to myself they turned (since none puts by
The curtain I have drawn for you, but I)
And seemed as they would ask me, if they durst,
How such a glance came there; so, not the first
Are you to turn and ask thus. Sir, 't was not
Her husband's presence only, called that spot
Of joy into the Duchess' check: perhaps
Frà Pandolf chanced to say, "Her mantle laps
Over my lady's wrist too much," or "Paint
Must never hope to reproduce the faint
Half-flush that dies along her throat:" such stuff
Was courtesy, she thought, and cause enough
For calling up that spot of joy. She had
A heart — how shall I say? — too soon made glad,
Too easily impressed: she liked whate'er
She looked on, and her looks went everywhere.
Sir, 't was all one! My favor at her breast,
The dropping of the daylight in the West,
The bough of cherries some officious fool
Broke in the orchard for her, the white mule
She rode with round the terrace — all and each
Would draw from her alike the approving speech,
Or blush, at least. She thanked men, — good! but thanked
Somehow — I know not how — as if she ranked
My gift of a nine-hundred-years-old name
With anybody's gift. Who'd stoop to blame
This sort of trifling? Even had you skill
In speech — (which I have not) — to make your will

Quite clear to such an one, and say, "Just this
Or that in you disgusts me; here you miss,
Or there exceed the mark"—and if she let
Herself be lessoned so, nor plainly set
Her wits to yours, forsooth, and made excuse,
—E'en then would be some stooping; and I choose
Never to stoop. Oh sir, she smiled, no doubt,
Whene'er I passed her; but who passed without
Much the same smile? This grew; I gave commands;
Then all smiles stopped together. There she stands
As if alive. Will 't please you rise? We'll meet
The company below, then. I repeat,
The Count your master's known munificence
Is ample warrant that no just pretence
Of mine for dowry will be disallowed;
Though his fair daughter's self, as I avowed
At starting, is my object. Nay, we'll go
Together down, sir. Notice Neptune, though,
Taming a sea-horse, thought a rarity,
Which Claus of Innsbruck cast in bronze for me!

One may ask in surprise did not society at that late date object even to a Duke's murdering his wife upon such slight grounds? On the contrary, society condoned the murder of a wife who was faithless or suspected of faithlessness. The law took cognizance of the fact, but always considered that there were extenuating circumstances. The murder of a sister who brought disgrace upon her family in any way was also condoned. In fact during the last three quarters of the sixteenth century violent crimes of all sorts committed by individuals for personal ends were on the increase.

The general state of society is horrible to contemplate, for it became the custom for people of quality to keep a retinue of "knights errant," as they were euphoniously called, to do their cruel jobs for them. They had only to "give commands" as the Duke did, whenever they wanted "smiles" to cease. This dismal state of affairs was probably the working out of the cruel, warlike spirit which had been engendered by the centuries of political struggle. Now as Symonds puts it, "the broad political and religious contests which had torn the country in the first years of the sixteenth century, were pacified, Foreign armies had ceased to dispute the provinces of Italy. The victorious powers of Spain, the church, and the protected principalities, seemed secure in the possession of their gains. But those international quarrels which kept the nation in unrest through a long period of municipal wars, ending in the horrors of successive invasions, were now succeeded by an almost universal discord between families and persons. Each province, each city, each village became the theater of private feuds and assassinations. Each household was the scene of homicide and empoisonment. Italy presented the spectacle of a nation, armed against itself, not to decide the issue of antagonistic political principles by civil strife, but to gratify lawless passions — cupidity, revenge, resentment — by deeds of personal high-handedness. Among the common people of the country and the towns, crimes of brutality and bloodshed were of daily occurrence; every man bore weapons for self-defense and for attack upon his neighbor. The aristocracy and the upper classes of the *bourgeoisie* lived in a perpetual state of mutual mistrust, ready upon the slightest occasion of fancied affront to blaze forth into murder."

The Church, instead of frowning upon these practises, countenanced them and even used them for their own ends; particularly the Jesuits encouraged assassination for reasons which they considered sacred.

The Medici, whom we have seen before as the patrons of learning and art connoisseurs, have a record of eleven murders in their family in a space of fifty years.

"In Cenciaja" Browning plunges into a discussion, it must be confessed not exactly poetic, of certain details of the Cenci story. The criminology of this family furnishes as good an example as any of the sort of family history possible at that time. In the story as usually told, Beatrice arouses sympathy for the crime in which she was implicated with her brothers of the murder of their father because of her father's outrageous treatment of her. Browning takes Shelley's "Cenci" as his starting point, and begs leave to tell how it came to pass that at the last the clemency of the Pope was changed to sternness.

CENCIAJA

Ogni cencio vuol entrare in bucato

— *Italian Proverb*

May I print, Shelley, how it came to pass
That when your Beatrice seemed — by lapse
Of many a long month since her sentence fell —
Assured of pardon for the parricide —
By intercession of stanch friends, or, say,
By certain pricks or conscience in the Pope
Conniver at Francesco Cenci's guilt, —
Suddenly all things changed and Clement grew
"Stern," as you state, "nor to be moved nor bent,
But said these three words coldly '*She must die;*'
Subjoining '*Pardon? Paolo Santa Croce*
Murdered his mother also yestereve,
And he is fled: she shall not flee at least!'"
— So, to the letter, sentence was fulfilled?
Shelley, may I condense verbosity
That lies before me, into some few words
Of English, and illustrate your superb
Achievement by a rescued anecdote,
No great things, only new and true beside?
As if some mere familiar of a house
Should venture to accost the group at gaze

Before its Titian, famed the wide world through,
And supplement such pictured masterpiece
By whisper, "Searching in the archives here,
I found the reason of the Lady's fate,
And how by accident it came to pass
She wears the halo and displays the palm:
Who, haply, else had never suffered — no,
Nor graced our gallery, by consequence."
Who loved the work would like the little news:
Who lauds your poem lends an ear to me
Relating how the penalty was paid
By one Marchese dell' Oriolo, called
Onofrio Santa Croce otherwise,
For his complicity in matricide
With Paolo his own brother, — he whose crime
And flight induced "those three words — 'She must die'."
Thus I unroll you then the manuscript.

"God's justice" — (of the multiplicity
Of such communications extant still,
Recording, each, injustice done by God
In person of his Vicar-upon-earth,
Scarce one but leads off to the selfsame tune) —
"God's justice, tardy though it prove perchance,
Rests never on the track until it reach
Delinquency. In proof I cite the case
Of Paolo Santa Croce."

Many times
The youngster, — having been importunate
That Marchesine Costanza, who remained
His widowed mother, should supplant the heir
Her elder son, and substitute himself
In sole possession of her faculty, —

And meeting just as often with rebuff, —
Blinded by so exorbitant a lust
Of gold, the youngster straightway tasked his wits,
Casting about to kill the lady — thus.

He first, to cover his inquity,
Writes to Onofrio Santa Croce, then
Authoritative lord, acquainting him
Their mother was contamination — wrought
Like hell-fire in the beauty of their House
By dissoluteness and abandonment
Of soul and body to impure delight.
Moreover, since she suffered from disease,
Those symptoms which her death made manifest
Hydroptic, he affirmed were fruits of sin
About to bring confusion and disgrace
Upon the ancient lineage and high fame
O' the family, when published. Duty bound,
He asked his brother — what a son should do?

Which when Marchese dell' Oriolo heard
By letter, being absent at his land,
Oriolo, he made answer, this, no more:
"It must behoove a son, — things haply so, —
To act as honor prompts a cavalier
And son, perform his duty to all three,
Mother and brothers" — here advice broke off.

By which advice informed and fortified,
As he professed himself — since bound by birth
To hear God's voice in primogeniture —
Paolo, who kept his mother company
In her domain Subiaco, straightway dared
His whole enormity of enterprise,

And, falling on her, stabbed the lady dead;
Whose death demonstrated her innocence,
And happened, — by the way, — since Jesus Christ
Died to save man, just sixteen hundred years.
Costanza was of aspect beautiful
Exceedingly, and seemed, although in age
Sixty about, to far surpass her peers
The coëtaneous dames, in youth and grace.

Done the misdeed, its author takes to flight,
Foiling thereby the justice of the world:
Not God's however, — God, be sure, knows well
The way to clutch a culprit. Witness here!
The present sinner, when he least expects,
Snug-cornered somewhere i' the Basilicate,
Stumbles upon his death by violence.
A man of blood assaults a man of blood
And slays him somehow. This was afterward:
Enough, he promptly met with his deserts,
And, ending thus, permits we end with him,
And push forthwith to this important point —
His matricide fell out, of all the days,
Precisely when the law-procedure closed
Respecting Count Francesco Cenci's death
Chargeable on his daughter, sons and wife.
"Thus patricide was matched with matricide,"
A poet not inelegantly rhymed:
Nay, fraticide — those Princes Massimi! —
Which so disturbed the spirit of the Pope
That all the likelihood Rome entertained
Of Beatrice's pardon vanished straight,
And she endured the piteous death.

Now see
The sequel — what effect commandment had

For strict inquiry into this last case,
When Cardinal Aldobrandini (great
His efficacy — nephew to the Pope)
Was bidden crush — ay, though his very hand
Got soil i' the act — crime spawning everywhere!
Because, when all endeavor had been used
To catch the aforesaid Paolo, all in vain —
"Make perquisition," quoth our Eminence,
"Throughout his now deserted domicile!
Ransack the palace, roof and floor, to find
If haply any scrap of writing, hid
In nook or corner, may convict — who knows? —
Brother Onofrio of intelligence
With brother Paolo, as in brotherhood
Is but too likely: crime spawns everywhere."

And, every cranny searched accordingly,
There comes to light — O lynx-eyed Cardinal! —
Onofrio's unconsidered writing-scrap,
The letter in reply to Paolo's prayer,
The word of counsel that — things proving so,
Paolo should act the proper knightly part,
And do as was incumbent on a son,
A brother — and a man of birth, be sure!

Whereat immediately the officers
Proceeded to arrest Onofrio — found
At football, child's play, unaware of harm,
Safe with his friends, the Orsini, at their seat
Monte Giordano; as he left the house
He came upon the watch in wait for him
Set by the Barigel, — was caught and caged.

News of which capture being, that same hour,
Conveyed to Rome, forthwith our Eminence

Commands Taverna, Governor and Judge,
To have the process in especial care,
Be, first to last, not only president
In person, but inquisitor as well,
Nor trust the by-work to a substitute:
Bids him not, squeamish, keep the bench, but scrub
The floor of Justice, so to speak, — go try
His best in prison with the criminal:
Promising, as reward for by-work done
Fairly on all-fours, that, success obtained
And crime avowed, or such connivency
With crime as should procure a decent death —
Himself will humbly beg — which means, procure —
The Hat and Purple from his relative
The Pope, and so repay a diligence
Which, meritorious in the Cenci-case,
Mounts plainly here to Purple and the Hat.

Whereupon did my lord the Governor
So masterfully exercise the task
Enjoined him, that he, day by day, and week
By week, and month by month, from first to last
Toiled for the prize: now, punctual at his place,
Played Judge, and now, assiduous at his post,
Inquisitor — pressed cushion and scoured plank,
Early and late. Noon's fervor and night's chill,
Naught moved whom morn would, purpling, make amends!
So that observers laughed as, many a day,
He left home, in July when day is flame,
Posted to Tordinona-prison, plunged
Into a vault where daylong night is ice,
There passed his eight hours on a stretch, content,
Examining Onofrio: all the stress
Of all examination steadily

Converging into one pin-point, — he pushed
Tentative now of head and now of heart.
As when the nut-hatch taps and tries the nut
This side and that side till the kernel sound, —
So did he press the sole and single point
— "What was the very meaning of the phrase
'*Do as beseems an honored cavalier?*'"

Which one persistent question-torture, — plied
Day by day, week by week, and month by month,
Morn, noon and night, — fatigued away a mind
Grown imbecile by darkness, solitude,
And one vivacious memory gnawing there
As when a corpse is coffined with a snake:
— Fatigued Onofrio into what might seem
Admission that perchance his judgment groped
So blindly, feeling for an issue — aught
With semblance of an issue from the toils
Cast of a sudden round feet late so free,
He possibly might have envisaged, scarce
Recoiled from — even were the issue death
— Even her death whose life was death and worse!
Always provided that the charge of crime,
Each jot and tittle of the charge were true.
In such a sense, belike, he might advise
His brother to expurgate crime with . . . well,
With blood, if blood, must follow on "*the course
Taken as might beseem a cavalier.*"

Whereupon process ended, and report
Was made without a minute of delay
To Clement, who, because of those two crimes
O' the Massimi and Cenci flagrant late,
Must needs impatiently desire result.

Result obtained, he bade the Governor
Summon the Congregation and despatch.
Summons made, sentence passed accordingly
— Death by beheading. When his death-decree
Was intimated to Onofrio, all
Man could do — that did he to save himself.
'T was much, the having gained for his defense
The Advocate o' the Poor, with natural help
Of many noble friendly persons fain
To disengage a man of family,
So young too, from his grim entanglement:
But Cardinal Aldobrandini ruled
There must be no diversion of the law.
Justice is justice, and the magistrate
Bears not the sword in vain. Who sins must die.

So, the Marchese had his head cut off,
With Rome to see, a concourse infinite,
In Place Saint Angelo beside the Bridge:
Where, demonstrating magnanimity
Adequate to his birth and breed, — poor boy! —
He made the people the accustomed speech,
Exhorted them to true faith, honest works,
And special good behavior as regards
A parent of no matter what the sex,
Bidding each son take warning from himself.
Truly, it was considered in the boy
Stark staring lunacy, no less, to snap
So plain a bait, be hooked and hauled ashore
By such an angler as the Cardinal!
Why make confession of his privity
To Paolo's enterprise? Mere sealing lips —
Or, better, saying "When I counseled him
'*To do as might beseem a cavalier,*'

What could I mean but '*Hide our parent's shame*
As Christian ought, by aid of Holy Church!
Bury it in a convent — ay, beneath
Enough dotation to prevent its ghost
From troubling earth!'" Mere saying thus, — 't is plain,
Not only were his life the recompense.
But he had manifestly proved himself
True Christian, and in lieu of punishment
Got praise of all men! — so the populace.

Anyhow, when the Pope made promise good
(That of Aldobrandini, near and dear)
And gave Taverna, who had toiled so much,
A Cardinal's equipment, some such word
As this from mouth to ear went saucily:
"Taverna's cap is dyed in what he drew
From Santa Croce's veins!" So joked the world.

I add: Onofrio left one child behind,
A daughter named Valeria, dowered with grace
Abundantly of soul and body, doomed
To life the shorter for her father's fate.
By death of her, the Marquisate returned
To that Orsini House from whence it came:
Oriolo having passed as donative
To Santa Croce from their ancestors.

And no word more? By all means! Would you know
The authoritative answer, when folk urged
"What made Aldobrandini, hound-like stanch,
Hunt out of life a harmless simpleton?"
The answer was — "Hatred implacable,
By reason they were rivals in their love."
The Cardinal's desire was to a dame

Whose favor was Onofrio's. Pricked with pride,
The simpleton must ostentatiously
Display a ring, the Cardinal's love-gift,
Given to Onofrio as the lady's gage:
Which ring on finger, as he put forth hand
To draw a tapestry, the Cardinal
Saw and knew, gift and owner, old and young;
Whereon a fury entered him — the fire
He quenched with what could quench fire only — blood.
Nay, more: "there want not who affirm to boot,
The unwise boy, a certain festal eve,
Feigned ignorance of who the wight might be
That pressed too closely on him with a crowd.
He struck the Cardinal a blow: and then,
To put a face upon the incident,
Dared next day, snug as ever, go pay court
I' the Cardinal's antechamber. Mark and mend,
Ye youth, by this example how may greed
Vainglorious operate in worldly souls!"

So ends the chronicler, beginning with
"God's justice, tardy though it prove perchance,
Rests never till it reach delinquency."
Ay, or how otherwise had come to pass
That Victor rules, this present year, in Rome?"

In a manuscript volume containing the "Relations of the Cenci affair with other memorials of Italian crime," Browning found what he called the "Cenciaja," namely, a story which divulges the true reason of the sudden change of attitude toward Beatrice. It was lent to him by Sir J. Simeon; who, he writes, "published the Cenci narrative with notes, in the series of the Philobiblon Society. It was a better copy of the 'Relation' than that used by Shelley, differing at least in a few particulars."

The poem tells the story that Browning found in this manuscript.

The title of the poem as the poet explains, means "a bundle of rags" — a "trifle"; the termination "Aja," is generally an accumulative yet depreciative one. The meaning of the proverb with which he heads the poem "Ogni cencio vuol entrare in bucato," is, "Every poor creature will be pressing into the company of his betters," which he says "I used to depreciate the notion that I intended anything of the kind."

It may be questioned whether the poetizing of this piece of information is worth while except for the light it throws upon the possible iniquities of the clergy at that time.

More to the point, however unpleasant it may be to contemplate, is the truth about Beatrice, whose story is now said to have been fabricated by Prospero Farinaccio, the lawyer engaged in her defense. He established a theory of enormous cruelty and unspeakable outrages committed upon her person by her father, in order to mitigate the guilt of parricide. He also tried to make out that her brother, Bernado, was half-witted, but there is other evidence to prove that he was a young man of ordinary intelligence, while nothing remains to prove the Beatrice legend. Perhaps the worst blow to our sentiments is the fact that the Guido Reni portrait of Beatrice in prison in one of the Roman palaces is most certainly not Beatrice, for Guido did not come to Rome until 1608, nine years after her death.

There can be no doubt, however, that old Cenci was anything but a delightful father to have around. Fines for brutal conduct toward servants seem to have been a constant feature of his daily life. At one time he was prosecuted for an attempt to murder a cousin, at another he was outlawed from the states of the church, and at another time we find him spending six months in prison for crimes of one kind and another. Everybody in those days seems to have been implicated in vice — cardinals, prelates, princes, professional men, and people of the lowest rank. If they were poor, they might be sent to the stake; if rich they could buy themselves off. Cenci, for example, paid 100,000 crowns to free himself from one of the crimes of which he was accused. After this he decided to settle down a second time. He married a second wife, Lucrezia, and proceeded to look after his family.

His elder sons seem to have been true sons of their father. The eldest, Giacomo, married against his father's will and proceeded to support himself by raising money through forging obligations. His father brought several lawsuits against him, in one of which he was accused of having plotted against his father's life. The second son, Cristoforo, was assassinated, during the course of a love affair with the wife of a Trasteverine fisherman, by a Corsican, Paolo Bruno. The third son, Rocco, was distinguished for street adventures. He had a devoted friend, Monsignore Querro, a cousin, and important in court circles, who helped him carry off all the plate and portable property from his father's palace. He was finally killed by Amilcare Orsini in a night brawl. "The young men met, Cenci attended by three armed servants, Orsini by two. A single pass of rapiers, in which Rocco was pierced through the right eye ended the affair," as this midnight tragedy has tersely been related.

The older sons were so bad that Cenci treated all the younger ones with strictness, not to say cruelty, as is sometimes said. Finally, the family rebelled, and they deliberately decided to remove the old count. His wife, Lucrezia, his eldest son, Giacomo, his daughter, Beatrice, and a younger son, Bernardo, were all implicated in the crime, which was carried out in a particularly horrible manner. On the night of September 9, at the Rocca di Petrella in the Abruzzi, two hired cutthroats, Olimpio Calvetti and Marzio Catalani, "entered the old man's bedroom, drove a nail into his head and flung the corpse out from the gallery." It was some time before suspicion fell upon his own family, but finally the government of Naples, where, and at Rome, the sons had taken out letters for the administration of their father's property, — was informed that proceedings ought to be taken against the Cenci and their cutthroats. Against Olimpio and Marzio a ban was immediately published. Giacomo and his friend Querro, with the assistance of three desperados, fell upon Olimpio and killed him, but Marzio was arrested and his evidence caused the arrest of the Cenci. It seems that they were tortured and none of them denied the accusation, so that the only course left to their advocates was to plead extenuating circumstances, and thus arose the Beatrice "legend."

Although the episode upon which Browning's great masterpiece, "The Ring and the Book" is founded did not occur until the end of the seventeenth century, a state of society still existed at that time in which wife-murder under certain circumstances was condoned. What such circumstances might be and how a despicable nature might misinterpret facts and manufacture others in order to give himself an excuse under the law for murdering his wife, is the story told in "The Ring and the Book."

In the poem itself, Browning describes how he found the old square yellow book, containing the records of this crime and the trial. In those days before newspapers, the "Relations" of things of this nature were frequently printed in books and pamphlets. The information in the old square yellow book was supplemented by an old pamphlet which Browning found in London. The account of the finding of the book is well worth quoting for the vivid picture it gives of a street scene in Florence to-day, as well as the description of the methods by which justice was enforced in the seventeenth century.

"That memorable day,
(June was the month, Lorenzo named the Square),
I leaned a little and overlooked my prize
By the low railing round the fountain-source
Close to the statue, where a step descends;
While clinked the cans of copper, as stooped and rose
Thick-ankled girls who brimmed them, and made place
For marketmen glad to pitch basket down,
Dip a broad melon-leaf that holds the wet,
And whisk their faded fresh. And on I read
Presently, though my path grew perilous
Between the outspread straw-work, piles of plait

Soon to be flapping, each o'er two black eyes
And swathe of Tuscan hair, on festas fine:
Through fire-irons, tribes of tongs, shovels in sheaves,
Skeleton bedsteads, wardrobe-drawers agape,
Rows of tall slim brass lamps with dangling gear, —
And worse, cast clothes a-sweetening in the sun:
None of them took my eye from off my prize.
Still read I on, from written title-page
To written index, on, through street and street,
At the Strozzi, at the Pillar, at the Bridge;
Till, by the time I stood at home again
In Casa Guidi by Felice Church,
Under the doorway where the black begins
With the first stone-slab of the staircase cold,
I had mastered the contents, knew the whole truth
Gathered together, bound up in this book,
Print three-fifths, written supplement the rest,
'*Romana Homicidiorum*' — nay,
Better translate — 'A Roman murder-case:
Position of the entire criminal cause
Of Guido Franceschini nobleman,
With certain Four the cutthroats in his pay,
Tried, all five, and found guilty and put to death
By heading or hanging as befitted ranks,
At Rome on February Twenty Two,
Since our salvation Sixteen Ninety Eight:
Wherein it is disputed if, and when,
Husbands may kill adulterous wives, yet 'scape
The customary forfeit.'

Word for word,

So ran the title-page: murder or else
Legitimate punishment of the other crime,
Accounted murder by mistake, — just that
And no more, in a Latin cramp enough

When the law had her eloquence to launch,
But interfilleted with Italian streaks
When testimony stooped to mother-tongue, —
That, was this old square yellow book about.

Now, as the ingot, ere the ring was forged,
Lay gold, (beseech you, hold that figure fast!)
So, in this book lay absolutely truth,
Fanciless fact, the documents indeed,
Primary lawyer-pleadings for, against,
The aforesaid Five; real summed-up circumstance
Adduced in proof of these on either side,
Put forth and printed, as the practice was,
At Rome, in the Apostolic Chamber's type,
And so submitted to the eye o' the Court
Presided over by His Reverence
Rome's Governor and Criminal Judge, — the trial
Itself, to all intents, being then as now
Here in the book and nowise out of it;
Seeing, there properly was no judgment-bar,
No bringing of accuser and accused,
And whoso judged both parties, face to face
Before some court, as we conceive of courts.
There was a Hall of Justice; that came last:
For Justice had a chamber by the hall
Where she took evidence first, summed up the same,
Then sent accuser and accused alike,
In person of the advocate of each,
To weigh its worth, thereby arrange, array
The battle. 'Twas the so-styled Fisc began,
Pleaded (and since he only spoke in print
The printed voice of him lives now as then)
The public Prosecutor — 'Murder's proved;
With five . . . what we call qualities of bad,

Worse, worst, and yet worse still, and still worse yet;
Crest over crest crowning the cockatrice,
That beggar hell's regalia to enrich
Count Guido Franceschini: punish him!'
Thus was the paper put before the court
In the next stage, (no noisy work at all,)
To study at ease. In due time like reply
Came from the so-styled Patron of the Poor,
Official mouthpiece of the five accused
Too poor to fee a better, — Guido's luck
Or else his fellows', — which, I hardly know, —
An outbreak as of wonder at the world,
A fury-fit of outraged innocence,
A passion of betrayed simplicity:
'Punish Count Guido? For what crime, what hint
O' the color of a crime, inform us first!
Reward him rather! Recognize, we say,
In the deed done, a righteous judgment dealt!
All conscience and all courage, — there's our Count
Charactered in a word; and, what's more strange,
He had companionship in privilege,
Found four courageous conscientious friends:
Absolve, applaud all five, as props of law,
Sustainers of society! — perchance
A trifle over-hasty with the hand
To hold her tottering ark, had tumbled else;
But that's a splendid fault whereat we wink,
Wishing your cold correctness sparkled so!'
Thus paper second followed paper first,
Thus did the two join issue — nay, the four,
Each pleader having an adjunct. 'True, he killed
— So to speak — in a certain sort — his wife,
But laudably, since thus it happed!' quoth one:
Whereat, more witness and the case postponed.

'Thus it happed not, since thus he did the deed,
And proved himself thereby portentousest
Of cutthroats and a prodigy of crime,
As the woman that he slaughtered was a saint,
Martyr and miracle!' quoted the other to match:
Again, more witness, and the case postponed.
'A miracle, ay — of lust and impudence;
Hear my new reasons:' interposed the first:
'— Coupled with more of mine!' pursued his peer.
'Beside, the precedents, the authorities!'
From both at once a cry with an echo, that!
That was a firebrand at each fox's tail
Unleashed in a cornfield: soon spread flare enough,
As hurtled thither and there heaped themselves
From earth's four corners, all authority
And precedent for putting wives to death,
Or letting wives live, sinful, as they seem.
How legislated, now, in this respect,
Solon and his Athenians? Quote the code
Of Romulus and Rome! Justinian speak!
Nor modern Baldo, Bartolo be dumb!
The Roman voice was potent, plentiful;
Cornelia de Sicariis hurried to help
Pompeia de Parricidiis; Julia de
Something-or-other jostled *Lex* this-and-that;
King Solomon confirmed Apostle Paul;
That nice decision of Dolabella, eh?
That pregnant instance of Theodoric, oh!
Down to that choice example Ælian gives
(An instance I find much insisted on)
Of the elephant who, brute-beast though he were,
Yet understood and punished on the spot
His master's naughty spouse and faithless friend;
A true tale which has edified each child,

Much more shall flourish favored by our court!
Pages of proof this way, and that way proof,
And always — once again the case postponed.

Thus wrangled, brangled, jangled they a month,
— Only on paper, pleadings all in print,
Nor ever was, except i' the brains of men,
More noise by word of mouth than you hear now —
Till the court cut all short with 'Judged, your cause.
Receive our sentence! Praise God! We pronounce
Count Guido devilish and damnable:
His wife Pompilia in thought, word and deed,
Was perfect pure, he murdered her for that:
As for the Four who helped the One, all Five —
Why, let employer and hirelings share alike,
In guilt and guilt's reward, the death their due!'

So was the trial at end, do you suppose?
'Guilty you find him, death you doom him to?
Ay, were not Guido, more than needs, a priest,
Priest and to spare!' — this was a shot reserved:
I learn this from epistles which begin
Here where the print ends, — see the pen and ink
Of the advocate, the ready at a pinch! —
'My client boasts the clerkly privilege,
Has taken minor orders many enough,
Shows still sufficient chrism upon his pate
To neutralize a blood-stain: *presbyter,*
Primæ tonsuræ, subdiaconus,
Sacerdos, so he slips from underneath
Your power, the temporal, slides inside the robe
Of mother Church; to her we make appeal
By the Pope, the Church's head!'

A parlous plea,
Put in with noticeable effect, it seems:
'Since straight,' — resumes the zealous orator,
Making a friend acquainted with the facts, —
'Once the word "clericality" let fall,
Procedure stopped and freer breath was drawn
By all considerate and responsible Rome.'
Quality took the decent part, of course;
Held by the husband, who was noble too:
Or, for the matter of that, a churl would side
With too-refined susceptibility,
And honor which, tender in the extreme,
Stung to the quick, must roughly right itself
At all risks, not sit still and whine for law
As a Jew would, if you squeezed him to the wall,
Brisk-trotting through the Ghetto. Nay, it seems,
Even the Emperor's Envoy had his say
To say on the subject; might not see, unmoved,
Civility menaced throughout Christendom
By too harsh measure dealt her champion here.
Lastly, what made all safe, the Pope was kind,
From his youth up, reluctant to take life,
If mercy might be just and yet show grace;
Much more unlikely then, in extreme age,
To take a life the general sense bade spare.
'T was plain that Guido would go scatheless yet.

But human promise, oh, how short of shine!
How topple down the piles of hope we rear!
How history proves . . . nay, read Herodotus!
Suddenly starting from a nap, as it were,
A dog-sleep with one shut, one open orb,
Cried the Pope's great self, — Innocent by name
And nature too, and eighty-six years old,

Antonio Pignatelli of Naples, Pope
Who had trod many lands, known many deeds,
Probed many hearts, beginning with his own,
And now was far in readiness for God,
'T was he who first bade leave those souls in peace,
Those Jansenists, re-nicknamed Molinists,
('Gainst whom the cry went, like a frowsy tune,
Tickling men's ears — the sect for a quarter of an hour
I' the teeth of the world which clown-like, loves to chew
Be it but a straw 'twixt work and whistling-while,
Taste some vituperation, bite away,
Whether at marjoran-spring or garlic-clove,
Aught it may sport with, spoil, and then spit forth,)
'Leave them alone,' bade he, 'those Molinists!
Who may have other light than we perceive,
Or why is it the whole world hates them thus?'
Also he peeled off that last scandal-rag
Of Nepotism; and so observed the poor
That men would merrily say, 'Halt, deaf and blind,
Who feed on fat things, leave the master's self
To gather up the fragments of his feast,
These be the nephews of Pope Innocent! —
His own meal costs but five carlines a day,
Poor-priest's allowance, for he claims no more.'
— He cried of a sudden, this great good old Pope,
When they appealed in last resort to him,
'I have mastered the whole matter: I nothing doubt.
Though Guido stood forth priest from head to heel,
Instead of, as alleged, a piece of one, —
And further, were he, from the tonsured scalp
To the sandāled sole of him, my son and Christ's.
Instead of touching us by finger-tip
As you assert, and pressing up so close
Only to set a blood-smutch on our robe, —

I and Christ would renounce all right in him.
Am I not Pope, and presently to die,
And busied how to render my account,
And shall I wait a day ere I decide
On doing or not doing justice here?
Cut off his head to-morrow by this time,
Hang up his four mates, two on either hand,
And end one business more!'

So said, so done —
Rather so writ, for the old Pope bade this,
I find, with his particular chirograph,
His own no such infirm hand, Friday night;
And next day, February Twenty Two,
Since our salvation Sixteen Ninety Eight,
— Not at the proper head-and-hanging-place
On bridge-foot close by Castle Angelo,
Where custom somewhat staled the spectacle,
('T was not so well i' the way of Rome, beside,
The noble Rome, the Rome of Guido's rank)
But at the city's newer gayer end, —
The cavalcading promenading place
Beside the gate and opposite the church
Under the Pincian gardens green with Spring,
'Neath the obelisk 'twixt the fountains in the Square,
Did Guido and his fellows find their fate,
All Rome for witness, and — my writer adds —
Remonstrant in its universal grief,
Since Guido had the suffrage of all Rome."

The contents of this book have been reduced by Mrs. Orr to an abstract of the story which she enlarged again with quotations from the pamphlet found in London. Though this is easily accessible either in Mrs. Orr's Handbook or in the Camberwell edition of Browning, it is given here in order that the subject under discussion may be as fully illustrated as possible.

"There lived in Rome in 1679 Pietro and Violante Comparini, an elderly couple of the middle class, fond of show and good living, and who in spite of a fair income had run considerably into debt. They were, indeed, at the period in question, in receipt of a papal bounty, employed in the relief of the needy who did not like to beg. Creditors were pressing and only one expedient suggested itself: they must have a child; and thus enable themselves to draw on their capital, now tied up for the benefit of an unknown heir-at-law. The wife conceived this plan and also carried it out, without taking her husband into her confidence. She secured beforehand the infant of a poor and not very reputable woman, announced her expectation, half miraculous at her past fifty years, and became, to all appearance, the mother of a girl, the Francesca Pompilia of the story.

"When Pompilia had reached the age of thirteen, there was also in Rome Count Guido Franceschini, an impoverished nobleman of Arezzo and the elder of three brothers, of whom the second, Abate Paola, and the third, Canon Girolamo, also play some part in the story. Count Guido himself belonged to the minor ranks of the priesthood and had spent his best years in seeking preferment in it. Preferment had not come and the only means of building up the family fortunes in his own person, was now a moneyed wife. He was poor, fifty years old, and personally unattractive. A contemporary chronicle describes him as short, thin, and pale, and with a projecting nose. He had nothing to offer but his rank; but in the case of a very obscure heiress, this might suffice, and such a one seemed to present herself in Pompilia Comparini. He heard of her at the local center of gossip, the barber's shop; received an exaggerated estimate of her dowry and made proposals for her hand; being supported in his suit by the Abate Paul. They did not, on their side, understate the advantages of the connection. They are, indeed, said to have given as their yearly income a sum exceeding their capital, and Violante was soon dazzled into consenting to it. Old Pietro was more wary. He made inquiries as to the state of the Count's fortune, and declined, under plea of his daughter's extreme youth, to think of him as a son-in-law.

"Violante pretended submission, secretly led Pompilia to a church, the very church of San Lorenzo in Lucina, where four years later the murdered bodies of all three were to be displayed, and brought her back as Count Guido's wife. Pietro could only accept the accomplished fact; and he so far resigned himself to it that he paid down an instalment of his daughter's dowry, and made up the deficiency by transferring to the newly married couple all that he actually possessed. This left him no choice but to live under their roof, and the four removed together to the Franceschini abode at Arezzo. The arrangement proved disastrous; and at the end of a few months Pietro and Violante were glad to return to Rome, though with empty pockets, and on money lent them for the journey by their son-in-law.

"We have conflicting testimony as to the cause of this rupture. The Governor of Arezzo, writing to the Abate Paul in Rome, lays all the blame of it on the Comparini, whom he taxes with vulgar and aggressive behavior; and Mr. Browning readily admits that at the beginning there may have been faults on their side. But popular judgment, as well as the balance of evidence, were in favor of the opposite view; and curious details are given by Pompilia and by a servant of the family, a sworn witness on Pompilia's trial, of the petty cruelties and privations to which both parents and child were subjected.

"So much, at all events, was clear; Violante's sin had overtaken her; and it now occurred to her, apparently for the first time, to cast off its burden by confession. The moment was propitious, for the Pope had proclaimed a jubilee in honor of his eightieth year and absolution was to be had for the asking. But the Church in this case made conditions. Absolution must be preceded by atonement. Violante must restore to her legal heirs that of which her pretended motherhood had defrauded them. The first step toward this was to reveal the fraud to her husband; and Pietro lost no time in making use of the revelation. He repudiated Pompilia, and with her all claims on her husband's part. The case was carried into court. The Court decreed a compromise. Pietro appealed from the decree, and the question remained unsettled.

"The chief sufferer by these proceedings was Pompilia herself. She already had reason to dread her husband as a tyrant — he to dislike her as a victim; and his discovery of her base birth, with the threatened loss of the greater part of her dowry, could only result, with such a man, in increased aversion towards her. From this moment his one aim seems to have been to get rid of his wife, but in such a manner as not to forfeit any pecuniary advantage he might still derive from their union. This could only be done by convicting her of infidelity; and he attacked her so furiously and so persistently, on the subject of a certain Canon Giuseppe Caponsacchi, whom she barely knew, but whose attentions he declared her to have challenged, that at last she fled from Arezzo with this very man.

"She had appealed for protection against her husband's violence to the Archbishop and to the Governor. She had striven to enlist the aid of his brother-in-law, Conti. She had implored a priest in confession to write for her to her parents and induce them to fetch her away. But the whole town was in the interest of the Franceschini, or in dread of them. Her prayers were useless, and Caponsacchi, whom she had heard of as a 'resolute man,' appeared her last resource. He was, as she knew, contemplating a journey to Rome; an opportunity presented itself for speaking to him from her window, or her balcony, and she persuaded him, though not without difficulty, to assist her escape and conduct her to her old home. On a given night she slipped away from her husband's side and joined the Canon where he awaited her with a carriage. They traveled day and night till they reached Castelnuovo, a village within four hours of the journey's end. There they were compelled to rest, and there also the husband overtook them. They were not together at the moment; but the fact of the elopement was patent; and if Franceschini had killed his wife there, in the supposed excitement of the discovery, the law might have dealt leniently with him. But it suited him best for the time being to let her live. He procured the arrest of the fugitives, and after a short confinement on the spot, they were conveyed to the New Prisons in Rome (Carceri Nuove) and tried on the charge of adultery.

"It is impossible not to believe that Count Guido had been working toward this end. Pompilia's verbal communications with Caponsacchi had been supplemented by letters, now brought to him in her name, now thrown or let down from her window as he passed the house. They were written, as he said, on the subject of the flight, and, as he also said, he burned them as soon as read, not doubting their authenticity. But Pompilia declared, on examination, that she could neither write nor read; and setting aside all presumption of her veracity, this was more than probable. The writer of the letters must, therefore, have been the Count, or some one employed by him for the purpose. He now completed the intrigue by producing eighteen or twenty more of a very incriminating character, which he declared to have been left by the prisoners at Castelnuovo; and these were not only disclaimed with every appearance of sincerity by both the persons accused, but bore the marks of forgery within themselves.

"Pompilia and Caponsacchi answered all the questions addressed to them simply and firmly; and though their statements did not always coincide, these were calculated on the whole to create a moral conviction of their innocence; the facts on which they disagreed being of little weight. But moral conviction was not legal proof; the question of false testimony does not seem to have been even raised; and the Court found itself in a dilemma, which it acknowledged in the following way: it was decreed that for his complicity in 'the flight and deviation of Francesca Comparini,' and too great intimacy with her, Caponsacchi should be banished for three years to Civita Vecchia; and that Pompilia, on her side, should be relegated, for the time being, to a convent. That is to say the prisoners were pronounced guilty; and a merely nominal punishment was inflicted upon them.

"The records of this trial contain almost everything of biographical or even dramatic interest in the original book. They are, so far as they go, the complete history of the case; and the result of the trial, ambiguous as it was, supplied the only argument on which an even formal defense of the subsequent murder could be based. The substance of these records appears in full in Mr. Browning's work; and his readers can judge for themselves whether the letters which were intended to substantiate Pompilia's guilt, could, even if she had possessed the power of writing, have been written by a woman so young and so uncultured as herself. They will also see that the Count's plot against his wife was still more deeply laid than the above-mentioned circumstances attest.

"Count Guido was of course not satisfied. He wanted a divorce; and he continued to sue for it by means of his brother, the Abate Paul, then residing in Rome; but before long he received news which was destined to change his plans. Pompilia was about to become a mother; and in consideration of her state she had been removed from the convent to her paternal home, where she was still to be ostensibly a prisoner. The Comparini then occupied a small villa outside one of the city gates. A few months later, in this secluded spot, the Countess Franceschini gave birth to a son, whom her parents lost no time in conveying to a place of concealment and safety. The murder took place a fortnight after this event. I give the rest of the story in an almost literal translation from a contemporary narrative, which was published immediately after the Count's execution, in the form of a pamphlet [1] — the then current substitute for a newspaper.

"Being oppressed by various feelings, and stimulated to revenge, now by honor, now by self-interest, yielding to his wicked thoughts, he (Count Guido) devised a plan for killing his wife and her nominal parents; and having enlisted in his enterprise four other ruffians,' — laborers on his property,— started with them from Arezzo, and on Christmas-eve arrived in Rome and took up his abode at Ponte Milvio, where there was a villa belonging to his brother and where he concealed himself with his followers till the fitting moment for the execution of his design had arrived. Having therefore watched from thence all the movements of the Comparini family, he proceeded on Thursday, the 2d of January, at one o'clock of the night,[2] with his companions to the Com-

[1] This pamphlet has supplied Mr. Browning with some of his most curious facts. It fell into his hands in London.

[2] The first hour after sunset.

parini's house; and having left Biagio Agostinelli and Domenico Gambasini at the gate, he instructed one of the others to knock at the house-door, which was opened to him on his declaring that he brought a letter from Canon Caponsacchi at Civita Vecchia. The wicked Franceschini, supported by two other of his assassins, instantly threw himself on Violante Comparini, who had opened the door, and flung her dead upon the ground. Pomilia, in this extremity, extinguished the light, thinking thus to elude her assassins, and made for the door of a neighboring blacksmith, crying for help. Seeing Franceschini provided with a lantern, she ran and hid herself under the bed, but being dragged from under it, the unhappy woman was barbarously put to death by twenty-two wounds from the hand of her husband, who, not content with this, dragged her to the feet of Comparini, who, being similarly wounded by another of the assassins, was crying, '*confession.*'

"At the noise of this horrible massacre people rushed to the spot; but the villains succeeded in flying, leaving behind, however, in their haste, one his cloak, and Franceschini his cap, which was the means of betraying them. The unfortunate Francesca Pompilia, in spite of all the wounds with which she had been mangled, having implored of the Holy Virgin the grace of being allowed to confess, obtained it, since she was able to survive for a short time and describe the horrible attack. She also related that after the deed, her husband asked the assassin who had helped him to murder her *if she were really dead;* and being assured that she was, quickly rejoined, *let us lose no time, but return to the vineyard;*[1] and so they escaped. Meanwhile the police (Forza) having been called, it arrived with its chief officer (Bargello), and a confessor was soon procured, together with a surgeon

[1] "Villa" is often called "vineyard" or "vigna," on account of the vineyard attached to it.

who devoted himself to the treatment of the unfortunate girl.

"Monsignore the Governor, being informed of the event, immediately despatched Captain Patrizj to arrest the culprits, but on reaching the vineyard the police officers discovered that they were no longer there, but had gone toward the high road an hour before. Patrizj pursued his journey without rest, and having arrived at the inn was told by the landlord that Franceschini had insisted upon obtaining horses, which were refused to him because he was not supplied with the necessary order; and had proceeded therefore on foot with his companions toward Baccano. Continuing his march and taking the necessary precautions, he arrived at the Merluzza inn, and there discovered the assassins, who were speedily arrested, their knives still stained with blood, a hundred and fifty scudi in coin being also found in Franceschini's person. The arrest, however, cost Patrizj his life, for he had heated himself too much, and having received a slight wound, died in a few days.

"The knife of Franceschini was on the Genoese pattern, and triangular; and was notched at the edge, so that it could not be withdrawn from the wounded flesh without lacerating it in such a manner as to render the wound incurable.

"The criminals being taken to Ponte Milvio, they went through a first examination at the inn there at the hands of the notaries and judges sent thither for the purpose, and the chief points of a confession were obtained from them.

"When the capture of the delinquents was known in Rome, a multitude of the people hastened to see them as they were conveyed bound on horses into the city. It is related that Franceschini having asked one of the police officers in the course of the journey *how ever the crime had been discovered*, and being told *that it had been revealed by his wife, whom they had found still living*, was almost stupefied by the intelligence. Toward twenty-three o'clock (the last hour before sunset) they arrived at the prisons. A certain Francesco Pasquini, of Città di Castello, and Allessandro Baldeschi, of the same town, both twenty-years of age, were the assistants of Guido Franceschini in the murder of the Comparini; and Gambasini and Agnostinelli were those who stood on guard at the gate.

"Meanwhile the corpses of the assassinated Comparini were exposed at San Lorenzo in Lucina, but so disfigured, and especailly Franceschini's wife, by their wounds in the face, that they were no longer recognizable. The unhappy Francesca, after taking the sacrament, forgiving her murderers, under seventeen years of age, and after having made her will, died on the sixth day of the month, which was that of the Epiphany; and was able to clear herself of all the calumnies which her husband had brought against her. The surprise of the people in seeing these corpses was great, from the atrocity of the deed, which made one really shudder, seeing two septuagenarians and a girl of seventeen so miserably put to death.

"The trial proceeding meanwhile, many papers were drawn up on the subject, bringing forward all the most incriminating circumstances of this horrible massacre; and others also were written for the defense with much erudition, especially by the advocate of the poor, a certain Monsignor Spreti, which had the effect of postponing the sentence; also because Baldeschi persisted in denial though he was tortured with the rope and twice fainted under it. At last he confessed, and so did the others, who also revealed the fact that they had intended in due time to murder Franceschini himself, and take his money, because he had not kept his promise of paying them the moment they should have left Rome.

"On the twenty-second of February there appeared on the Piazza del Popolo a large platform with a guillotine and two gibbets, on which the culprits were to be executed. Many stands were constructed for the convenience of those who were curious to witness such a terrible act of justice; and the concourse was so great that some windows fetched as much as six dollars each. At eight o'clock Franceschini and his companions were summoned to their death, and having been placed in the Consorteria and there assisted by the Abate Panciatici and the Cardinal Acciajuoli, forthwith disposed themselves to die well. At twenty o'clock the Company of Death and the Misericordia reached the dungcons and the condemned were let down, placed on separate carts, and conveyed to the place of execution."

"It is further stated that Franceschini showed the most intrepidity and cold blood of them all, and that he died with the name of Jesus on his lips. He wore the same clothes in which he had committed the crime: a close fitting garment (*juste-au-corps*) of gray cloth, a loose black shirt (*camiciuola*), a goat's hair cloak, a white hat, and a cotton cap.

"The attempt made by him to defraud his accomplices, poor and helpless as they were, has been accepted by Mr. Browning as an indication of character which forbade any lenient interpretations of his previous acts. Pompilia, on the other hand, is absolved, by all the circumstances of her protracted death, from any doubt of her innocence which previous evidence might have raised. Ten different persons attest, not only her denial of any offence against her husband, but, what is of far more value, her Christian gentleness, and absolute maiden modesty, under the sufferings of her last days, and the medical treatment to which they subjected her. Among the witnesses are a doctor of theology (Abate Liberato Barberito), the apothecary and his assistant and a number of monks or priests; the first and most circumstantial deposition being that of an Augustine, Frà Celestino Angelo di Sant' Anna, and concluding with these words: 'I do not say more, for fear of being taxed with partiality. I know well that God alone can examine the heart. But I know also that from the abundance of the heart the mouth speaks; and that my great St. Augustine says: "As the life was, so is its end."'

"It needed all the evidence in Pompilia's favor to secure the full punishment of her murderer, strengthened, as he was, by social and ecclesiastical position, and by the acknowledged rights of marital jealousy. We find curious proof of the sympathies which might have prejudiced his wife's cause, in the marginal notes appended to her depositions, and which repeatedly introduce them as lies.

'F. *Lie concerning the arrival at Castelnuovo.*'

'H. *New lies to the effect that she did not receive the lover's letters, and does not know how to write,*' etc., etc.[1]

"The significant question, 'Whether and when a husband may kill his unfaithful wife,' was in the present case not thought to be finally answered till an appeal had been made from the ecclesiastical tribunal to the Pope himself. It was Innocent XII who virtually sentenced Count Franceschini and his four accomplices to death."

Browning has developed each one of the important characters, Guido, Pompilia, Caponsacchi, the two lawyers, the Pope, in separate monologues, as well as giving three views of public opinion in "Half-Rome," "The Other Half-Rome" and "Tertium Quid."

The panorama of human life centering around

[1] It is difficult to reconcile this explicit denial of Pompilia's statements with the belief in her implied in her merely nominal punishment: unless we look on it as a part of the formal condemnation which circumstances seemed to exact.

Piazza del Popolo, Rome.

a few strong personalities that results is, of course, far more than a portrayal of social conditions and individual life as it existed in Rome at that time; it becomes a sort of phantasy of universal human nature ranging from the saint-like yet wholly human beauty of Pompilia to the inhuman monster Guido, with all gradations of weakness and of strength, of wisdom and of intellect lying between.

Although typical human nature is everywhere depicted in this poem, opinions and actions are deeply colored by the environment as reflected in the part played by the church, by law, and by the social usage of the time. Very decided "local" color is also given by the constant references to the doctrines of Miguel Molinos, a Spanish priest who was the founder of a theology called "Quietism." His principles divided the Rome of the day as positively as the rights and wrongs of the Guido trial divide it in Browning's poem.

In 1675 he published his "Spiritual Guide," which appealed so strongly to many of the religious minds of the time that the Church felt it necessary to take measures against Molinos and his followers. Quotations from this remarkable book will give the best idea of his ideals, which, though lofty in conception seem to have been open to misinterpretations that led some of his followers into rather devious paths and brought accusations upon Molinos himself which were probably entirely unfounded.

"The Divine Majesty knows very well that it is not by the means of one's own ratiocination or industry that a soul draws near to Him and understands the divine truths, but rather by silent and humble resignation. The patriarch Noah gave a great instance of this, who, after he had been by all men reckoned a fool, floating in the middle of a raging sea wherewith the whole world was overflowed, without sails or oars, and environed by wild beasts that were shut up in the ark, walked by faith alone, not knowing nor understanding what God had a mind to do with him."

Virtues, according to Molinos, were not to be acquired by much abstinence, maceration of the body, mortification of the senses, rigorous penances, wearing sackcloth, chastising the flesh by discipline, going in quest of sensible affections and fervent sentiments, thinking to find God in them. Molinos regarded such practises as the way of beginners. He called it the external way and declared it could never conduct them to perfection, "nor so much as one step toward it, as experience shows in many, who, after fifty years of this external exercise, are void of God, and full of themselves (of spiritual pride), having nothing of a spiritual man but the name."

"The truly spiritual men, on the other hand, are those whom the Lord, in his infinite mercy, has called from the outward way in which they had been wont to exercise themselves; who had retired into the interior part of their souls; who had resigned themselves into the hand of God, totally putting off and forgetting themselves, and always going with an elevated spirit to the presence of the Lord, by means of pure faith, without image, form, or figure, but with great assurance founded in tranquillity and rest internal. These blessed and sublimated souls take no pleasure in anything of the world, but in contempt of it, in being alone, forsaken and forgotten by everybody, keeping always in their hearts a great lowliness and contempt of themselves; always humbled in the depths of their own unworthiness and vileness. In the same manner they are always quiet, serene and even-minded, whether under extraordinary graces and favor, or under the most rigorous and bitter torments. No news makes them afraid. No success makes them glad. Tribulations never disturb them, nor the interior, continual Divine communications make them vain and conceited; they always remain full of holy and filial fear, in a wonderful peace, constancy, and serenity."

Again "The Lord has repose nowhere but in quiet souls, and in those in which the fire of tribulation and temptation hath burned up the dregs of passions, and with the bitter water of afflictions hath washed off the filthy spots of inordinate appetites; in a word, this Lord reposes only where quiet reigns and self-love is banished."

"By the way of nothing thou must come to lose thyself in God (which is the last degree of perfection), and happy wilt thou be if thou canst so lose thyself. In this same shop of nothing, simplicity is made, interior and infused recollection is possessed, quiet is obtained, and the heart is cleansed from all imperfection."

Molinos had been in Rome some little time when he published this book (1675), which immediately gained him great popularity. It besides received the formal approbation of five famous doctors, four of them Inquisitors and one a Jesuit, and within six years passed through twenty editions, in most European tongues. Bigelow in his book on Molinos describes how "Its author's acquaintance and friendship was sought by people in the greatest credit, not only at Rome, but in other parts of Europe by correspondence. Among his followers were three followers of the Oratoire, who soon after received cardinal's hats, and even the popes who successively occupied the pontifical chair during his residence in Rome took particular notice of him. The Cardinal Odescalchi was no sooner raised to the pontificate as Innocent XI, than he provided Molinos with lodgings at the Vatican, and such was his esteem for him that he is said to have formed the purpose of making him a cardinal, and to have actually selected him for a time as his spiritual director."

It is of interest to note that the Pope in the "Ring and the Book" is certainly touched with the enlightened views of Molinos, though it was really Innocent XII who passed sentence upon Guido. Browning seems to have combined in his good old pope characteristics belonging to both of these pontiffs.

Among his distinguished followers there was none more conspicuous than Queen Christina of Sweden, who at this time was a great lioness at Rome, because of her abdication. She had given up her crown in order that she might be free to enter the Roman church, and upon doing so she took Molinos for her especial guide, and is described as making his gifts and his piety a favorite theme of her extensive correspondence. Cardinal d'Estrées, even, the representative of Louis XIV, thought it worth while to be in the fashion and identify himself with the movement, and went so far as to put Molinos in correspondence with important people in France. Later, Louis XIV and d'Estrées were chiefly responsible, upon the instigation of the Jesuits, for bringing him under the ban of the Inquisition. Another important follower was Father Petruci, who wrote many letters, and one or more treatises in favor of the contemplative life as taught by Molinos for the edification of nuns.

We get a breath of the uprising against Molinos and his doctrines which was to come, in a letter of Bishop Gilbert Burnet, who being in Italy in 1685 wrote home, "The new method of Molinos doth so much prevail at Naples that it is believed he hath above twenty thousand followers in the city. He hath writ a book which is entitled *Il Guida Spirituale*, which is a short abstract of the Mystical Divinity, the substance of the whole is reduced to this, that, in our prayers and other devotions, the best methods are to retire the mind from all gross images, and so to form an act of Faith, and thereby to present ourselves before God, and then to sink into a silence and cessation of new acts and to let God act upon us and so to follow his conduct. This way he prefers to the multiplication of many new acts and different forms of devotion, and he makes small account of corporal austerities, and reduces all the exercises of religion to this simplicity of mind. He thinks this is not only to be proposed to such as live in religious houses, but even to secular persons, and by this he hath proposed a great reformation of men's minds and manners. He hath many priests in Italy, but chiefly in Naples that dispose those who confess themselves to them to follow his methods. The Jesuits have set themselves much against this conduct as foreseeing it may weaken the empire that superstition hath over the minds of the people; that it may make religion become a more plain and simple thing, and may also open the door to enthusiasms. They also pretend that his conduct is factious and seditious, that this may breed a schism in the Church. And because he saith in some places of his book that the mind may rise up to such simplicity in its acts that it may rise in some of its devotions to God immediately, without contemplating the humanity of Christ, they have accused him as intending to lay aside the doctrine of Christ's humanity, though it is plain that he speaks only of the purity of some single acts. Upon all those heads they have set themselves much against Molinos, and they have also pretended that some of his disciples have infused it into their penitents that they may go and communicate as they find themselves disposed without going first to confession, which they thought weakened much the yoke by which the priests subdue the consciences of the people to their conduct. Yet he was much supported, both in the Kingdom of Naples and Sicily. He hath also many friends and followers at Rome. So the Jesuits, as a provincial of the Order assured me, finding they could not ruin him by their own force, got a great King, that is now extremely in the interests of their Order, to interpose and to represent to the Pope the danger of such innovations. It is certain the Pope understands the matter very little, and that he is possessed of a great opinion of Molinos' sanctity; yet, upon the complaints of some cardinals that seconded the zeal of the King, he and some of his followers were clapt into the Inquisition, where they have been now some months, but still they are well used, which is believed to flow from the good opinion that the Pope hath of him, who saith still that 'he may err, yet he is still a good man!'"

It is needless to say that once the Jesuits were aroused against Molinos they did not rest until they had him convicted of heresies and imprisoned for life. He was finally brought to trial after twenty-two months' close imprisonment, on the third of September, 1687. Among the accusations against him were that he taught divers doctrines which treated as lawful the commission of various unseemly acts, also with having taught the lawfulness of detraction, resentment toward one's neighbor, anger, blasphemy, with cursing God and the saints, and with execrating the consecrated robes. He is said to have assigned for his excuse that these acts were the works of the devil, who operated as God's instrument, and that such violence should be regarded as necessary. "Moreover, that they were not called to do penance for acts thus provoked, neither ought they to praise them nor to confess them, but to leave them unpunished, and if scruples on account of such acts came, to make no account of them because they were done without the consent of the higher nature, but solely by the force of the devil."

Such doctrines as these, of course, led to accusations of wilful sinning on the one hand, and on the other hand later to the doctrine of predestination as held by Johannes Agricola and Calvin. Molinos, like many other fathers of the Church, was seeking for a spiritual truth. He was trying to reconcile the omnipotence of God with the facts of sin and the human will, and the only way he could see out was in the utter passivity of man. The more passive a man was the more holy he would finally become, though God might take him through sin on the way to everlasting redemption. Practically it is equivalent to abandoning one's self to every impulse whether good or bad and having faith that the good will finally predominate and that even the bad impulses cannot touch the integrity of the soul. He emphasized a truth that was needed, namely, that sin may be a means of development, and in so doing he took religious conceptions several steps forwards, but he did not see the complementary truth that sin can only be a means of development if it is struggled against by the active human will. Although he was accused of various sins he absolutely denied most of the accusations, and his followers refused to believe the reports against him.

It was not, however, a war on the part of the Jesuits against evil doing or even heretical doctrines, it was a war against an influence which was usurping their own, and which they foresaw would break the power of the Church with its machinery of intercession and confession, and penitential vows.

A vivid picture of the scene when the judgment against Molinos was given is drawn by Bigelow:

"On the morning of the third of September, 1687, the church of Santa Maria Sopra Minerva, at Rome, was thronged at an early hour. The stalls, or *palchi*, of which a large number had been erected for the occasion, were filled by the nobility and with prelates of distinction. The college of cardinals, the General of the Inquisition and all his officers, were there, too, seated opposite each other upon a platform reserved for them. Every remaining place to sit or stand upon in that vast temple was occupied, for had it not been posted upon all the churches in Rome that on that day and in that church the officers of the Inquisition were to proclaim the result of their inquiries into the alleged heresies of Molinos? To insure a large attendance and to give to the impending ceremonies as much as possible the air of a popular manifestation against the accused and his followers, the public had been also notified, several days before, that an indulgence would be accorded of fifteen years to all, and of forty years to some, who should assist at the ceremonies of this *auto da fé*.

"It was a gala day for Rome and all its population, from the highest to the lowest, seemed to have been condensed within the walls of this famous church which resounded with the murmur of conversation, with the flutter of dresses and of fans, and which within the memory of men then living had witnessed the humiliation of Galileo. In the curiosity excited by every new or conspicuous arrival, in the gayety of the scene, in the pleasure of unexpected meetings and joyous greetings, in the quickened wit and lively repartee, which are the familiar incidents of an unoccupied crowd, the occasion which had brought the assembly was almost forgotten. Suddenly the noise is hushed, the motion of fans is suspended and all eyes are directed towards a side door nearest the platform occupied by the Inquisitors. An aged monk, attended by an officer, was approaching with a slow and solemn pace. His hands in manacles were held in front of him. In one of them he bore a candle. With a self-possessed, though somewhat severe expression, he walked slowly towards the place assigned him by his attendant, fronting at once the cardinals and the Grand Inquisitors.

"Molinos, the man upon whom now every eye in the vast and breathless assembly was fixed, was about sixty years of age. His frame was robust, his movement dignified and majestic. A settled expression of melancholy sat upon his face; his complexion was quite dark and his nose was both long and sharp. He wore the frock of his Order, descending to his heels and having the soiled and shabby look which daily use during nearly two years' confinement in prison sufficiently explained. The scene in which he bore so conspicuous a part seemed to find no reflection in his face. It expressed no emotion, but said in language more eloquent than words, 'This is your hour and the power of darkness.'"

A letter written in Rome on the very day by Estiennot gives another lifelike glimpse of this remarkable man:

"Molinos was conducted to the platform facing the cardinals and the tribunal of the Holy Office, consisting of consulting prelates, of the General of the Dominican Order, of the Commissioner, of some of the Qualifiers who qualified the propositions, and other agents of the Holy Office. Molinos stood with a policeman by his side, who from time to time wiped his face. In his hands which were manacled he held a burning candle. From the pulpit near the criminal, one of the fathers of St. Dominick read in a loud voice an abstract of the trial. It was observed that his face while this lasted, about three hours, as when he entered and left, was full of contempt and defiance, especially at the commotion of the people who as they heard the account of some of his graver villainies shouted boisterously, 'To the stake! to the stake!' During all this Molinos did not even change color, but made his feeling of contempt only the more conspicuous.

"To the guard who bound and brought him through the street to the Holy Office he said that he was the special agent of God and that he (the guard) would be punished. After the reading of the trial was over he was stripped of the long frock of the priest and clothed with the garment of penance with the cross on the back, showing through all the ceremony of excommunication his accustomed intrepidity and contempt. He was condemned to close confinement for the rest of his life, to wear the garment of penance, with the cross on his breast, to confess four times a year, — at Christmas, Easter, Pentecost, and All Saints' Day, — and besides to recite the *credo* every day, a third part of the rosary and to meditate the mysteries. All his writings, as well manuscript as printed, are proscribed under the heaviest penalties."

Nothing more is known of Molinos, personally, except that he continued to drag out a solitary existence in the cell to which he was taken from the church and died in ten years on Holy Innocents' Day, December 28, 1696, in the seventieth year of his age.

At the time of the episode related in "The Ring and the Book," 1692 or 93, the trial and condemnation of Molinos would have been a thing of the past. His disciples alarmed by the movement against Quietism fell silent, every scrap of a letter or a paper that could be found was burned. The Jesuits followed up their advantage, and compelled every one suspected of harboring any leanings toward Molinos to join in the hue and cry against Quietism, which had been started by the rabble in the church of Minerva upon the memorable day of the trial.

It is this atmosphere that comes out everywhere in "The Ring and the Book." The characters one after another have their fling at Molinism.

Take first from "Half-Rome" the description of the placing of the dead bodies on view in the church, this sort of exhibition being a custom of the time. An old fellow who comes up to see the sight thinks that such deeds along with the sin of Molinism show the degeneracy of the time:

"Sir, do you see,
They laid both bodies in the church, this morn
The first thing, on the chancel two steps up,
Behind the little marble balustrade;
Disposed them, Pietro the old murdered fool
To the right of the altar, and his wretched wife
On the other side. In trying to count stabs,
People supposed Violante showed the most,
Till somebody explained us that mistake;
His wounds had been dealt out indifferent where,
But she took all her stabbings in the face,
Since punished thus solely for honor's sake,
Honoris causâ, that's the proper term.
A delicacy there is, our gallants hold,

When you avenge your honor and only then,
That you disfigure the subject, fray the face,
Not just take life and end, in clownish guise.
It was Violante gave the first offense,
Got therefore the conspicuous punishment:
While Pietro, who helped merely, his mere death
Answered the purpose, so his face went free.
We fancied even, free as you please, that face
Showed itself still intolerably wronged;
Was wrinkled over with resentment yet,
Nor calm at all, as murdered faces use,
Once the worst ended: an indignant air
O' the head there was — 'tis said the body turned
Round and away, rolled from Violante's side
Where they had laid it loving-husband-like.
If so, corpses can be sensitive,
Why did not he roll right down altar-step,
Roll on through nave, roll fairly out of church,
Deprive Lorenzo of the spectacle,
Pay back thus the succession of affronts
Whereto this church had served as theatre?
For see: at that same altar where he lies,
To that same inch of step, was brought the babe
For blessing after baptism, and there styled
Pompilia, and a string of names beside,
By his bad wife, some seventeen years ago,
Who purchased her simply to palm on him,
Flatter his dotage and defraud the heirs.
Wait awhile! Also to this very step
Did this Violante, twelve years afterward,
Bring, the mock-mother, that child-cheat full-grown,
Pompilia, in pursuance of her plot,
And there brave God and man a second time
By linking a new victim to the lie.

Church of San Lorenzo, Rome.

There, having made a match unknown to him,
She, still unknown to Pietro, tied the knot
Which nothing cuts except this kind of knife;
Yes, made her daughter, as the girl was held,
Marry a man, and honest man beside,
And man of birth to boot, — clandestinely
Because of this, because of that, because
O' the devil's will to work his worst for once, —
Confident she could top her part at need
And, when her husband must be told in turn,
Ply the wife's trade, play off the sex's trick
And, alternating worry with quiet qualms,
Bravado with submissiveness, prettily fool
Her Pietro into patience: so it proved.
Ay, 'tis four years since man and wife they grew,
This Guido Franceschini and this same
Pompilia, foolishly thought, falsely declared
A Comparini and the couple's child:
Just at this altar where beneath the piece
Of Master Guido Reni, Christ on cross,
Second to naught observable in Rome,
That couple lie now, murdered yestereve.
Even the blind can see a providence here.

From dawn till now that it is growing dusk,
A multitude has flocked and filled the church,
Coming and going, coming back again,
Till to count crazed one. Rome was at the show.
People climbed up the columns, fought for spikes
O' the chapel-rail to perch themselves upon,
Jumped over and so broke the wooden work
Painted like porphyry to deceive the eye;
Serve the priests right! The organ-loft was crammed,
Women were fainting, no few fights ensued,

In short, it was a show repaid your pains:
For, though their room was scant undoubtedly,
Yet they did manage matters, to be just,
A little at this Lorenzo. Body o' me!
I saw a body exposed once . . . never mind!
Enough that here the bodies had their due.
No stinginess in wax, a row all round,
And one big taper at each head and foot.

So, people pushed their way, and took their turn,
Saw, threw their eyes up, crossed themselves, gave place
To pressure from behind, since all the world
Knew the old pair, could talk the tragedy
Over from first to last: Pompilia too,
Those who had known her — what 'twas worth to them!
Guido's acquaintance was in less request;
The Count had lounged somewhat too long in Rome,
Made himself cheap; with him were hand and glove
Barbers and blear-eyed, as the ancient sings.
Also he is alive and like to be:
Had he considerately died, — aha!
I jostled Luca Cini on his staff,
Mute in the midst, the whole man one amaze,
Staring amain, and crossing brow and breast.
'How now?' asked I. ''Tis seventy years,' quoth he,
'Since I first saw, holding my father's hand,
Bodies set forth: a many have I seen,
Yet all was poor to this I live and see.
Here the world's wickedness seals up the sum:
What with Molinos' doctrine and this deed,
Antichrist surely comes and doomsday's near.
May I depart in peace, I have seen my see.'
'Depart then,' I advised, 'nor block the road
For youngsters still behindhand with such sights!'

'Why no,' rejoins the venerable sire,
'I know it's horrid, hideous past belief,
Burdensome far beyond what eye can bear;
But they do promise when Pompilia dies
I' the course o' the day, — and she can't outlive night, —
They'll bring her body also to expose
Beside the parents, one, two, three abreast;
That were indeed a sight which, might I see,
I trust I should not last to see the like!'
Whereat I bade the senior spare his shanks,
Since doctors give her till to-night to live,
And tell us how the butchery happened. 'Ah,
But you can't know!' sighs he, 'I'll not despair:
Beside I'm useful at explaining things —
As, how the dagger laid there at the feet,
Caused the peculiar cuts: I mind its make,
Triangular i' the blade, a Genoese,
Armed with those little hook-teeth on the edge
To open in the flesh nor shut again:
I like to teach a novice: I shall stay!'
And stay he did, and stay be sure he will."

In contrast to this venerable man a bright young fellow, the curate, tells the crowd the story of the murder and declares such deeds to be the result of Molinos' tares sown for wheat. And having introduced the subject he seems to have enlarged upon it and the cardinal who wrote about it, probably referring to Cardinal d'Estrées, who wrote several books on Molinism.

"A personage came by the private door
At noon to have his look: I name no names:

Well then, His Eminence the Cardinal,
Whose servitor in honorable sort
Guido was once, the same who made the match,
(Will you have the truth?) whereof we see effect.
No sooner whisper ran he was arrived
Than up pops Curate Carlo, a brisk lad,
Who never lets a good occasion slip,
And volunteers improving the event.
We looked he'd give the history's self some help,
Treat us to how the wife's confession went
(This morning she confessed her crime, we know)
And, maybe, throw in something of the Priest —
If he's not ordered back, punished anew,
The gallant, Caponsacchi, Lucifer
I' the garden where Pompilia, Eve-like, lured
Her Adam Guido to his fault and fall.
Think you we got a sprig of speech akin
To this from Carlo with the Cardinal there?
Too wary he was, too widely awake, I trow.
He did the murder in a dozen words;
Then said that all such outrages crop forth
I' the course of nature, when Molinos' tares
Are sown for wheat, flourish and choke the Church:
So slid on to the abominable sect
And the philosophic sin — we've heard all that,
And the Cardinal too, (who book-made on the same)
But, for the murder, left it where he found.
Oh but he's quick, the Curate, minds his game!"

"Half-Rome" shows us the scene at the Church of San Lorenzo. "The Other Half-Rome" shows us Pompilia, lying on her death-bed visited by the lawyers, by a confessor, by many who suddenly found themselves friends, and by an artist. Here again the thought of Molinism is ever present. The speaker describes Pompilia as a miracle to tell these Molonists:

"Another day that finds her living yet,
Little Pompilia, with the patient brow
And lamentable smile on those poor lips,
And, under the white hospital-array,
A flower-like body, to frighten at a bruise
You'd think, yet now, stabbed through and through again
Alive i' the ruins. 'T is a miracle.
It seems that, when her husband struck her first,
She prayed Madonna just that she might live
So long as to confess and be absolved;
And whether it was that, all her sad life long
Never before successful in a prayer,
This prayer rose with authority too dread, —
Or whether, because earth was hell to her,
By compensation, when the blackness broke
She got one glimpse of quiet and the cool blue,
To show her for a moment such things were, —
Or else, — as the Augustinian Brother thinks,
The friar who took confession from her lip, —
When a probationary soul that moved
From nobleness to nobleness, as she,
Over the rough way of the world, succumbs,
Bloodies its last thorn with unflinching foot,
The angels love to do their work betimes,
Stanch some wounds here nor leave so much for God.
Who knows? However it be, confessed, absolved,
She lies, with overplus of life beside

To speak and right herself from first to last,
Right the friend also, lamb-pure, lion-brave,
Care for the boy's concerns, to save the son
From the sire, her two-weeks' infant orphaned thus,
And — with best smile of all reserved for him —
Pardon that sire and husband from the heart.
A miracle, so tell your Molinists!"

There is some one at Pompilia's bedside also to explain the cause of such crimes on the score of Molinism. Possibly the same curate already met with at the church.

"Somebody at the bedside said much more,
Took on him to explain the secret cause
O' the crime: quoth he, 'Such crimes are very rife,
Explode nor make us wonder nowadays,
Seeing that Antichrist disseminates
That doctrine of the Philosophic Sin:
Molinos' sect will soon make earth too hot!'
'Nay,' groaned the Augustinian, 'what's there new?
Crime will not fail to flare up from men's hearts
While hearts are men's and so born criminal;
Which one fact, always old yet ever new,
Accounts for so much crime that, for my part,
Molinos may go whistle to the wind
That waits outside a certain church, you know!'

Though really it does seem as if she here,
Pompilia, living so and dying thus,
Has had undue experience how much crime
A heart can hatch. Why was she made to learn
— Not you, not I, not even Molinos' self —
What Guido Franceschini's heart could hold?

Thus saintship is effected probably;
No sparing saints the process! — which the more
Tends to the reconciling us, no saints,
To sinnership, immunity and all."

Guido, again, must bring Molinos into his argument by telling a piece of gossip about the Cardinal's tract which illustrates his ideas of the ways and means by which one may "get on" in life. The story is of a clown who

"'. . . dressed vines on somebody's estate
His boy recoiled from muck, liked Latin more,
Stuck to his pen and got to be a priest,
Till one day . . . don't you mind that telling tract
Against Molinos, the old Cardinal wrote?
He penned and dropped it in the patron's desk,
Who, deep in thought and absent much of mind.
Licensed the thing, allowed it for his own;
Quick came promotion, — *suum cuique*, Count!
Oh, he can pay for coach and six, be sure!'
' — Well, let me go, do likewise: war 's the word —
That way the Franceschini worked at first,
I'll take my turn, try soldiership.' — 'What, you?
The eldest son and heir and prop o' the house,
So do you see your duty? Here's your post,
Hard by the hearth and altar' (Roam from roof,
This youngster, play the gypsy out of doors,
And who keeps kith and kin that fall on us?)
Stand fast, stick tight, conserve your gods at home!'
'Well — then, the quiet course, the contrary trade!
We had a cousin amongst us once was Pope,
And minor glories manifold. Try the Church,
The tonsure, and, — since heresy's but half-slain

Even by the Cardinal's tract he thought he wrote, —
Have at Molinos!' — 'Have at a fool's head!
You a priest? How were marriage possible?
There must be Franceschini till time ends —
That's your vocation. Make your brothers priests,
Paul shall be porporate, and Girolamo step
Red-stockinged in the presence when you choose,
But save one Franceschini for the age!
Be not the vine but dig and dung its root,
Be not a priest but gird up priesthood's loins,
With one foot in Arezzo stride to Rome,
Spend yourself there and bring the purchase back!
Go hence to Rome, be guided!"

Caponsacchi relates how he was told by the judges the priest's duty — to "labor to pluck tares and weed the corn of Molinism," and how when he, through the awakening influence of Pompilia, found his society life flat, stale and unprofitable and decided never to write another canzonet, his patron spoke abrupt:

"'Young man, can it be true
That after all your promise to sound fruit,
You have kept away from Countess young or old
And gone play truant in church all day long?
Are you turning Molinist?'
I answered quick:
'Sir, what if I turned Christian? It might be.
The fact is I am troubled in my mind,
Beset and pressed hard by some novel thoughts.
This your Arezzo is a limited world;
There's a strange Pope, — 'tis said, a priest who thinks.

Rome is the port, you say: to Rome I go.
I will live alone, one does so in a crowd,
And look into my heart a little.'"

Pompilia, as one would expect, only quotes what the priest said in regard to Molinism.

"'For see —
If motherhood be qualified impure,
I catch you making God command Eve sin!
— A blasphemy so like these Molinists,
I must suspect you dip into their books.'"

Each of the lawyers refers to the Molinists. To illustrate his argument, Hyacinthus de Archangelis declares:

"Yea, argue Molinists who bar revenge —
Referring just to what makes out our case!
Under old dispensation, argue they,
The doom of the adulterous wife was death,
Stoning by Moses' law."

Bottinius, on the other hand, would like to impress the Molinists as he would every one else with his own importance:

"Rome, that Rome whereof — this voice
Would it might make our Molinists observe,
That she is built upon a rock nor shall
Their powers prevail against her! — Rome, I say,
Is all but reached."

From the references of these various characters to Molinism it would be quite impossible to discover the truth in regard to this sect. Each one uses it as a stalking horse for any evil he wishes to account for or any opinion he wishes to combat. There could not be a better way of showing what a pervasive influence Molinism had become in the Roman world at the same time that, once having fallen under the ban of the Church, all sorts of lies about its tenets would gain credence.

Browning, however, has been clever enough to show the influence for good in the ideas of Molinos, indirectly in the independent and enlightened vision of Caponsacchi and Pompilia and directly in a passage in the "Pope," where the Pope says:

"Must we deny, — do they, these Molinists,
At peril of their body and their soul, —
Recognized truths, obedient to some truth
Unrecognized yet, but perceptible? —
Correct the portrait by the living face,
Man's God, by God's God in the mind of man?
Then, for the few that rise to the new height,
The many that must sink to the old depth
The multitude found fall away! A few,
E'en ere new law speak clear, may keep the old,
Preserve the Christian level, call good good
And evil evil, (even though razed and blank
The old titles,) helped by custom, habitude,
And all else they mistake for finer sense
O' the fact that reason warrants, — as before,
They hope perhaps, fear not impossibly."

. . . .

"Here comes the first experimentalist
In the new order of things, — he plays a priest;
Does he take inspiration from the Church,
Directly make her rule his law of life?
Not he: his own mere impulse guides the man —
Happily sometimes, since ourselves allow
He has danced, in gayety of heart, 'i the main
The right step through the maze we bade him foot.
But if his heart had prompted him break loose
And mar the measure? Why, we must submit,
And thank the chance that brought him safe so far,
Will he repeat the prodigy? Perhaps.
Can he teach others how to quit themselves,
Show why this step was right while that were wrong?
How should he? 'Ask your hearts as I ask mine,
And get discreetly through the Morrice too;
If your hearts misdirect you, — quit the stage,
And make amends, — be there amends to make!'"

This lenient attitude toward impulse, especially such an impulse as that of Caponsacchi's, in saving Pompilia by flying with her to Rome, and so outraging churchly and social proprieties, shows the influence of the teachings of Molinos in regard to sin not having any effect upon the soul, which might safely be left in the hands of God. The whole passage is really an interpretation on the part of the poet indicating that the sins Molinos thought unimportant were really the sins against imperfect human conceptions of right and wrong, and that these imperfect conceptions of right and wrong could only be changed to something better by following human vision without regard to the Church. Pompilia reaches the greatest height in her attitude toward sin in her forgiveness of Guido:

"We shall not meet in this world nor the next,
But where will God be absent? In His face
Is light, but in His shadow healing too:
Let Guido touch the shadow and be healed!

. . . .

Nothing about me but drew somehow down
His hate upon me, — somewhat so excused
Therefore, since hate was thus the truth of him, —
May my evanishment for evermore
Help further to relieve the heart that cast
Such object of its natural loathing forth!
So he was made; he nowise made himself:
I could not love him, but his mother did.

. . . .

Whatever he touched is rightly ruined: plague
It caught, and disinfection it had craved
Still but for Guido; I am saved through him
So as by fire; to him — thanks and farewell!"

We may add to this pervasive atmosphere of the time that envelops the poem, a few special illustrations of customs which were then rife. The resort to torture to extract truth from criminals was still practised and Guido gives graphically his experience of the torture to which he was subjected:

"Thanks, Sir, but, should it please the reverend Court,
I feel I can stand somehow, half sit down
Without help, make shift to even speak, you see,
Fortified by the sip of . . . why, 't is wine,
Velletri, — and not vinegar and gall,
So changed and good the times grow! Thanks, kind Sir!
Oh, but one sip's enough! I want my head
To save my neck, there's work awaits me still.
How cautious and considerate . . . aie, aie, aie,
Nor your fault, sweet Sir! Come, you take to heart
An ordinary matter. Law is law.
Noblemen were exempt, the vulgar thought,
From racking; but, since law thinks otherwise,
I have been put to the rack: all's over now,
And neither wrist — what men style, out of joint:
If any harm be, 'tis the shoulder-blade,
The left one, that seems wrong i' the socket, — Sirs,
Much could not happen, I was quick to faint,
Being past my prime of life, and out of health.
In short, I thank you, — yes, and mean the word.
Needs must the Court be slow to understand
How this quite novel form of taking pain,
This getting tortured merely in the flesh,
Amounts to almost an agreeable change
In my case, me fastidious, plied too much
With opposite treatment, used (forgive the joke)
To the rasp-tooth toying with this brain of mine,
And, in and out my heart, the play o' the probe.
Four years have I been operated on
I' the soul, do you see — its tense or tremulous part —
My self-respect, my care for a good name,
Pride in an old one, love of kindred — just
A mother, brothers, sisters, and the like,
That looked up to my face when days were dim,

And fancied they found light there — no one spot,
Foppishly sensitive, but has paid its pang.
That, and not this you now oblige me with,
That was the Vigil-torment, if you please!"

Caponsacchi's account of his life reveals what the life of a priest at that time might be, without arousing criticism on the part of the Church. The slackness was due to Jesuitical influence. They winked at anything by means of which they could serve their own ambitions for the aggrandizement of their order.

"I begin.
Yes, I am one of your body and a priest.
Also I am a younger son o' the House
Oldest now, greatest once, in my birth-town
Arezzo, I recognize no equal there —
(I want all arguments, all sorts of arms
That seem to serve, — use this for a reason, wait!)
Not therefore thrust into the Church, because
O' the piece of bread one gets there. We were first
Of Fiesole, that rings still with the fame
Of Capo-in-Sacco our progenitor:
When Florence ruined Fiesole, our folk
Migrated to the victor-city, and there
Flourished, — our palace and our tower attest,
In the Old Mercato, — this was years ago,
Four hundred, full, — no, it wants fourteen just.
Our arms are those of Fiesole itself,
The shield quartered with white and red: a branch
Are the Salviati of us, nothing more.
That were good help to the Church? But better still —

Not simply for the advantage of my birth
I' the way of the world, was I proposed for priest;
But because there's an illustration, late
I' the day, that's loved and looked to as a saint
Still in Arezzo, he was bishop of,
Sixty years since: he spent to the last doit
His bishop's-revenue among the poor,
And used to tend the needy and the sick,
Barefoot, because of his humility.
He it was, — when the Granduke Ferdinand
Swore he would raze our city, plough the place
And sow it with salt, because we Aretines
Had tied a rope about the neck, to hale
The statue of his father from its base
For hate's sake, — he availed by prayers and tears
To pacify the Duke and save the town.
This was my father's father's brother. You see,
For his sake, how it was I had a right
To the selfsame office, bishop in the egg,
So, grew i' the garb and prattled in the school,
Was made expect, from infancy almost,
The proper mood o' the priest; till time ran by
And brought the day when I must read the vows,
Declare the world renounced, and undertake
To become priest and leave probation, — leap
Over the ledge into the other life,
Having gone trippingly hitherto up to the height
O'er the wan water. Just a vow to read!

I stopped short awe-struck. 'How shall holiest flesh
Engage to keep such vow inviolate,
How much less mine? I know myself too weak,
Unworthy! Choose a worthier stronger man!'
And the very Bishop smiled and stopped my mouth

In its mid-protestation. 'Incapable?
Qualmish of conscience? Thou ingenuous boy!
Clear up the clouds and cast thy scruples far!
I satisfy thee there's an easier sense
Wherein to take such vow than suits the first
Rough rigid reading. Mark what makes all smooth,
Nay, has been even a solace to myself!
The Jews who needs must, in their synagogue,
Utter sometimes the holy name of God,
A thing their superstition boggles at,
Pronounce aloud the ineffable sacrosanct, —
How does their shrewdness help them? In this wise;
Another set of sounds they substitute,
Jumble so consonants and vowels — how
Should I know? — that there grows from out the old
Quite a new word that means the very same —
And o'er the hard place slide they with a smile.
Giuseppe Maria Caponsacchi mine,
Nobody wants you in these latter days
To prop the Church by breaking your backbone, —
As the necessary way was once, we know,
When Diocletian flourished and his like.
That building of the buttress-work was done
By martyrs and confessors; let it bide,
Add not a brick, but, where you see a chink,
Stick in a sprig of ivy or root a rose
Shall make amends and beautify the pile!
We profit as you were the painfullest
O' the martyrs, and you prove yourself a match
For the cruellest confessor ever was,
If you march boldly up and take your stand
Where their blood soaks, their bones yet strew the soil,
And cry 'Take notice, I the young and free
And well-to-do i' the world, thus leave the world,

Cast in my lot thus with no gay young world
But the grand old Church: she tempts me of the two!'
Renounce the world? Nay, keep and give it us!
Let us have you, and boast of what you bring.
We want the pick o' the earth to practise with,
Not its offscouring, halt and deaf and blind
In soul and body. There's a rubble-stone
Unfit for the front o' the building, stuff to stow
In a gap behind and keep us weather-tight;
There 's porphyry for the prominent place. Good lack!
Saint Paul has had enough and to spare, I trow,
Of ragged runaway Onesimus:
He wants the right-hand with the signet-ring
Of King Agrippa, now, to shake and use.
I have a heavy scholar cloistered up,
Close under lock and key, kept at his task
Of letting Fénelon know the fool he is,
In a book I promise Christendom next Spring.
Why, if he covets so much meat, the clown,
As a lark's wing next Friday, or, any day,
Diversion beyond catching his own fleas,
He shall be properly swinged, I promise him.
But you, who are so quite another paste
Of a man, — do you obey me? Cultivate
Assiduous that superior gift you have
Of making madrigals — (who told me? Ah!
Get done a Marinesque Adoniad straight
With a pulse o' the blood a-pricking here and there,
That I may tell the lady, 'And he's ours!'"

So I became a priest: those terms changed all,
I was good enough for that, nor cheated so;
I could live thus and still hold head erect.
Now you see why I may have been before

A fribble and coxcomb, yet, as priest, break word
Nowise, to make you disbelieve me now.
I need that you should know my truth. Well, then,
According to prescription did I live,
— Conformed myself, both read the breviary
And wrote the rhymes, was punctual to my place
I' the Pieve, and as diligent at my post
Where beauty and fashion rule. I throve apace,
Sub-deacon, Canon, the authority
For delicate play at tarocs, and arbiter
O' the magnitude of fan-mounts: all the while
Wanting no whit the advantage of a hint
Benignant to the promising pupil, — thus:
'Enough attention to the Countess now,
The young one; 't is her mother rules the roast,
We know where, and puts in a word: go pay
Devoir to-morrow morning after mass!
Break that rash promise to preach, Passion-week!
Has it escaped you the Archbishop grunts
And snuffles when one grieves to tell his Grace
No soul dares treat the subject of the day
Since his own masterly handling it (ha, ha!)
Five years ago, — when somebody could help
And touch up an odd phrase in time of need,
(He, he!) — and somebody helps you, my son!
Therefore, don't prove so indispensable
At the Pieve, sit more loose i' the seat, nor grow
A fixture by attendance morn and eve!
Arezzo's just a haven midway Rome —
Rome's the eventual harbor — make for port,
Crowd sail, crack cordage! And your cargo be
A polished presence, a genteel manner, wit
At will, and tact at every pore of you!
I sent our lump of learning, Brother Clout,

And Father Slouch, our piece of piety,
To see Rome and try suit the Cardinal.
Thither they clump-clumped, beads and book in hand,
And ever since 'tis meat for man and maid
How both flopped down, prayed blessing on bent pate
Bald many an inch beyond the tonsure's need,
Never once dreaming, the two moony dolts,
There's nothing moves his Eminence so much
As — far from all this awe at sanctitude —
Heads that wag, eyes that twinkle, modified mirth
At the closet-lectures on the Latin tongue
A lady learns so much by, we know where.
Why, body o' Bacchus, you should crave his rule
For pauses in the elegiac couplet, chasms
Permissible only to Catullus! There!
Now go to duty: brisk, break Priscian's head
By reading the day's office — there's no help.
You've Ovid in your poke to plaster that;
Amen's at the end of all: then sup with me!'

Well, after three or four years of this life,
In prosecution of my calling, I
Found myself at the theatre one night
With a brother Canon, in a mood and mind
Proper enough for the place, amused or no:
When I saw enter, stand, and seat herself
A lady, young, tall, beautiful, strange and sad.
It was as when, in our cathedral once,
As I got yawningly through matin-song,
I saw *facchini* bear a burden up,
Base it on the high-altar, break away
A board or two, and leave the thing inside
Lofty and lone: and lo, when next I looked,
There was the Rafael! I was still one stare,

When — 'Nay, I'll make her give you back your gaze' —
Said Canon Conti; and at the word he tossed
A paper-twist of comfits to her lap,
And dodged and in a trice was at my back
Nodding from over my shoulder. Then she turned,
Looked our way, smiled the beautiful sad strange smile."

Pompilia's view of the Carnival will be an exquisite passage to close the glimpses of seventeenth century Italy, given in "The Ring and the Book:"

"I had been miserable three drear years
In that dread palace and lay passive now,
When I first learned there could be such a man.
Thus it fell: I was at a public play,
In the last days of Carnival last March,
Brought·there I knew not why, but now know well.
My husband put me where I sat, in front;
Then crouched down, breathed cold through me from behind,
Stationed i' the shadow, — none in front could see, —
I, it was, faced the stranger-throng beneath,
The crowd with upturned faces, eyes one stare,
Voices one buzz. I looked but to the stage,
Whereon two lovers sang and interchanged
'True life is only love, love only bliss:
I love thee — thee I love!' then they embraced.
I looked thence to the ceiling and the walls, —
Over the crowd, those voices and those eyes, —
My thoughts went through the roof and out, to Rome
On wings of music, waft of measured words, —
Set me down there, a happy child again,
Sure that to-morrow would be festa day,

Hearing my parents praise past festas more,
And seeing they were old if I was young,
Yet wondering why they still would end discourse
With 'We must soon go, you abide your time,
And, — might we haply see the proper friend
Throw his arm over you and make you safe!'
Sudden I saw him; into my lap there fell
A foolish twist of comfits, broke my dream
And brought me from the air and laid me low,
As ruined as the soaring bee that's reached
(So Pietro told me at the Villa once)
By the dust-handful. There the comfits lay:
I looked to see who flung them, and I faced
This Caponsacchi, looking up in turn.
Ere I could reason out why, I felt sure,
Whoever flung them, his was not the hand, —
Up rose the round face and good-natured grin
Of one who, in effect, had played the prank,
From covert close beside the earnest face, —
Fat waggish Conti, friend of all the world.
He was my husband's cousin, privileged
To throw the thing: the other, silent, grave,
Solemn almost, saw me, as I saw him."

A characteristic episode of Renaissance Italy is shown in "The Statue and the Bust," in which there is the usual jealous husband and a lover. The husband in this case vindicates sixteenth century notions of authority by subjecting his wife to lifelong imprisonment and lifelong torture. He places her in a room where she can see her lover pass daily. She plans to escape and join the lover, he plans to carry her off, but day by day something prevents; their whole life passes and nothing is accomplished; only his statue in the square and her bust in the window tell of their love. The legend is connected with the Statue of Duke Ferdinand I of Florence, whose equestrian statue, executed by the sculptor John of Douay, was placed by him in the Piazza dell Annunciata so that he might forever gaze toward the old Riccardi palace where the lady lived.

Confusion sometimes arises because of the fact that the Riccardi Palace in the Piazza dell Annunciata where the lady lived is now the Palazzo Antinori, while the palace now known as the Riccardi was then the Medici Palace, where the Duke lived. It is in the Via Larga and Browning refers to it as "the pile which the mighty shadow makes," a shadow not merely of bulk, but because of its connection with the name of Medici, the family who in the person of Cosimo and Lorenzo committed the crime of destroying the political liberty of Florence. Browning uses the story merely as a fable upon which to hang a moral. That moral has caused a good deal of discussion among Browning students and any one who cares to decide upon the pros and cons of the matter may follow it up in the various books of Browning criticism.

Statue of Duke Ferdinand, Florence.

The remaining poems to be considered in this pleasant search for the historical, artistic, and social aspects of Italian life which Browning has chosen to draw upon in his work, carry us for the first time to Venice, whose history furnishes one of the most interesting and instructive chapters in the fascinating labyrinth of Italy's political and social growth.

"In a Gondola" belongs to that Venice which had lost its early liberties. The history of Venice is that of a gradual evolution into a Republic of an oligarchical form. The struggles of the Doges in the first place to convert themselves into hereditary princes caused a curtailment of their power until they became little more than symbols of the state. The general assembly of the people who elected the Doge and from among whom the Doge invited councillors to advise him, was changed to an elected assembly of four hundred and eighty members holding office for a year. Finally the people were disfranchised altogether and the Great Council elected and chose by lot according to its own sweet will, though it must be said that its will was to guard elections with the most complicated *red-tapism.* Next a Council of Ten is evolved, the Great Council being too cumbrous to manage special affairs. Lastly a Council of Three, elected from the Ten, and these councils between them wielded autocratic power and became the engines of the horrible injustices and cruelties so often secretly perpetrated in the palmy days of Venice. The Three were especially invested with inquisitorial powers which they exercised in spying into the morals of the Venetian subjects, and as these morals were similar to those of the rest of Italy at that time they soon rendered themselves hateful to a corrupt nobility. The story of "In a Gondola" is a typical example of the romantic episodes of the time. In it the lover refers to the "Three" more than once, by which he probably meant the ladies' relations, husband and brothers perhaps — Gian, Paul, Himself, but the speaking of them as the "Three," by which name the Council of Three was always designated, is too significant in the connection for Browning not to have had in mind these inquisitorial guards of morality and he probably wished to imply that the Lover had them in mind also.

IN A GONDOLA

He sings.

I SEND my heart up to thee, all my heart
  In this my singing.
For the stars help me, and the sea bears part;
  The very night is clinging
Closer to Venice' streets to leave one space

Above me, whence thy face
May light my joyous heart to thee its dwelling-place.

She speaks.

Say after me, and try to say
My very words, as if each word
Came from you of your own accord,
In your own voice, in your own way:
"This woman's heart and soul and brain
Are mine as much as this gold chain
She bids me wear; which" (say again)
"I choose to make by cherishing
A precious thing, or choose to fling
Over the boat-side, ring by ring."
And yet once more say . . . no word more!
Since words are only words. Give o'er!

Unless you call me, all the same,
Familiarly by my pet name,
Which if the Three should hear you call,
And me reply to, would proclaim
At once our secret to them all.
Ask of me, too, command me, blame —
Do, break down the partition-wall
'Twixt us, the daylight world beholds
Curtained in dusk and splendid folds!
What's left but — all of me to take?
I am the Three's; prevent them, slake
Your thirst! 'Tis said, the Arab sage,
In practising with gems, can loose
Their subtle spirit in his cruce
And leave but ashes: so, sweet mage,
Leave them my ashes when thy use
Sucks out my soul, thy heritage!

He sings.

Past we glide, and past, and past!
  What's that poor Agnese doing
Where they make the shutters fast?
  Gray Zanobi's just a-wooing
To his couch the purchased bride:
  Past we glide!

Past we glide, and past, and past!
  Why's the Pucci Palace flaring
Like a beacon to the blast?
  Guests by hundreds, not one caring
If the dear host's neck were wried:
  Past we glide!

She sings.

The moth's kiss, first!
Kiss me as if you made believe
You were not sure, this eve,
How my face, your flower, had pursed
Its petals up; so, here and there
You brush it, till I grow aware
Who wants me, and wide ope I burst.

The bee's kiss, now!
Kiss me as if you entered gay
My heart at some noonday,
A bud that dares not disallow
The claim, so all is rendered up,
And passively its shattered cup
Over your head to sleep I bow.

He sings.

What are we two?
I am a Jew.

VENICE.

And carry thee, farther than friends can pursue,
To a feast of our tribe;
Where they need thee to bribe
The devil that blasts them unless he imbibe
Thy . . . Scatter the vision forever! And now,
As of old, I am I, thou art thou!

Say again, what we are?
The sprite of a star,
I lure thee above where the destinies bar
My plumes their full play
Till a ruddier ray
Than my pale one announce there is withering away
Some . . . Scatter the vision forever! And now,
As of old, I am I, thou art thou!

He muses.

Oh, which were best, to roam or rest?
The land's lap or the water's breast?
To sleep on yellow millet-sheaves,
Or swim in lucid shallows just
Eluding water-lily leaves,
An inch from Death's black fingers, thrust
To lock you, whom release he must;
Which life were best on Summer eves?

He speaks, musing.

Lie back; could thought of mine improve you?
From this shoulder let there spring
A wing; from this, another wing;
Wings, not legs and feet, shall move you!
Snow-white must they spring, to blend
With your flesh, but I intend
They shall deepen to the end,

Broader, into burning gold,
Till both wings crescent-wise enfold
Your perfect self, from 'neath your feet
To o'er your head, where lo, they meet
As if a million sword-blades hurled
Defiance from you to the world!

Rescue me thou, the only real!
And scare away this mad ideal
That came, nor motions to depart!
Thanks! Now, stay ever as thou art!

Still he muses.

What if the Three should catch at last
Thy serenader? While there's cast
Paul's cloak about my head, and fast
Gian pinions me, Himself has past
His stylet through my back; I reel;
And . . . is it thou I feel?
They trail me, these three godless knaves,
Past every church that saints and saves,
Nor stop till, where the cold sea raves
By Lido's wet accursed graves,
They scoop mine, roll me to its brink,
And . . . on thy breast I sink!

She replies, musing.

Dip your arm o'er the boat-side, elbow-deep,
As I do: thus: were death so unlike sleep,
Caught this way? Death's to fear from flame or steel,
Or poison doubtless; but from water — feel!

Go find the bottom! Would you stay me? There!
Now pluck a great blade of that ribbon-grass

To plait in where the foolish jewel was,
I flung away: since you have praised my hair,
'T is proper to be choice in what I wear.

He speaks.

Row home? must we row home? Too surely
Know I where its front's demurely
Over the Giudecca piled;
Window just with window mating,
Door on door exactly waiting,
All's the set face of a child:
But behind it, where 's a trace
Of the staidness and reserve,
And formal lines without a curve,
In the same child's playing-face?
No two windows look one way
O'er the small sea-water thread
Below them. Ah, the autumn day
I, passing, saw you overhead!
First, out a cloud of curtain blew,
Then a sweet cry, and last came you —
To catch your lory that must needs
Escape just then, of all times then,
To peck a tall plant's fleecy seeds,
And make me happiest of men.
I scarce could breathe to see you reach
So far back o'er the balcony
To catch him ere he climbed too high
Above you in the Smyrna peach,
That quick the round smooth cord of gold,
This coiled hair on your head, unrolled,
Fell down you like a gorgeous snake
The Roman girls were wont, of old,
When Rome there was, for coolness' sake

To let lie curling o'er their bosoms,
Dear lory, may his beak retain
Ever its delicate rose stain
As if the wounded lotus-blossoms
Had marked their thief to know again!

Stay longer yet, for other's sake
Than mine! What should your chamber do?
— With all its rarities that ache
In silence while day lasts, but wake
At night-time and their life renew,
Suspended just to pleasure you
Who brought against their will together
These objects and, while day lasts, weave
Around them such a magic tether
That dumb they look: your harp, believe,
With all the sensitive tight strings
Which dare not speak, now to itself
Breathes slumberously, as if some elf
Went in and out the chords, his wings
Make murmur wheresoe'er they graze,
As an angel may, between the maze
Of midnight palace-pillars, on
And on, to sow God's plagues, have gone
Through guilty glorious Babylon.
And while such murmurs flow, the nymph
Bends o'er the harp-top from her shell
As the dry limpet for the lymph
Come with a tune he knows so well.
And how your statues' hearts must swell!
And how your pictures must descend
To see each other, friend with friend!
Oh, could you take them by surprise,
You'd find Schidone's eager Duke

Saint Mark's, Venice, Before the Fall of the Tower.

Doing the quaintest courtesies
To that prim saint by Haste-thee-Luke!
And, deeper into her rock den,
Bold Castelfranco's Magdalen
You'd find retreated from the ken
Of that robed counsel-keeping Ser —
As if the Tizian thinks of her,
And is not, rather, gravely bent
On seeing for himself what toys
Are these, his progeny invent,
What litter now the board employs
Whereon he signed a document
That got him murdered! Each enjoys
Its night so well, you cannot break
The sport up, so, indeed must make
More stay with me, for others' sake.

She speaks.

To-morrow, if a harp-string, say,
Is used to tie the jasmine back
That overfloods my room with sweets,
Contrive your Zorzi somehow meets
My Zanze! If the ribbon's black,
The Three are watching: keep away!

Your gondola — let Zorzi wreathe
A mesh of water-weeds about
Its prow, as if he unaware
Had struck some quay or bridge-foot stair!
That I may throw a paper out
As you and he go underneath.

There's Zanze's vigiliant taper; safe are we.
Only one minute more to-night with me?

Resume your past self of a month ago!
Be you the bashful gallant, I will be
The lady with the colder breast than snow.
Now bow you, as becomes, nor touch my hand
More than I touch yours when I step to land,
And say, "All thanks, Siora!" —
Heart to heart
And lips to lips! Yet once more, ere we part,
Clasp me and make me thine, as mine thou art!

He is surprised, and stabbed.

It was ordained to be so, sweet! — and best
Comes now, beneath thine eyes, upon thy breast.
Still kiss me! Care not for the cowards! Care
Only to put aside thy beauteous hair
My blood will hurt! The Three, I do not scorn
To death, because they never lived: but I
Have lived indeed, and so — (yet one more kiss) — can die!"

A "Toccata of Galuppi's" takes us farther along the road of the political and social degeneracy of Venice, when she had arrived at a point where it was necessary to dance to keep her courage up. The picture given by Horatio E. Brown in his "Sketch of Venice" parallels remarkably that conjured up in the poet's mind by the cold, dead music of Galuppi. He writes:

"The decline of the Republic, the failure of her vital force, did not interrupt the flow of pleasure nor check the flaunting glories of the civic state. Amusement, ease of life, when business and battles were over was still sought for and found. The political effacement of the Republic and the rigid prohibition of politics as a topic, left Venetian society with little but the trivialities of life to engage the attention. The Illustrissimi, in periwig and crimson cloak and sword sauntered on the Liston, at the foot of the Campanile, in the square. The ladies over their chocolate tore each others characters to shreds. They might discuss with ribald tongues the eccentric tastes of the great Procuratore Andrea Trou, but if they ventured to suggest a remedy for financial embarrassments, if they dared to contemplate a reform, deportation to Verona stared them in the face. And so life was limited to the Liston, the café, the casino, to a first night at the Teatro San Moise or San Sarunele, to a cantata at the Mendicante, the Pieta or Incurabili. Their excitements were scandal and gambling, varied by the interest that might be aroused by a battle-royal between Goldoni and Lozzi, or the piquant processo of Piu Antonio Graturol. Sometimes the whole city would be thrown into a flutter by the arrival of some princes incogniti like the counts of the North, when the ladies would put on their finest dresses, and fight with each other outside the royal box for the honor of presentation.

"Tripolo painted their houses with hues as delicate, evanescent, aerial as the miracle of a sirocco day on the lagoon; Longhi depicted their lives in the Ridotto, in the parlor of a convent, in the alcove; Chiusi, Goldoni, Gozzi, Buratti, or Baffo wrote for them; Galuppi, Jouelli, Hasse, Faustina, Bordone, made music to them in their conservatories. There was taste — though rococo; there was wit — though malicious, in their salons, where the *cicisbeo* and the *abbatino* ruffled their laces, toyed with tea cups, learned to carry their hat upon their hip while leaning on the back of a lady's chair. An easy, elegant, charming life the Venetians spent in their beautiful chambers, stuccoed in low relief and tinted with mauve and lemon, with pistaccio green and salmon; there they read their Baffo, their Buratti, their Calmo; and thence late at night, or rather in the early morning, they were wont to pass across the lagoon to the Lido, where they made a matutinal supper and paid their orisons to the rising sun."

The causes for this sinking of a great state into the slough of incompetence and frivolity were to be found in the raising of that three-headed hydra of destruction, ambition, prosperity, and the consequent arousing of envy. Ambition led Venice to extend her dominions beyond her lagoons to the mainland, prosperity brought upon her responsibilities as a great nation (the war with the Turks, for example,)

Interior of St. Mark's, Venice.

which she could not sustain single-handed; and envy set the other states of Italy upon her, for as one writer says, while the Republic was actually hurling headlong to ruin, the outward pomp, the glory, the splendor of her civilization were for the first time attracting the eyes of Europe. There is something splendid as well as pitiful about the manner in which Venice, with all her wantonness and her frivolity, put up a brave front to the world and gave up at last only to the all-devouring grasp of Napoleon. Browning finds a deeper reason for the decay of Venice in her lack of spiritual aspiration, which is reflected only too surely in the deadness of Galuppi's music. The fires of the Renaissance had burned out because of the smoke of selfish ambition that had become mingled with the flame.

A TOCCATA OF GALUPPI'S

I

Oh Galuppi, Baldassaro, this is very sad to find!
I can hardly misconceive you; it would prove me deaf and blind;
But although I take your meaning, 'tis with such a heavy mind!

II

Here you come with your old music, and here's all the good it brings.

What, they lived once thus at Venice where the merchants were the kings,
Where Saint Mark's is, where the Doges used to wed the sea with rings?

III

Ay, because the sea's the street there; and 'tis arched by . . . . what you call
. . . . Shylock's bridge with houses on it, where they kept the Carnival.
I was never out of England — it's as if I saw it all.

IV

Did young people take their pleasure when the sea was warm in May?
Balls and masks begun at midnight, burning ever to mid-day,
When they made up fresh adventures for the morrow, do you say?

V

Was a lady such a lady, cheeks so round and lips so red, —
On her neck the small face buoyant, like a bell-flower on its bed,
O'er the breast's superb abundance where a man might base his head?

VI

Well, and it was graceful of them — they'd break talk off and afford
— She, to bite her mask's black velvet — he, to finger on his sword,
While you sat and played Toccatas, stately at the clavichord?

VII

What? Those lesser thirds so plaintive, sixths diminished, sigh on sigh,
Told them something? Those suspensions, those solutions — "Must we die?"
Those commiserating sevenths — "Life might last! we can but try!"

VIII

"Were you happy?" — "Yes." — "And are you still as happy?" — "Yes. And you?"
— "Then, more kisses!" — "Did I stop them, when a million seemed so few?"
Hark, the dominant's persistence till it must be answered to!

IX

So, an octave struck the answer. Oh, they praised you, I dare say!
"Brave Galuppi! that was music! good alike at grave and gay!
I can always leave off talking when I hear a master play!"

X

Then they left you for their pleasure: till in due time, one by one,
Some with lives that came to nothing, some with deeds as well undone,
Death stepped tacitly and took them where they never see the sun.

XI

But when I sit down to reason, think to take my stand nor swerve,
While I triumph o'er a secret wrung from nature's close reserve,

In you come with your cold music till I creep thro' every nerve.

XII

Yes, you, like a ghostly cricket, creaking where a house was burned:
"Dust and ashes, dead and done with, Venice spent what Venice earned.
The soul, doubtless, is immortal — where a soul can be discerned.

XIII

"Yours for instance: you know physics, something of geology,
Mathematics are your pastime; souls shall rise in their degree:
Butterflies may dread extinction, — you'll not die, it cannot be!

XIV

"As for Venice and her people, merely born to bloom and drop,
Here on earth they bore their fruitage, mirth and folly were the crop:
What of soul was left, I wonder, when the kissing had to stop?

XV

"Dust and ashes!" So you creak it, and I want the heart to scold.
Dear dead women, with such hair, too — what's become of all the gold
Used to hang and brush their bosoms? I feel chilly and grown old.

The Rialto — "Shylock's Bridge," Venice.

"Pippa Passes" has already been referred to in connection with the historical section of our subject. Of social life it gives some glimpses which merely reinforce those already dwelt upon. There is the selfishness leading to crime in the murder of old Luca by Sebald and Ottima, there is the infamous group of young artists who play their disgraceful trick upon Jules and Phene, and last, there are the machinations of a degenerate group of clergy. These are situations all possible in the Italy which was in its last stages of Austrian domination; but that good seed was sprouting for the regeneration of Italy is shown in the characters of Jules and of Luigi. It is very probable that no such little paragon of a silk-winder as Pippa ever existed, but she symbolizes the eternally good that sooner or later must show evil its own ugly features.

The idea of a personality going through life and by its innate, unconscious goodness exerting a powerful influence upon those about it had long been in Browning's thoughts, as he has himself expressed it, a being passing through the world obscure and unnameable, but molding the destinies of others to mightier and better issues. This idea he gave form to in the little silk-winder of Asolo — "his first love among Italian cities." The Italian life, vividly as the characters are portrayed, is not drawn primarily for itself, but rather as a world in which his ideal being may move. Certainly, he could not have chosen any world in which such a being could move and touch so many universal forces in so short a space of time as that Italy in which for centuries the problems of social life, of art, of politics, and of the Church, had been agitating the human spirit; nor any world more greatly in need at this especial epoch of the light-bringing power of pure goodness.

Printed in the United States
104477LV00001B/165/A

9 781406 779240